Elections, Parties and Political Traditions

German Historical Perspectives Series
General Editors:
Gerhard A. Ritter, Werner Pöls, Anthony J. Nicholls

German Historical Perspectives/IV

Elections, Parties and Political Traditions
Social Foundations of German Parties and Party Systems, 1867–1987

Edited by
KARL ROHE

BERG
New York / Oxford / Munich
Distributed exclusively in the US and Canada by
St. Martin's Press, New York

First published in 1990 by
Berg Publishers Limited
Editorial Offices:
165 Taber Avenue, Providence RI 02906, USA
150 Cowley Road, Oxford OX4 1JJ, UK
Westermühlstraße 26, 8000 München 5, FRG

The editors and publishers wish to thank the Stiftverband für die Deutsche
Wissenschaft for generous assistance with the publication of this volume.

Library of Congress Cataloging-in-Publication Data

Elections, parties, and political traditions: Social Foundations of German Parties and
Party Systems, 1867–1987
edited by Karl Rohe.
   p.   cm. — (German historical perspectives: 4)
Includes bibliographical references.
ISBN 0–85496–619–6
   1. Germany—Politics and government—1870– 2. Political
parties–Germany—History. 3. Elections—Germany—History. I. Rohe. Karl.
II. Series.
DD221.E48 1990
320.943—dc20
                                                                89–18033
                                                                CIP

British Library Cataloguing in Publication Data

Elections, Parties and political traditions in Germany,
1867–1987. — (German historical perspectives; 4)
1. Germany.   Politics, History
I. Rohe, Karl   II. Series
320 943

ISBN 0–85496–619–6

Printed in Great Britain by Billing and Sons Ltd, Worcester

Contents

List of Tables and Figures

Tables

Figures

Editorial Preface

The purpose of this series of books is to present the results of research by German historians and social scientists to readers in English-speaking countries. Each of the volumes has a particular theme which will be handled from different points of view by specialists. The series is not limited to the problems of Germany but will also involve publications dealing with the history of other countries, with the general problems of political, economic, social and intellectual history as well as international relations and studies in comparative history.

The aim of the series is to help overcome the language barrier which experience has shown obstructs the rapid appreciation of German research in English-speaking countries.

The publication of the series is closely associated with the German Visiting Fellowship at St Antony's College, Oxford, which has existed since 1965, having been originally funded by the Stiftung Volkswagenwerk, later by the British Leverhulme Foundation and, since 1982, by the Ministry of Education and Science in the Federal Republic of Germany. Each volume will be based on a series of seminars held in Oxford, which will have been conceived and directed by the Visiting Fellow and organized in collaboration with St Antony's College.

The editors wish to thank the Stifterverband für die Deutsche Wissenschaft for meeting the expenses of the original lecture series and for generous assistance with the publication. They hope that this enterprise will help to overcome national introspection and to further international academic discourse and co-operation.

Gerhard A. Ritter   **Werner Pöls**   **Anthony J. Nicholls**

KARL ROHE

Foreword

The following collection of articles originated from a seminar held at St Antony's College in the spring of 1988. Gerhard A. Ritter analyses the social bases of German political parties between 1867 and 1920. His article may well serve as a second introduction, in addition to the more general and conceptual introduction given by the editor. Jürgen W. Falter summarizes his long-term research on the social foundations of the NSDAP. The somewhat ironic title, 'The First German *Volkspartei*', takes up the question of whether the rise of the NSDAP marks the end or at least the beginning of the end of the traditional German system of regionally based *Milieuparteien* described by Gerhard A. Ritter and other authors in this volume.

The regional pattern of German electoral behaviour and party politics, which is crucial to understanding German political traditions, is dealt with by three contributors. Merith Niehuss concentrates on party configurations in state and municipal elections in southern Germany before 1914. What emerges very clearly from her research is that in southern Germany both the social-cultural environments of political parties and their mutual relationships differed greatly from those in Prussia and north Germany. The next articles, one written by the editor and one by Alf Mintzel, deal with the contrasting cases of Bavaria and the Ruhr. Both studies come to the conclusion that different regional party and electoral developments must always be seen as the complex outcome of social and cultural conditions on the one hand and strategic decisions taken by political elites on the other.

Karl Schmitt, whose findings are based on a major piece of research, tackles what is perhaps the most characteristic and at the same time the least understood problem of German political society, namely that of religious affiliation. To the embarrassment of analysts outside and inside Germany it is the confessional allegiance which again and again proves to be the most important factor in 'explaining' electoral behaviour in the Federal Republic. As Karl Schmitt suggests, one of the reasons for the enduring importance of religion may well be that the meaning of this religious factor has changed considerably over time.

Franz Urban Pappi gives his assessment of future party political development in Germany based on ongoing research into the relationships between new social movements and the traditional party system. He comes to the conclusion that the Greens are basically a party of the left competing for votes mainly with the Social Democrats, and that it will depend on the SPD and its ability to integrate old and new left elements whether or not the Greens will remain an option within the German party system.

Pappi's article was written before the 1989 Berlin elections, the municipal elections in Hesse and the European elections took place. It is still a matter of debate whether we are witnessing the emergence of a new party system in West Germany. The latter possibility is not unlikely to materialize. After all it should not be overlooked that the party system of the Federal Republic as it gradually developed after the Second World War was at least partly the result of some very special political circumstances. As a consequence of the Nazi regime the extreme right was politically and culturally discredited after 1945 and the extreme left was soon going to become discredited as well, due to the establishment of a Communist regime in East Germany. What we experience at the moment, and what we have experienced in the last few years with the emergence of a new left party, may well be a kind of 'normalization' of German political culture. So there are good reasons at the moment to think anew about the historical roots of German political parties and about the political traditions which shaped them in different regions of the Federal Republic after the Second World War.

I wish to thank all co-authors of this volume, and Gerhard A. Ritter and Tony Nicholls, the editors of the series *German Historical Perspectives*. The Stifterverband für die Deutsche Wissenschaft provided the financial means which allowed us to invite German colleagues to Oxford. I am very much indebted to this institution and to Marion Berghahn for publishing the book. I also want to thank Leo E. Caron, Tony Nicholls and Hartmut Pogge von Strandmann who went through the articles and made some very helpful suggestions for transforming an often somewhat Germanic English into something more readable.

KARL ROHE

German Elections and Party Systems in Historical and Regional Perspective: An Introduction

Regional Contexts and Voting: Towards a Cultural Analysis of Voting Behaviour in Imperial Germany

In an influential statement the historical German party system has been described as a system of regionally based *Milieuparteien*.[1] Political parties in Imperial Germany, so the argument runs, had neither a clear religious nor a clear class base but must be looked at as political expressions of complex constellations of social, religious and regional factors which had been merged into comparatively stable socio-cultural milieus. This interpretation has been questioned with some reason as being too ahistorical and too narrow;[2] but it may nevertheless be taken as a useful point of departure.

1. M. Rainer Lepsius, 'Parteiensystem und Sozialstruktur. Zum Problem der Demokratisierung der deutschen Gesellschaft', in Gerhard A. Ritter (ed.), *Die deutschen Parteien vor 1918*, Cologne, 1973, p. 67.
2. See, for example, James J. Sheehan, 'Klasse und Partei im Kaiserreich: Einige Gedanken zur Sozialgeschichte der deutschen Politik', and David Blackbourn, 'Die Zentrumspartei und die deutschen Katholiken während des Kulturkampfs und danach', both in Otto Pflanze (ed.), *Innenpolitische Probleme des Bismarck-Reiches*, Munich and Vienna, 1983, pp. 1–24 and pp. 73–94, esp. p. 21 and pp. 76–7. See also Stanley Suval, *Electoral Politics in Wilhelmine Germany*, Chapel Hill and London, 1985, pp. 60–2. This introductory article covers such a wide field that it would take too many pages to mention even all major contributions by historians and political scientists. For further literature on German elections and the social bases of German political parties in the nineteenth and twentieth centuries see the select bibliography and the other articles collected in

1

What precisely is meant by region? Are we to consider individual states of the Reich, or provinces within states or large areas such as southern Germany as compared to northern Germany as appropriate regional units? The answer is somewhat difficult. Firstly, regions are historical phenomena, that is to say they are phenomena the size, salience and meaning of which can vary according to time and space. So the political importance not only of individual regions but that of the regional factor as such cannot simply be taken for granted. Secondly, the choice of regional units very much depends on the questions one wants to raise and to answer. Thus one needs a broad understanding and flexible use of the term; region may be everything below the national and, as a rule, above the local level. Taking a regional view means to look at elections and parties from a spatial or territorial perspective.

For pragmatic reasons, but partly from theoretical considerations as well, Reichstag constituencies will often be referred to as regions in the following chapter. Due to the existing Law of Association in Prussia[3] and due to the electoral system which like all majority systems stressed regionality rather than national party, it was the Reichstag constituencies which were to become important political units when the popular foundations of the German party system were laid in the late 1860s and early 1870s.

If one wants to grasp the regional dimensions of party and electoral politics in Imperial Germany, one must first consider the fact that political parties differed considerably in their regional political strength. This is, of course, not to say that regional political differences simply reflected some regionally specific factors. Conventional wisdom tells us that regional factors may be nothing else but general structural factors in disguise and that only if there remains a 'regional residuum', having first controlled for factors such as class and religion, is one allowed to claim that a regional factor is operating.

Even if one accepts this position, which is, as will be argued below, too narrow an approach, regional factors will not disappear. Numerous 'regional residua' can be found in the Kaiserreich. For most of the nineteenth and twentieth centuries catholic constituencies, such as the

---

this volume; see further the most useful 'Wahlgeschichtlichen Arbeitsbücher' by Gerhard A. Ritter, *Wahlgeschichtliches Arbeitsbuch. Materialien zur Statistik des Kaiserreiches 1871–1918*, Munich, 1980; Jürgen W. Falter, Thomas Lindenberger and Siegfried Schumann, *Wahlen und Abstimmungen in der Weimarer Republik. Materialien zum Wahlverhalten 1919–1933*, Munich, 1986; Gerhard A. Ritter and Merith Niehuss, *Wahlen in der Bundesrepublik Deutschland. Bundestags- und Landtagswahlen 1946–1987*, Munich, 1987.

3. See the chapter by Gerhard A. Ritter in this volume, pp. 27–52.

Allgäu or Munich, were represented by Liberals or even Social Democrats in the Reichstag. On the other hand there are industrial regions with high degrees of proletarization, like the Ruhr, where up to the end of the nineteenth century the SPD failed to win a single Reichstag seat – even if the constituency was not predominantly catholic. In 1898 the Centre Party was still able to mobilize 80.6% of catholic voters in the Ruhr, but only 59.7% in Cologne and 31.4% in Munich.

So we have to think anew. One possibility is to refer to structural variables hitherto not accounted for; the other to allude to cultural variables. What really matters, one would argue from a cultural perspective, is not the social characteristics of individuals – such as being a catholic or being an industrial worker – but cultural characteristics: mentalities and ways of life. We have to know how catholics and workers think and how they live if we want to know how they are most likely to behave politically. Cultures, however, do not emerge overnight. They are not only shaped by present constellations but by historical traditions as well. Thus the more one gets involved in comparative cultural analysis of regional voting patterns in Imperial Germany the more one is inclined to raise questions such as the following: was there a catholic or protestant revivalism in the nineteenth century? Was there a catholic enlightenment in the eighteenth century? Moreover, one is often tempted to go even further back and have a close look at the regional circumstances under which reformation and counter-reformation took place in order to understand why a strong anticlericalism can be found in some catholic regions and not in others. Accordingly, cultural analysis necessarily includes an historical perspective.

So far, emphasis has been deliberately laid on religion rather than on class. From the beginning of mass politics up until the present[4] religion has proved to be the most important influence in German electoral and party politics. And it is the aspect of confession, and not simply that of religious convictions, which has to be stressed and which is of key significance when explaining why religion tends to have a stronger influence on party choice than class when both factors play a role.[5] Religion, as a rule, stands for already existing social communities, whereas class, as measured by the percentage of industrial workers, may represent nothing more than the raw materials out of which

4. See the chapter by Karl Schmitt in this volume, pp. 179–202.
5. See in general A. Lijphart, 'Religious vs. Linguistic vs. Class Voting: The Crucial Experiment of Comparing Belgium, Canada, South Africa and Switzerland', *American Political Science Review*, vol. 73, 1979, pp. 442–58.

communities might be built. No doubt both dimensions of religiosity, the belief aspect as well as the community aspect, counted politically. The ideal type of SPD voter, not to speak of the ideal type of SPD member, was secular-minded.[6] But there are regional exceptions. If one tries to find out why the SPD was successful in some catholic villages in the Ruhr and not in others, it turns out that it is the aspect of social and cultural integration into a local catholic community which accounts best for political differences.[7]

A cultural perspective does not necessarily imply the notion of a particular regional culture as such. In a way, region may be nothing but a specific spatial allocation of general cultural variables. But often it is precisely this specific regional allocation of general cultural variables in past or present which accounts for qualitative cultural differences between regions. As can be shown again and again, the spatial constellation of denominations or classes has, as a rule, a great impact on the way members of a class or a denomination think and behave. Consequently, any attempt to reduce the regional factor to a 'regional residuum' – having first considered variables such as class, religion, etc. – is highly questionable if it is not controlled itself in the light of historical knowledge. From this would follow that not only variables but also methods and techniques of electoral research have to be put into historical context.[8]

Deviant regional cases, as have been mentioned above, can serve as valuable guides if one wants to avoid creating ahistorical artefacts. The lesson to be drawn from them is not that only when political behaviour cannot be fully 'explained' by structural factors should cultural variables also be considered, but rather the reverse. They are to be seen as clues which tell us something about what variables like class and religion really 'mean'. It is somewhat absurd to assume that cultural variables should only count in some cases and not in all. In reality they count in all, but become visible only in some. Thus the general conclusion is that all variables have to be defined in cultural and

6. See Gerhard A. Ritter, *Die deutschen Parteien 1830–1914. Parteien und Gesellschaft im konstitutionellen Regierungssystem*, Göttingen, 1985, p. 61; Adelheid v. Saldern, 'Wer ging in die SPD? Zur Analyse der Parteimitgliedschaft in wilhelminischer Zeit', in Gerhard A. Ritter (ed.), *Der Aufstieg der sozialistischen Arbeiterorganisationen zur Massenbewegung im deutschen Kaiserreich*, Munich, 1990.

7. See Karl Rohe, 'Konfession, Klasse und lokale Gesellschaft als Bestimmungsfaktoren des Wahlverhaltens. Überlegungen und Problematisierungen am Beispiel des historischen Ruhrgebiets', in L. Albertin and W. Link (eds), *Politische Parteien auf dem Weg zur parlamentarischen Demokratie in Deutschland. Festschrift für Erich Matthias*, Düsseldorf, 1981.

8. See Karl Rohe, 'Wahlanalyse im historischen Kontext. Zu Kontinuität und Wandel von Wahlverhalten', *Historische Zeitschrift*, vol. 234, 1982, pp. 337–57, esp. p. 350.

thereby in historical terms. There is no social structure as such but only structures which in one way or the other are shaped by cultures.

Without doubt, different manifestations of culture have to be distinguished. This can best be done by referring to Max Weber's famous dictum about the interplay of interests (material and non-material), *Weltbilder* and ideas: 'Interests (material and non-material), not: ideas, directly govern men's behaviour. But: "*Weltbilder*", which had been created by "ideas", very often functioned as pointsmen determining the frameworks in which the dynamics of interests moved men's actions.'[9] What Max Weber understands by non-material or 'symbolic' interests is by no means clear. But it makes sense to relate the distinction between material and non-material interests to another important distinction made by Weber, namely that between *Klassenlagen* (class positions) and *ständischen Lagen* (status positions) along which societies can differentiate. Thus material interests are to be related to class position, and non-material interests to status position, or, more generally, to ways of life which, in fact, do not exist without a material base but which in the last instance are founded on non-material interests.

Accordingly, three different kinds of cultural objectivation can be distinguished, which differ in their relation to social structure and social action:

(1) Ways of life, that is to say ideas or designs for living which do not belong to the realm of 'superstructure' but have become an integrated part of social structure. The non-material interests related to them are, therefore, as real and rational as material ones. And, as men are, after all, social beings and not simply rational calculators, it might even be argued that rational people primarily defend their ways of life rather than their material well-being.[10]

(2) *Weltbilder* or mentalities, that is to say ideas which have become an integrated part of people's heads and which constitute a frame of mind by which men's thinking, feelings and actions are conditioned.

(3) And finally ideas proper, that is to say those cultural meanings

---

9. Max Weber, *Gesammelte Aufsätze zur Religionssoziologie*, vol. 1, Tübingen, 1920, p. 252.

10. See Aaron Wildavsky, 'Choosing Preferences by Constructing Institutions: A Cultural Theory of Preference Formation', *American Political Science Review*, vol. 81, 1987, pp. 3–22.

which are produced, reproduced and communicated in society and which together make up a group's culture in the narrow sense of the word – so to speak its 'superstructure' as contrasted with other manifestations of culture which have become an integrated part of social structures or mentalities.

Weber generally assumes that men's actions are determined by their interests. This may seem too narrow an approach at first sight. It does, however, not mean that ideas – whether produced by intellectuals for others or by people's own historical experiences with social and political institutions – play no role. *Weltbilder* can be shaped by them and thereby not only the interpretation of interests, but social structures as well. What is excluded, indeed, is the notion that men are moved purely by abstract ideas. And it is at least arguable that only ideas which respond to people's mentalities and material and non-material interests are politically important. People must be able to recognize themselves with their own interests and aspirations if ideas are to attain actual force.

It has, however, to be stressed that a direct and not only an indirect influence of ideas on social and political behaviour should be taken into account. Cultural hegemony, which is not necessarily identical with a dominant *Weltbild* or mentality, matters in politics. Voting behaviour apparently is not only influenced by what people actually think in private, that is to say by their political mentalities, but also by what can be said and done in public, that is to say by prevailing public philosophies. What are basically the same political mentalities can, therefore, lead to a different voting behaviour, due to different cultural hegemonies at regional or national levels.

Accordingly, voting behaviour can be influenced by cultural factors in many ways. Following Weber, interests and situations are to be interpreted in the light of *Weltbilder* which, for example, depend very much on how much emphasis is laid either on short-term or long-term interests or on material and non-material factors. From this would follow that it is highly arbitrary to assume that material interests – regardless of time and space – are more important than non-material ones in determining social and political behaviour, and that the latter only count when the former have been satisfied. Secularized *Weltbilder*, in fact, may be structured like that, but this cannot simply be assumed without historical reasoning. It should, however, be noted that the relative political importance of non-material interests as compared to material ones depends not only on *Weltbilder*, and thereby on subjective interpretations of reality, but on objective social conditions as well. Non-material interests are always related to ways of life shared with others. It is, however, conceivable that historical situations and constellations are structured in such a way that no common ways of life have developed or are thought of. Thus it always depends on subjective *Weltbilder* and objective positions and situations whether and to what extent non-material interests are likely to influence political behaviour. It is, therefore, the specific historical constellation of *Weltbilder* and *Lagen* which have to be studied carefully if one wants to understand and explain political behaviour.

It is especially culture as a way of life and the related concept of non-material interests which perhaps can make us understand the rationale behind 'milieu voting' and other kinds of expressive voting which too easily are conceived of as non-rational forms of electoral behaviour. Milieu means basically nothing more than a distinct way of life shared with others and reproduced by daily practice. As a rule, the territorial aspect of grouping is stressed. But a 'milieu' is not necessarily a territorially defined community of individuals living in close proximity. What is, however, crucial when the term milieu is used in a meaningful way is that people should have something essential in common – not only in the way they think but in the way that they live. Ideologies may be important in making people more aware of their common non-material interests and in shaping their ways of life. But it should be noted that in principle milieus can exist without ideologies, which become more important when different milieus are to be integrated. Milieu, therefore, is a more restricted and specific concept than the concept of *Lager* or (sub)culture. Both do not necessarily imply the notion of a specific way of life. (Sub)cultures may be spoken of when a particular set of beliefs and values can be identified which is typical only of a certain grouping; or when ideas and symbols are produced which are only exchanged and communicated within the narrow confines of a subculture and which are basically ignored by a wider public. Culture as mentally-based orientations and culture as 'superstructure' are both politically important cultural institutions, but they have to be clearly distinguished from culture as a way of life.

Culture can also help us understand why some social cleavages were successfully translated into a stable party system and others not. If one takes a closer look at the cleavages in the Rokkan/Lipset tradition, one gets the impression that at the root of all cleavages which made a major political impact lie clashes between different cultures – at the root not only of the conflict between state and church, but also of class conflicts.

Material interests without cultural integration tend, it seems, to behave like prostitutes who change their masters according to time and circumstances and do not provide a basis on which enduring political coalitions can be built.

Political Parties and Regional Milieus in the Kaiserreich: A Complex Relationship

Until now, emphasis has exclusively been laid on the social and cultural sides of politics. It was thereby tacitly assumed that only the regional environments of party and electoral politics in the Kaiserreich differed, but that the same political animals were competing for votes in all regions. This position cannot be upheld. First of all, there were political parties based on regionalist movements like, for example, the *Welfenpartei* in the former independent kingdom of Hanover;[11] and there were others, like, for example, the Centre Party in the Rhineland, which, if not in name then certainly in substance, undoubtedly had some anti-Prussian regionalist connotations.[12] So political regionalism was a more widespread political phenomenon in the Kaiserreich than it may seem at first sight. It affected not only individual parties but regional party systems as a whole. For the foundation of political parties based on real or supposed regional or ethnic interests and sentiments or on those of a religious minority, such as the catholics, usually led to the emergence of regional party systems structured along the centre–periphery cleavage or, to put it more generally, along the conflict-lines between a dominant culture and a minority culture. This was a regional cleavage constellation in which by and large the National Liberal Party or its regional variations, like the *Deutsche Partei* in Württemberg[13] or the *Nationale Lager* in the Ruhr,[14] were the rallying points of all forces belonging to the dominant culture.

11. Michael John, 'Liberalism and Society in Germany, 1850–1880: The Case of Hanover', *English Historical Review*, vol. 102, 1987, pp. 579–98.
12. See on the Centre Party in the Rhineland Rudolf Morsey, 'Die Zentrumspartei in Rheinland und Westfalen', in Walter Förster (ed.), *Politik und Landschaft. Beiträge zur neueren Landesgeschichte des Rheinlandes und Westfalens*, vol. 3, Cologne, 1969, pp. 11–50; see, for an interesting contemporary Social Democratic view on this question, Walter Wehner (ed.), *Die Arbeiterbewegung im Ruhrgebiet. Eine Gabe an den Parteitag 1907 vom Sozialdemokratischen Verein Kreis Essen*, Essen, 1981, pp. 15–16. On the anti-Prussian liberal People's Party in Württemberg see James Clark Hunt, *The People's Party in Württemberg and Southern Germany 1890–1914*, Stuttgart, 1975.
13. On the particularities of the Württemberg party system see Wolfgang Schulte, *Struktur und Entwicklung des Parteisystems im Königreich Württemberg. Versuche zu einer quantitativen Analyse der Wahlergebnisse*, Ph.D. Mannheim, 1970.
14. See my chapter in this volume (pp. 107–44) and Karl Rohe, *Vom Revier zum*

Thus political parties, even if they were operating on a national scale, often greatly reflected a specific regional conflict constellation which undoubtedly was shaped by national issues as well. Accordingly, the political 'meaning' of a vote, especially for liberal parties, which were notorious for presenting different images in different regions, could differ tremendously from region to region – from sometimes being mainly an anti-catholic, an anti-separatist or an anti-socialist vote to being primarily a liberal vote in a proper and narrower sense of the word.[15] It can rightly be said that more or less all political parties in the Kaiserreich, even if they did not represent regional interests, had a distinctive regional character. To some extent this holds true of the SPD as well,[16] although it was by and large the only truly national party in Imperial Germany. Accordingly, political parties' strengths and weaknesses in different regions cannot be properly measured and analysed without referring to their regional shape and character, which enabled them to build up 'political coalitions' with different social strata and mentalities in different regions. So one has to be very careful when one relates regional election results to the national average, because it always has to be asked whether like is being compared with like.

In a sense the party system of the early Kaiserreich is to be understood as a loosely connected system of regional party systems which in many ways resembled the party system of Western Europe today as represented in the Strasburg assembly. This system was gradually transformed in the course of the nineteenth and early twentieth centuries. National issues came to dominate the political arena. At the end of the Kaiserreich in every other electoral district run-off elections had to be held. Political parties spread more evenly over the country and penetrated regions where hitherto they had been virtually non-existent. And in the Reichstag, there finally emerged a fairly stable five-party system consisting of the Conservatives, the catholic Centre Party, the National Liberals, the Left Liberals and the Social Democrats.[17] Some

Ruhrgebiet. Wahlen – Parteien – Politische Kultur, Essen, 1986; Karl Rohe in collaboration with Wolfgang Jäger and Uwe Dorow, 'Politische Gesellschaft und politische Kultur an der Ruhr 1848/49–1987', in Dietmar Petzina et al. (eds), *Das Ruhrgebiet im Industriezeitalter*, Düsseldorf, 1990.
15. See James Sheehan, *German Liberalism in the Nineteenth Century*, Chicago, 1978.
16. For south Germany see the chapter by Merith Niehuss in this volume, pp. 83–106. See also Merith Niehuss, 'Zur Schichtungsanalyse der SPD-Wähler in Bayern, 1890–1900', in Peter Steinbach (ed.), *Probleme politischer Partizipation im Modernisierungsprozeß*, Stuttgart, 1982, pp. 217f.
17. See Stefan Immerfall and Peter Steinbach, 'Politisierung und Nationalisierung

essential features of a regionally based party system, however, survived. The five-party system which had developed at the top level existed virtually nowhere at a regional level, where often a kind of three-party system gradually emerged, the specific configurations of which varied according to regional conditions and traditions.[18] It could range from a party system which was made up of the Centre Party, the SPD and a third political party, in most cases the National Liberal Party, which represented the *Nationale Lager*, to a party system as, for example, in the Hagen Reichstag constituency consisting of the Left Liberals, the National Liberals and the Socialists.

As has been convincingly demonstrated elsewhere,[19] the emergence of a popularly based party system in the 1860s and 1870s was not simply the 'natural' outcome of given cultural divisions in German society but the result of a complex interplay of social and political forces. Most cleavages, as it seems, originated from political manoeuvres, although they only became enduring cleavages when there was a receptive social base. Political calculations of the balance of power and strategic decisions by political elites, however, had to be taken not only at the national level but at regional levels as well. Given regional socio-cultural milieus were political potentials which still had to be realized. And this required not only strategic decisions about which conflict should be emphasized and which one not, but also what might be called political mechanisms. That is to say: means of political communication and mobilization which in principle may range from party organizations, mass media and organized interest groups to informal networks and local notables. There are examples, like the case of the SPD in the Ruhr during the era of the anti-socialist laws, which show how much the almost total lack of 'political mechanisms' at the local and regional levels greatly contributed to political failure;[20] and

deutscher Regionen im Kaiserreich', in Dirk Berg-Schlosser and Jakob Schissler (eds), *Politische Kultur in Deutschland. Bilanz und Perspektiven der Forschung*, Opladen, 1987, pp. 68–79.

18. See Brett Fairbairn, *The German Elections of 1898 and 1903*, Ph.D. Oxford, 1987, pp. 12–13, who summarizes the findings of other authors. For more information about possible political configurations in Reichstag constituencies and their explanation see the forthcoming dissertation by Stefan Immerfall, *Territorium und Wahlverhalten. Zur Erklärungskraft geoökonomischer und geopolitischer Entwicklungsprozesse*, Passau, 1990.

19. William Claggett et al., 'Political Leadership and the Development of Political Cleavages: Imperial Germany, 1871–1912', *American Journal of Political Science*, vol. 26, 1982, pp. 643–64. Heinrich Best, 'Politische Eliten, Wahlverhalten und Sozialstruktur: theoretische Aspekte historisch und interkulturell vergleichender Analysen', in idem (ed.), *Politik und Milieu. Wahl- und Elitenforschung im historischen und interkulturellen Vergleich*, St Katharinen, 1989, especially pp. 15–17.

20. As a case-study for the Ruhr see Karl Rohe, 'Die "verspätete Region". Thesen und Hypothesen zur Wahlentwicklung im Ruhrgebiet vor 1914', in Peter Steinbach

there are others, like the belated foundation of the Centre Party in Württemberg,[21] which demonstrate how much depended on strategic decisions made by regional elites. So it might be argued in general that it was always the regional constellation of milieus, elites and available political mechanisms which explains the emergence of specific regional party systems and which made for political failure or political success.

Political mechanisms are not only crucial for communicating the ideology and the character of a political party to potential voters; they also provide means by which given interests and mentalities to some extent can be changed. In principle, therefore, the necessary 'fit between the general character of a party and the voters' own general ideology' which 'best accounts for electoral choice'[22] can be attained either by a party adapting itself to a given social and cultural environment or by attempting to adapt the environment to a party's own ideology.

All parties in one way or the other had to come to terms with pre-existing cultural conditions in different regions if they wanted to be successful; but what the example of 'cultivator' parties, like the SPD and to a lesser degree that of the Centre Party, demonstrate is that regional milieus were not simply givens but could to some extent be politically made. Accordingly, the basic relationship between political parties and social milieus and the political mechanisms on which these connections were primarily founded could be very different. Social Democratic milieus in general and Centre Party milieus in urban areas very much depended on organizations and associations, whereas conservative and liberal milieus, as a rule, heavily relied on local notables and informal relations.

Even within the same party the relationship between party and milieu could be very different. Ratios between SPD voters on the one hand and figures of party membership and membership in socialist organizations on the other seem, for example, to indicate that the SPD in some parts of the Reich was, indeed, very much a socialist *Milieupartei* which reflected the milieus created around the socialist working-class movement and its organizations; in others, however, it might better be understood as a party which had been able to establish a stable 'political coalition' with pre-existing industrial workers' or miners'

(ed.), *Probleme politischer Partizipation im Modernisierungsprozeß*, Stuttgart, 1982, pp. 231–52.
   21. See Blackbourn, *Class, Religion*.
   22. Anthony Heath, Roger Jowell and John Curtice, *How Britain Votes*, Oxford, 1985, p. 9.

milieus without very much changing them. And in some parts of the Reich it has to be seen primarily as a broad and diffuse protest movement without stable milieu foundations at all.[23] The National Liberal Party, too, often was not a *Milieupartei* in the proper sense of the word but a broad *Sammlungsbewegung* collecting rather different social milieus and individuals whose only common feature was that they were neither attached to socialism nor to political catholicism or to regionalist movements.

Such findings suggest that we should qualify some assumptions about the milieu foundations of the German party system in the Kaiserreich. It has been rightly pointed out that there are apparently more variations in time and space and more changes over time than normally are thought of when one speaks of *Milieuparteien*.[24] Not only has a certain volatility in voting behaviour to be reckoned with but processes of de-alignment and re-alignment which took place between 1867 and 1912 must be taken into account as well.

Stability and change of individual voting behaviour is one thing; stability and change of political institutions is another. Surely, political programmes, like menus, will only be kept if people continue to select from them, but at least in principle this may be done by very different people. Thus, even if one accepts the fact that the percentage of 'affirming voters' amounted to about two-thirds of all voters in the Kaiserreich,[25] the changing generational composition of the electorate has to be borne in mind as well as the growing voting turn-outs. The 'affirmers' who created a popularly based party system in the 1870s were only partly identical with those who upheld it in 1912. While in 1871 almost 50% of the electorate were born between 1807 and 1830, this group amounted to only about 1% of the electorate in 1912.[26]

In order to understand and to explain these phenomena, it seems that concepts which go beyond the confines of individualistic approaches are required, such as the milieu concept. Milieu is a group concept of voting which, contrary to class concepts and related sociological approaches, stresses the cultural dimension of groups. In contrast to the cleavage concept, it emphasizes the overlapping of

23. See, for example, Karl Rohe, 'Die Ruhrgebietssozialdemokratie im Wilhelminischen Kaiserreich und ihr politischer und kultureller Kontext', in Ritter, *Der Aufstieg*; see in general Saldern, 'Wer ging in die SPD?'
24. See Sheehan, 'Klasse und Partei', p. 21.
25. Suval, *Electoral Politics*, p. 56.
26. See Monika Neugebauer-Wölk, *Wählergenerationen in Preußen zwischen Kaiserreich und Republik. Versuch zu einem Kontinuitätsproblem des protestantischen Preußen in seinen Kernprovinzen*, Berlin, 1987.

social, religious and regional factors and, in addition, is not bound to define groups in terms of polarities or conflict. Like the party identification model, it assumes that voters have developed a longstanding loyalty to a party which is expressed in the voting act. But contrary to the party identification model, it holds that voters do so not so much as individuals but rather as members of a group which has established a stable political coalition with a political party in the past. Consequently, voting is primarily to be seen as an expression, not of party identification, but of group identification.

The milieu concept has its shortcomings. One of its problematic aspects is that it tends to blind us to hidden changes which may have taken place in the basic relationship between party and society in the Kaiserreich and about which we know next to nothing. What originally started as a milieu foundation could well have ended up as a relationship primarily based on individual orientations, ideologies or material interests. Not the variables as such, but the 'meaning' of variables like the percentage of catholics or that of working-class members may have changed, and thereby the social foundations of party politics.

It is precisely for that reason that analytical distinctions between ways of life, mentalities and ideologies become crucial. Thus the milieu concept has always to be firmly put into historical context and to be seen as a tool for historical analysis to be used with some care. But it should not be abandoned altogether, since, properly understood and carefully used, it is still able to explain some essential features of political society in the Kaiserreich and beyond. One of its potential strengths is that by introducing concepts like ways of life and non-material interests it tries to provide a combined answer to the questions of how and why the party system was reproduced and political coalitions between political parties and parts of the electorate were upheld.

There is, however, a certain danger in the traditional notion of milieu that collective party identification is taken too much for granted. Alignments between social groupings and political parties are not a single act which can be forged once and for all at a moment when the 'seminal political accumulation' takes place. For, although there existed what might be called a law of political primacy and although it was difficult for a new political party to get in once stable political coalitions had been established in a region, it has to be stressed that stability and continuity of political alignment was not a 'natural' phenomenon. Political coalitions had to be carefully nurtured by elites.

This meant that political parties had to adapt to changing circumstances in order to keep up political alignments and to the interests of their potential voters.[27] Not all policies, however, were of equal importance. Despite the growing significance of interest politics, parties had primarily to be sensitive to those issues that tackled the cultural basis which the political coalition was originally built upon. More than that, they were more or less forced to reconstruct artificially the original cleavages and to renew their 'meanings' from time to time by symbolic politics – the more so the more imperatives of power politics in the constituencies and the daily routine of pragmatic politics threatened to make the cultural ties between parties and milieus less visible and less conscious.

By doing so, not only at election campaigns but more or less regularly by newspapers, associations and informal contacts, political parties were shaping and reshaping regional political cultures. Thus milieu parties not only have to been seen as products of regional cultures but as their producers as well, even if they were not 'cultivator' parties like the SPD. The permanent exposure to different parties and party systems and to the political symbols and political propaganda connected with them led to what might be called a regionally differentiated political education of the German people. The impact of political socialization carried out by parties and party systems should not be underestimated as German political parties were always not simply political teams competing for political power and influence but institutions which in one way or the other wanted to preach to people and to educate them. And at least political catholicism and the socialist working-class movement had the ability to do so, because they had built up powerful cultural institutions of their own, independent of state institutions, ranging from trade unions to leisure-time associations and to the socialist and catholic press.

In many ways the cultural influence exerted by these institutions was a transregional one. This holds true not only of the SPD, which perhaps rightly may be considered the only real 'national' influence in Imperial Germany outside state institutions, but of the Centre Party as well. Catholic institutions, such as the Volksverein für das katholische Deutschland founded in 1890, played a powerful role in creating more homogenized catholic milieus in Germany. It might even be said that regional and local traditions and constellations became less important and that accordingly the concept of a regionally defined milieu is less

---

27. This has especially been pointed out by David Blackbourn, *Class, Religion and Local Politics in Wilhelmine Germany. The Centre Party in Württemberg before 1914*, Wiesbaden, 1980.

convincing at the end of the Kaiserreich than at the beginning.[28]

The political arena, no doubt, became more nationalized. In the 1870s issues like, for example, the *Kulturkampf* had to be 'translated' in order to be understood in some protestant regions.[29] This was no longer the case by the end of the Kaiserreich, but there hardly developed what might be called a national political milieu, that is to say a national way of life. Recent research on political elites even seems to indicate that political class became more regionalized by the end of the period than it had been at the beginning.[30] And given the still highly regionalized party systems and the uneven regional distribution of socialist and catholic subcultures, it might even be argued that in the era of mass politics some cultural differences between regions became more articulate than before. The political notion of 'we' and 'they' and thereby the notion of which social cleavages were to be considered the most important ones in political life, those between 'Black', the colour which symbolised catholicism, and 'Blue', the colour representing protestantism, those between 'Blue' and 'Red' or those between 'Black' and 'Red', still showed strong regional variations. It should also not be overlooked that the different cultures, especially the catholic as compared to the dominant protestant-secularist culture, not only differed in their specific attitudes to the Kaiserreich but in their basic understanding of the state and its proper relationship to society. And if one further assumes that political orientations are shaped by political ideas and by historical experiences with institutions, some traces of this regionally diverse political socialization should be found in later times. Diachronic analyses of political language point in this direction. Former ways of life and former interpretations of reality can partly survive as political mentalities, even if neither the old institutions nor the former ideological indoctrination any longer exist. The Ruhr is a very good example of this.

28. See for a general discussion of this problem Karl Rohe, 'Das Parteiensystem in den preußischen Westprovinzen und in Lippe-Detmold 1877–1933', in Ulrich v. Alemann (ed.), *Parteien und Wahlen in Nordrhein-Westfalen*, Cologne, 1985, pp. 22–47, esp. pp. 31–3.

29. See Peter Steinbach, 'Historische Wahlforschung und regionalspezifische Politikrezeption. Diskussionsbeitrag über einen Forschungsansatz', in Otto Büsch (ed.), *Wählerbewegung in der europäischen Geschichte. Ergebnisse einer Konferenz*, Berlin, 1980, pp. 23–39.

30. See Heinrich Best, 'Politische Modernisierung und parlamentarische Führungsgruppen in Deutschland 1867–1918', *Historische Sozialforschung*, vol. 13, 1988, pp. 5–75.

From Weimar to Bonn: Persistence and Decline of *Milieuparteien*

Because of its constitutional arrangements and its electoral system of proportional representation which stressed party rather than territory, the Weimar Republic furthered tendencies which might be put under the heading: from region to nation. Some traditional political mechanisms no longer fitted the new political realities and 'modern' political mechanisms such as ideologies and organizations became crucial requirements if political parties were to survive. It is of no surprise that especially the liberals, who had heavily relied on local *Honoratioren* and informal structures in the past and proved more or less unable to develop new transregional media, soon encountered difficulties.

So, in a way, the decline of *Milieuparteien* preceded the rise of the Nazi Party which, as has been claimed,[31] marks the end of the traditional German system of *Milieuparteien*. But how far can this interpretation be upheld and in what sense was the NSDAP in fact an anti-*Milieupartei*? As far as the social basis of the NSDAP voters is concerned, much can be said for describing it as the first German *Volkspartei* (catch-all party).[32] But from a cultural perspective some qualifications have to be made.

The rise of the Nazi Party had a distinctive regional pattern.[33] One is in a better position to forecast the Nazi Party's regional strength if one knows not only the social composition of the regional electorate but its voting behaviour in the Kaiserreich and in the early Weimar Republic as well, that is to say its politico-cultural composition. From this would follow that the NSDAP, apparently, was much less of a cultural mix than it was a social one. Although it was partly successful among catholics and among workers as well, it never became what might be called a genuine political expression of catholic or working-class milieus. Except for a few cases, it was not really able to conquer and penetrate the local/regional milieus which were historically connected with political catholicism or the socialist working-class movement, in

---

31. Lepsius, 'Parteiensystem'.
32. See the chapter by Jürgen Falter in this volume (pp. 53–82). See also the most useful article by Falter, 'Die Wählerpotentiale politischer Teilkulturen 1920–1933', in Detlev Lehnert and Klaus Megerle (eds), *Politische Identität und nationale Gedenktage. Zur politischen Kultur in der Weimarer Republik*, Opladen, 1989, pp. 281–305.
33. See Nico Passchier, 'The Electoral Geography of the Nazi Landslide. The Need for Community Studies', in Stein U. Larsen et al. (eds), *Who were the Fascists? Social Roots of European Fascism*, Bergen, 1980, pp. 283–300.

contrast to milieus which were directly attached to the dominant protestant-secularist culture.

So in some regions and localities the NSDAP was an anti-*Milieupartei* par excellence which, not unlike the KPD,[34] relied heavily on those who were living at the fringes of local and regional societies. As a consequence of the First World War, of inflation and unemployment, the percentage of people who belonged to this category had greatly increased as compared to the Kaiserreich, especially among the younger generation.[35] In other regions and localities, however, the NSDAP represented the interests and feelings of traditional local milieus which did not crumble but only temporarily exchanged their political masters.[36] So from a cultural point of view the NSDAP as a whole appears to have been, similar to the National Liberal Party in some parts of Germany before the First World War, a broad national rally containing very different elements, namely parochial milieus under the leadership of local notables on the one hand and individuals who for one reason or the other no longer lived within the confines of traditional local and regional communities on the other.

From this would follow that the political impact of social milieus and thereby the era of *Milieuparteien* did not necessarily come to an end after 1945, despite the fact that, as a consequence of the Nazi era and the war as well as the social uprooting accompanied by them, the percentage of the electorate who were no longer integrated in local and regional societies had greatly increased. So the social and cultural foundations of the traditional system of *Milieuparteien* had been diminished indeed. But one would, nevertheless, grossly misunderstand postwar political developments in the Federal Republic without due regard to the regional and milieu dimension of party politics. In the first years after its foundation the CDU was essentially nothing other

34. See, for example, the interesting study by Günter Plum on the catholic milieu and its partial dissolution, *Gesellschaftsstruktur und politisches Bewußtsein in einer katholischen Region, 1928–1933. Untersuchung am Beispiel des Regierungsbezirk Aachen*, Stuttgart, 1972. This is not to say that the NSDAP was especially successful in mobilizing the unemployed.

35. See, for example, the articles by Geary, Rosenhaft and others in Richard J. Evans (ed.), *The German Unemployed: Experiences and Consequences of Mass Unemployment from the Weimar Republic to the Third Reich*, London, 1987; Detlev J. K. Peukert, 'Die Erwerbslosigkeit junger Arbeiter in der Weltwirtschaftskrise in Deutschland 1929–1933', in *Vierteljahresschrift für Sozial- und Wirtschaftsgeschichte*, vol. 72, 1985, pp. 305–28.

36. See the classical study of Rudolf Heberle, *Landbevölkerung und Nationalsozialismus*, Stuttgart, 1963. See also, for example, William S. Allen, *The Nazi Seizure of Power: The Experience of a Single German Town, 1922–1945*, rev. edn, New York, 1984; Rudy Koskar, *Social Life, Local Politics, and Nazism. Marburg, 1880–1935*, Chapel Hill and London, 1986, esp. pp. 204–5; Richard F. Hamilton, *Who Voted for Hitler?*, Princeton, 1982, esp. pp. 364–71. See also idem, 'Hitler's Electoral Support: Recent Findings and Theoretical Implications', *Canadian Journal of Sociology*, vol. 11, 1986, pp. 1–34, esp. p. 3.

than a national collection of regional milieus. In some parts of West Germany like Oldenburg, Württemberg and Franconia, however, not the CDU, but the FDP was the local *Milieupartei* which was supported by the *Honoratioren*. It should be noted that the FDP-founders had been divided on the issue of whether organized liberalism was better to be rebuilt on the model of a *nationale Sammlungsbewegung* or on that of a *Milieupartei*.[37]

At least in the first decade after 1945 political parties could and actually did develop very different regional characters. This holds especially true of the CDU which encompassed not only different regional milieus but different political traditions as well. Consequently the 'meaning' of a vote for the CDU in Sleswick-Holstein differed from that, let us say, in the Rhineland or in the Ruhr. In the Rhineland and in the Ruhr it was basically a successor party to political catholicism, in Sleswick-Holstein it attracted liberal and protestant regional traditions and milieus which had temporarily built up a 'political coalition' with the NSDAP. In other regions it was the FDP, and in some parts of Hesse and the Ruhr it was the SPD which became heir to traditions and milieus of the old *Nationale Lager*. So the much tabooed question of where the former Nazis went to after 1945 has to be answered differently according to region – and according to generation and social class as well.

There is today, it seems, a renewed interest among political scientists in the regional dimensions of electoral and party politics in West Germany. Some interesting research on continuity and change of regional political traditions after 1945 has, for example, been done on Lower Saxony,[38] on the Ruhr and North Rhine Westphalia[39] and on Bavaria.[40] In 1987, a Freiburg scholar published a book on Baden-Württemberg which tried to explain the remarkable regional weakness of the Württemberg SPD and the correspondingly unusual strength of the CDU.[41] In the same year a conference was held at the Bergsträsser Institute at Freiburg on parties and regional political cultures in the

37. See Dieter Hein, *Zwischen Milieupartei und nationaler Sammlungsbewegung. Gründung, Entwicklung und Struktur der Freien Demokratischen Partei 1945–1949*, Düsseldorf, 1985.

38. Wolfgang Gunther (ed.), *Sozialer und Politischer Wandel in Oldenburg, Studien zur Regionalgeschichte vom 17. bis 20. Jahrhundert*, Oldenburg, 1981; Wolfgang Günther (ed.), *Parteien und Wahlen in Oldenburg. Beiträge zur Landesgeschichte im 19. und 20. Jahrhundert*, Oldenburg, 1983.

39. See, for example, Herbert Kühr, 'Die CDU in Nordrhein-Westfalen. Von der Unionsgründung zur modernen Mitgliederpartei', in Alemann, *Parteien und Wahlen*, pp. 91–120 and other articles in this book.

40. See the chapter by Alf Mintzel in this volume (pp. 145–78); Alf Mintzel, *Die CSU. Anatomie einer konservativen Partei 1945–1972*, Opladen, 2nd edn, 1978.

41. Gerd Mielke, *Sozialer Wandel und politische Dominanz in Baden-Württemberg. Eine*

Federal Republic,[42] and a group of political scientists generally interested in political culture also did some very useful work on regional political cultures.[43] So there has emerged a new sensitivity and a new consciousness of the regional foundations of political parties in Germany and of the transformation which took place after 1945 at the regional and local levels.

What emerges very clearly from Naßmacher and his associates' research on Lower Saxony[44] is that the traditional system of *Milieuparteien* was quickly re-established after the war. This applies not only to the catholic and Social Democratic milieus but to the old liberal and Hanoverian party milieus as well. Although diminished in size the latter provided a convenient local base for the FDP or the *Deutsche Partei*, which were the parties originally supported by the local notables, whereas in the beginning the CDU had mainly to rely on newcomers and immigrants. This gradually changed. The CDU was able to integrate the milieus connected to the *Deutsche Partei*, whereas during the era of the Social–Liberal coalition in Bonn, the FDP more or less lost its traditional milieu foundations not only in Oldenburg, but also in Hesse, Franconia, Coburg-Gotha and Württemberg.

Naßmacher suggests that this political transformation, contrary to what happened in the 1930s, meant the end of the traditional German system of *Milieuparteien*, and that since then studying local milieus has become a question of 'political archeology'. His suggestions are very persuasive, especially if one further thinks of the impact which the drastic change in mass communication is likely to have had on local and regional milieus. However, more empirical research is needed before one definitely can answer the question why precisely the drift of the liberal voters to the NSDAP is to be understood as a temporary political occupation of a milieu, whereas the drift of the FDP-voters to the CDU should be interpreted as its dissolution.

The end of the *Milieuparteien*-thesis does not necessarily imply the notion that the political past no longer plays any role today. Former

---

politikwissenschaftliche Analyse des Zusammenhangs von Sozialstruktur und Wahlverhalten in einer ländlichen Region, Berlin, 1987.

42. The results of the conference have been published by Dieter Oberndörfer and Karl Schmitt under the title: *Parteien und regionale politische Traditionen in der Bundesrepublik Deutschland*, Berlin, 1990.

43. See Berg-Schlosser/Schissler, *Politische Kultur*, pp. 250–308.

44. See Karl-Heinz Naßmacher, 'Zerfall einer liberalen Subkultur – Kontinuität und Wandel des Parteiensystems in der Region Oldenburg', in Herbert Kühr (ed.), *Vom Milieu zur Volkspartei. Funktionen und Wandlungen der Parteien im kommunalen und regionalen Bereich*, Königstein, Ts., 1979, pp. 30–134; idem, *Parteien im Abstieg. Wiederbegründung und Niedergang von DP, DZP und FDP in Jahren 1945–1965*, Opladen, 1989.

ways of life can, so to speak, survive as mentalities. Just to illustrate the point: people can have lost all contacts with their churches but still stick to traditional christian values.[45] This may be one of the explanations why catholics who no longer belong to a catholic milieu still show a stronger preference for the CDU than their protestant equivalents.[46] At the same time, this would mean that the over-representation of catholics among CDU-voters today not so much reflects the old confessional cleavage but the higher preference of catholics for traditional values.[47]

In some regions, however, it was the SPD and not the CDU which was able to incorporate political traditions which had once existed outside the socialist camp. It is precisely this aspect which makes the Ruhr such an interesting case.[48] The regional party system and voters' political alignments changed dramatically; but so did the character of the Social Democratic Party in the Ruhr which rose from a marginal position before the war to unquestioned regional hegemony today. This was not simply due to social change. Consciously or unconsciously the SPD adapted to political mentalities which had been shaped by non-socialist forces in the past. Therefore, it has to be asked what changed more, the political party or its contexts, and whether a political party which now scores between 50% and 60% of the vote as compared to about 10–15% at the end of the Weimar Republic can still be considered the same party.

So there may be more continuity in voting behaviour in the Ruhr than at first sight appears, because what are basically the same cultural dispositions and preferences can be expressed by different political parties according to time and circumstances. From this would follow that traditional research on party systems and voting behaviour should be complemented by research on political traditions, cultures, milieus and mentalities and how they find their party political expressions in different historical situations. In a sense, the turn from the history of the working-class movement to the history of the workers and the working class could set the example which research on continuity and change of political parties should follow.

45. See, for example, Ursula Boos-Nünning and Egon Golomb, *Religiöses Verhalten im Wandel. Untersuchungen in einer Industriegesellschaft*, Essen, 1974.

46. See the chapter by Karl Schmitt in this volume (pp. 179–202).

47. See Franz Urban Pappi, 'Sozialstruktur, gesellschaftliche Wertorientierungen und Wahlabsicht. Ergebnisse eines Zeitvergleichs des deutschen Elektorats 1953 und 1976', in *Politische Vierteljahresschrift*, vol. 18, 1977, pp. 195–229; idem, 'Das Wahlverhalten sozialer Gruppen bei Bundestagswahlen im Zeitvergleich', in Hans-Dieter Klingemann and Max Kaase (eds), *Wahlen und politischer Prozeß. Analysen aus Anlaß der Bundestagswahl 1983*, Opladen, 1986, pp. 369–84.

48. See my chapter in this volume (pp. 107–44).

So regional and milieu factors directly or indirectly have influenced and still do influence party political developments in the Federal Republic. It can justly be claimed that taking a regional and historical view even today gives us a deeper insight and a better understanding of political life in West Germany. But it is also fair to say that regional traditions and milieus no longer play the same political role today as they played in the past.

New Milieus and New Regionalism?

Two further reservations, however, have to be made. During the last two decades West German society has envisaged the emergence of new milieus and new social movements which until now have found their main political expression in the 'Greens', although, as Franz Urban Pappi tries to show,[49] this may not necessarily be the case in the future. Alternative milieus certainly are milieus in the sense in which the term is used here, namely that they not only represent distinct ways of thinking but stand for distinct ways of life. To this extent they are similar to the old milieus. There are, however, two main differences. Traditional milieus never were simply territorial communities. They were always mixtures of territorial and functional identities[50] the relevance of which could vary in time and space. But the concept of regionally based *Milieuparteien*, nevertheless, rested on the assumption that territorial constellations and traditions were important and that it mattered politically where a catholic or a worker lived, in Saxony or in the Ruhr, in Cologne or in Essen. The new milieus, however, are not territorial communities but milieus which happened to have settled somewhere.[51] The territorial dimension is no longer constitutive.

To some extent this reminds us of the old socialist milieus and partly of the old catholic urban milieus as well, which displayed strong transregional features. But what makes for a decisive difference is the

---

49. See the chapter by Franz Urban Pappi in this volume, pp. 203–22. On the Greens as a *Milieupartei* and the problems connected with it see Hans-Joachim Veen, 'The Greens as a Milieu Party', in Eva Kolinsky (ed.), *The Greens in West Germany: Organisation and Policy Making*, Oxford, New York, Munich, 1989, pp. 31–59.
50. See for this distinction Seymour Lipset and Stein Rokkan, 'Cleavage Structures, Party Systems, and Voter Alignments: An Introduction', in Seymour Lipset and Stein Rokkan (eds), *Party Systems and Voter Alignments: Cross-National Perspectives*, London, 1967, pp. 1–64, esp. pp. 11–13.
51. See Rohe, 'Wahlanalyse'.

element of choice. Formerly, people were more or less born into a milieu, whereas the new milieus have to a high degree become a question of choice; today this even applies partly to the old milieus as well. Belonging to a catholic parish community or being a member of the local community has also widely become a matter of choice. So the old local and regional milieus have changed their character and diminished in size, but they still exist. It should not be overlooked that even today about 50% of the German population live in the same place as they were born, and that at least a proportion of the newcomers have become integrated members of local and regional communities by joining local associations. There still can be found what has been called *heimatbezogene Gemeinschaften*, that is to say local communities emotionally committed to *Heimat*. What has, however, to be studied with some care is whether and to what extent local communities still have preserved some of their former political salience which after all was the very precondition of the old system of *Milieuparteien*.

The same question has to be raised with regard to life styles.[52] Are political parties still rooted in milieus, life styles and different regional and local traditions? CDU/CSU and SPD are, of course, no longer *Milieuparteien* in the old meaning of the term. They have, however, not simply become catch-all parties, but are complex entities which reflect different historical stages of party development[53] and, it should be added, different regional traditions as well.

Is there a distinct milieu behind the new party of the Republikaner[54] which could be compared to that of the Greens? This party, which is overrepresented among young males, is still a somewhat diffuse political phenomenon. It partly reflects social protest in working-class districts and among peasants in the countryside and partly a kind of 'national' protest. That is to say, the party is to some extent an attempt

52. As to the concept of life styles or social milieus see: Sinus, *Planungsdaten für die Mehrheitsfähigkeit der SPD. Ein Forschungsprojekt des Vorstands der SPD*, Bonn, 1984. Sceptical of its political relevance Hans-Joachim Veen and Peter Gluchovski, 'Tendenzen der Nivellierung und Polarisierung in den Wählerschaften von CDU/CSU und SPD von 1959–1983. Eine Fortschreibung', *Zeitschrift für Parlamentsfragen*, vol. 14, 1983, pp. 545–55; see also Michael T. Greven, *Parteimitglieder. Ein empirischer Essay über das Alltagsbewußtsein in Parteien*, Opladen, 1987, p. 124.

53. See Gordon Smith, 'Europäische Parteiensysteme – Stationen einer Entwicklung?', in Jürgen W. Falter, Christian Fenner and Michael T. Greven (eds), *Politische Willensbildung und Interessenvermittlung*, Opladen, 1984, pp. 14–22.

54. See Dieter Roth, 'Sind die Republikaner die fünfte Partei?' and Norbert Lepzsy, 'Die Republikaner', both in *Aus Politik und Zeitgeschichte*, vol. B41–2, 1989, pp. 10–20 and 3–9. See also FORSA Analysen, *Rechtsanwälte in einer SRD-Hochburg – dargestellt am Beispiel des Dortmunder Nordens*, 15 July 1989, Dortmund. See in general Claus Leggewie, *Die Republikaner. Phantombild der neuen Rechten*, Berlin, 1989.

to revive the old national cleavage in German party politics which in the decade after the war was partly represented by the conflict between an Adenauer-CDU and a Schumacher-SPD. At the same time it is an anti-establishment movement which cannot be reduced to 'national' or social protest. It seems to have historical roots in populist traditions of some regions. This would partly explain why the Republikaner are not only overrepresented in some regions where the *Nationale Lager* in the nineteenth century and later the NSDAP were strong but also in some catholic regions where these parties were extremely weak. So it is still too early to answer the question whether there really exists what might be called a 'Republican' milieu, although some hints point in that direction.

The second point which makes one hesitate to give up the concept of region and milieu altogether is a growing tendency among German Länder governments to create or even to invent territorial identities and traditions of their own and to connect them to the ruling party in the land. The admired model, of course, is Bavaria. During the last Landtag election in North Rhine Westphalia, for example, the ruling SPD consciously imitated the CSU model and created the most successful slogan 'Wir in Nordrhein-Westfalen'.[55]

The idea behind this is certainly the search for new mechanisms upon which mass loyalties can be built – given the fact that class and religion are no longer as powerful as they were in the past. Regional identities based on Länder and traditional regional milieus are different phenomena. And there is often a certain tension between old regional identities and these new ones. Alf Mintzel has shown that Bavarian political culture which, as he claims, is basically a postwar phenomenon to a great extent masterminded by the Bavarian state-party, the CSU, tends to make traditional regional cultures within Bavaria more and more a matter of political folklore.[56] But still, in a way the oldest mechanism on which political loyalties were built upon, namely territory, comes in again at the very moment when the old political milieus are threatened with being 'folklorized' and new 'de-territorialized' milieus are emerging.

The prospects of this new kind of regional loyalty are a question of debate. It has primarily a political basis, not a cultural or an economic

55. See Lutz Niethammer et al. (eds), *'Die Menschen machen ihre Geschichte nicht aus freien Stücken, aber sie machen sie selbst.' Einladung zu einer Geschichte des Volkes in NRW*, Berlin, 1985.
56. See Alf Mintzel, 'Besonderheiten der Politischen Kultur Bayerns – Facetten und Etappen einer politisch-kulturellen Homogenisierung', in Berg-Schlosser/Schissler, *Politische Kultur*, pp. 295–308.

one, although a widening of the economic gulf between a rich south and a poor north could provide an economic basis as well. But on the whole, the Federal Republic is regionally fairly homogeneous and has not produced, except for the case of Bavaria, a regionalized party system like the Kaiserreich. Still, the federal structure of the political system in the Federal Republic is in many ways strongly reflected in the organizational structures of political parties and in the ways in which they recruit political elites. The German state parties (*Landesparteien*) are institutions of their own and influential organizations, although their influence is stronger within the CDU than in the SPD and although within the *Landesverbände* the older regional groupings often still play an important role.

There can, however, be no doubt that the *Landesparteien*, as a rule, have developed distinctive regional images and characters. The North Rhine Westphalian SPD, for example, is in many ways a different political animal, as compared to its Bavarian or Württemberg counterparts. There are several factors which explain this phenomenon, but among them are different political traditions not only of the respective political parties but of the regions as a whole, to which political parties had to adapt, especially when they became governing parties in the Land. And this leads on to a further point. There does exist what has been called 'political regionalism'.[57] Political contexts, that is to say political hegemony or minority status of a party over a long time, tend to become factors which influence the behaviour of voters, not to speak of the behaviour of power-seeking elites.

So a politically based Länder 'regionalism' is not necessarily without social foundations, although it is not rooted in a common way of life as the old regionally based milieus were. The experience of common government and administration, however, as has been proved in the past, is a possible source out of which regional identity can be built. And it must not be overlooked that even in the past political cultures and political milieus to some extent were politically made and that political coalitions between political parties and social milieus could differ from region to region. Thus one cannot exclude the possibility that the Länder, even if some of them are somewhat artificial creations without much historical foundation, might well become centres of regional loyalties and of party identifications based on them. Voting

---

57. Gerd Mielke, 'Sozialstruktur, politische Traditionen und Parteiensystem in Baden-Württemberg', in Oberndörfer, Schmitt and Mielke, *Parteien und regionale politische Kultur*.

behaviour at the last European and Bundestag elections seems to indicate that a Länder-based regional pattern, or what the Institute for Applied Social Science (Infas) called 'the peculiar political milieu of the Federal states',[58] is re-emerging in the Federal Republic.

58. Ursula Feist and Klaus Liepelt, 'Stärkung und Gefährdung der sozialliberalen Koalition. Das Ergebnis der Bundestagswahl vom 5. 10. 1980', in *Zeitschrift für Parlamentsfragen*, vol. 1, 1981, p. 35. See also idem, 'Volksparteien auf dem Prüfstand: Die SPD und ihre regionalen politischen Traditionen' (unpublished paper, 18 September 1989).

GERHARD A. RITTER

The Social Bases of the German Political Parties, 1867–1920

The social bases of the German parties in the period preceding the beginning of the Weimar Republic have received little study until now. This is due in part to the fact that most of the German parties in Imperial Germany were relatively disjointed organizations whose main focus of activity lay in the parliamentary bodies of the Reich and its constituent states. In the individual communities and electoral districts, an active group of party supporters nominated candidates for the forthcoming elections and supported these candidates in the election campaign. However, for quite a long period of time there did not exist a clearly defined party membership. To some extent this was a consequence of the Law of Association, which until 1899 forbade the formation of centralized political parties in Prussia, where approximately three-fifths of the national population lived, as well as in some other states. This law forced party organizations in communities and electoral districts to maintain only very loose links with each other and with the central bodies of the party.

However, the Law of Association alone did not shape party organizations. Even after the law's repeal, the lack of willingness on the part of supporters to associate themselves closely with a party, as well as concern on the part of parliamentary party leaders that they might lose control of their parties, deterred them from organizing party membership. This meant that the discussion of questions of party politics and even the mobilization of voters devolved mainly on to separate organizations allied with but detached from the parties.[1] Therefore, we have either no statistical record of party membership at all for the period preceding 1914 or only data limited to a few regions of the German Reich, as in the case of the Social Democrats until 1906.

Methods and Sources for the Study of the German Electorate

This chapter, therefore, limits itself to the study of party voters and is based on the systematic analysis of official election statistics, which have been published in relatively great detail.[2] The votes cast between 1874 and 1918 in the 397 electoral districts of the Reich or in the state legislative elections were correlated with the social, economic and denominational character of the states and the administrative districts of the German Reich. This information was obtained primarily from the statistics available on trade, occupation and religious persuasion. Also analysed were the statistical data available since 1898 on the vote in communities of various orders of size, namely rural communities, small towns and middle-sized to large cities.

Local and regional historical research, which has grown considerably in importance in the last decade, has greatly expanded our knowledge of the political processes at the microlevel and of their relationships to social, economic and denominational structures for individual regions and cities.

Some of the best of these studies have been carried out by Karl Rohe on the Ruhr area.[3] These and other studies have given a more definite

1. For the organization of German parties see the study by Thomas Nipperdey, *Die Organisation der deutschen Parteien vor 1918*, Düsseldorf, 1961.
2. See the bibliography in Gerhard A. Ritter with the co-operation of Merith Niehuss, *Wahlgeschichtliches Arbeitsbuch. Materialien zur Statistik des Kaiserreichs, 1871–1918*, Munich, 1980. The book summarizes and analyses the election results for the Reichstag of the German Reich and the parliaments of the most important German states, the Kingdoms of Prussia, Bavaria and Saxony.
3. Karl Rohe, 'Konfession, Klasse und lokale Gesellschaft als Bestimmungsfaktoren des Wahlverhaltens. Überlegungen und Problematisierungen am Beispiel des historischen Ruhrgebiets', in Lothar Albertin and Werner Link (eds), *Politische Parteien auf dem Weg zur parlamentarischen Demokratie in Deutschland. Entwicklungslinien bis zur Gegenwart*, Düsseldorf, 1981, pp. 109–26; idem, 'Die "verspätete" Region. Thesen und Hypothesen zur Wahlentwicklung im Ruhrgebiet vor 1914', in Peter Steinbach (ed.), *Probleme politischer Partizipation im Modernisierungsprozeß*, Stuttgart, 1982, pp. 231–52; idem, 'Vom alten Revier zum heutigen Ruhrgebiet. Die Entwicklung einer regionalen politischen Gesellschaft im Spiegel der Wahlen', in Karl Rohe and Herbert Kühr (eds), *Politik und Gesellschaft im Ruhrgebiet. Beiträge zur regionalen Politikforschung*, Königstein, 1979, pp. 21–73.

shape to our views of the everyday conduct of politics than was earlier the case. In this chapter it will be shown that a relatively precise description of the social bases of German parties is also possible on the macrolevel by means of a systematic compilation of dispersed data, as well as by means of reconstruction and careful interpretation of contemporary statistical material.

That certain regional and local characteristics are necessarily levelled down through such a process cannot be prevented. However, such characteristics can best be investigated by comparing the results of local and regional studies with the results at the national level. Therefore in this chapter I also aim to illuminate some aspects of links between social history and political history, and between national history and the histories of the constituent states, regions and localities. In addition, I would like to provide a means of bridging the gulf between a locally oriented 'people's history'[4] and a history of national-scale politics. The former type of history, which is often entrapped in its fascination for detail, sometimes ignores the broader considerations and does not question the typicality or atypicality of the subjects it describes, whereas the latter type does not pose the question of the social basis of politics and the interplay between the upper and lower echelons of society.

My study begins with the year 1867, the year of the foundation of the North German Confederation, whose constitution and voting rights were incorporated into the German Reich of 1871 with only minor changes. The foundation of the new national state constituted the prerequisite for the development of a national party system which during the era of Imperial Germany consisted of the Social Democrats, the Catholic Centre Party, the Left Liberals (represented under different names), the National Liberals, two conservative parties and several national and particularistic splinter parties. The chapter will conclude with the national Reichstag election of 1920. The inclusion of an analysis of the first two elections of the Weimar Republic should enable us, on the one hand, to explore the question of the continuity of the party system and of the parties of Imperial Germany even after the First World War. On the other hand, I shall exclude the question of the fundamental transformation of the party system as a result of hyperinflation, the Great Depression and the emergence of the National Socialist mass movement, whose supporters and membership have become the subject of intense historical research.

4. The German word for 'people's history' is *Alltagsgeschichte*, the history of everyday life.

Historical Foundations of the German Party System

Compared with, say, the United Kingdom, the United States and France, in Germany the political parties are characterized by their late formation. The German parties originated in the ideologies of conservatism and liberalism dating from the late eighteenth century. Later in the 1830s and 1840s, political catholicism, democratic radicalism and socialism emerged. However due to the long-delayed establishment of parliamentary institutions, the parties did not arise until the mid-nineteenth century as independent organizations, first inside parliament and later outside it. This occurred long after the creation of strong, bureaucratic and military organizations during the absolutist era of the seventeenth and eighteenth centuries. Neither in Imperial Germany nor during the Weimar Republic were the parties capable of bringing these powerful preparliamentary institutions under their control.

The relatively weak position of the German parties and many of the particularities of the German party system were conditioned by the political system of a dualistic, constitutional monarchy which existed until 1918. Within this system, the parliament and – via parliament – the parties had extensive influence on legislation and the determination of budgets. However, they did not have any direct influence on appointing the executive. This remained the responsibility of the emperor in the Reich and of the sovereigns of the constituent states in their respective states. Even control of military and foreign policy lay effectively beyond parliament's competence. The exclusion of parties from the appointment of the government and, with some exceptions, also from political patronage meant that the parties were not formed through the struggle for power and that they could not offer their leaders the chance to advance to governmental positions. This was one of the reasons why the Weimar Republic lacked a political elite equal to the new tasks confronting it. The institutional exclusion from political responsibility corresponded with the parties' deficient consciousness of responsibility and inadequate ability to govern. It also helped to explain their inability to integrate and lead.

A further characteristic of the German parties was their strong regionalism, which was naturally determined by the differences in religion and in the economic and social structure of each of the regions in the German Reich. This regionalism was maintained by the rise of the parties within the scope of the constituent states before the creation of the Reich and the mooring of federalism in its constitution. In the case of all the parties, including the Social Democrats, internal fractionalization within a party and the extensive autonomy of the party organization in each state was definitely caused by the federalist structure of the Reich. The regionalism of the German parties was also encouraged by the electoral system existing until 1918. According to this system victory in an electoral district was awarded to the candidate who secured an absolute majority of the votes cast in either the initial election or in a run-off election between the two strongest candidates. With the exception of the Social Democrats, the parties usually refrained from running candidates in electoral districts where their chances of winning were hopeless.[5]

The German Reich has often been referred to as an unfinished nation state. This holds true not only for the lack of identity of the nation as defined by language and culture and the nation as defined by the state, but also for the process of internal consolidation of the Reich. This process was laggardly, although there was undoubtedly a consensus in the population in favour of the nation state and the regional and territorial differences were being increasingly smoothed out. The primary cause of this faulted internal consolidation of the Reich was the delayed or insufficient political and social integration of broad sectors of the population.

To take one example, this was true for the national minorities of Poles, Danes and those coming from Alsace-Lorraine, who made up approximately 10% of the Reich's population in 1871. It was also true for the supporters of the so-called *reichsfeindliche* parties, those parties supposedly hostile to the nation state. Bismarck contended that such *Reichsfeinde* were primarily the Social Democratic and Centre parties but he also included some of the Left Liberals. The political and social integration in broad sectors of the population was unnecessarily delayed by the massive campaign levelled against these parties. The German catholics and their party succeeded in integrating themselves after the end of the so-called *Kulturkampf*, the campaign waged against the Catholic Church mainly in the 1870s, just as the Left Liberals later refrained from opposing the government over national issues of army and navy policy and accepted the fundamentals of the political–social system. Even the Social Democratic Party, which held to its basic criticism of the constitutional, social and economic system, was incorporated partly into the political system after 1890 upon the repeal of

5. For the number of candidates put up by the various parties in elections for the Reichstag from 1871 to 1912, see Ritter and Niehuss, *Wahlgeschichtliches Arbeitsbuch*, p. 121.

the so-called 'Socialist Law', which had been aimed at destroying it. This process of integration, which expressed itself, for example, in the rise of reformism inside the party, could have undoubtedly made much greater progress, even before the First World War, had the policies of social discrimination and political repression against the Social Democrats and the socialist unions not been continued after 1890 by police, administrative and judicial authorities.

The Political Mobilization of the Population

Characteristic of the history of Imperial Germany is the political mobilization of increasingly broader sectors of the population. The right to vote in Reichstag elections attained significance because with the usual exceptions (convicted criminals, receivers of poor aid, soldiers, etc.) it was universal for men over the age of 25 and was equal, secret and direct. The electoral system was thus more democratic than those of most European countries of the time (including the United Kingdom). Voter participation rose from approximately 50% in 1871 to roughly 85% in the Reichstag elections of 1907 and 1912.

Political mobilization progressed in stages. Put under pressure by the *Kulturkampf*, the first group to be mobilized was the catholic population, which the Centre Party increasingly attracted and led in opposition to the *Kulturkampf* laws. At first, voter participation in the catholic constituencies exceeded that in the protestant constituencies by about half of the latter's participation percentage.[6]

A second wave of political mobilization was set off by the Social Democrats, again in opposition to the state and its repressive measures against the political and trade union workers' organizations. Their success also led to an increasing mobilization of the political forces which were hostile to them. Thus, the advancement of the Social Democratic Party to a mass party ran parallel with an increase in voter participation in the major cities of Berlin and Hamburg. In 1871 the voter participation in these two cities was well under the national

6. In the Reichstag elections of 1874, in the 199 constituencies with a protestant majority of more than 75% only 50.3% of the voters took part. In the ninety-seven constituencies in which more than 75% of the population were catholics, 70.7% of the voters participated. The poll was particularly high, with 78.7%, in the forty-eight constituencies in which catholics made up from 50% to 75% of the population. The national average was 61.2%. See Gerhard A. Ritter, *Die deutschen Parteien 1830–1914. Parteien und Gesellschaft im konstitutionellen Regierungssystem*, Göttingen, 1985, pp. 17–18.

average; but by 1878 it had tripled, rising well above the national average.[7]

After 1890 the further politicization of the population was especially stimulated by new, emerging interest organizations and by national agitation associations.[8] The farmers, for example, were attracted by the League of Farmers (Bund der Landwirte), established in 1893, and by regional peasant leagues.[9]

Master artisans,[10] retail salesmen,[11] white-collar employees and the members of other occupations and branches of business were politically mobilized by an increasingly expanding network of interest organizations and through appeals to their economic and social interests. On the one hand, the social basis of the parties was thereby expanded; on the other hand, however, the integration of often divergent interests within the framework of their organizations and political co-operation with other parties were impeded.

This development reveals the fundamental change in the manner in which politics was conducted. Where politics earlier was solely the business of notables, now increasingly broad sectors of the population participated in shaping public opinion, within the scope of the specific interests of their station in life. Pressured by Social Democratic competition, the non-socialist parties expanded their organizations and developed themselves gradually from parties of notables, who were active only in parliament or during an election campaign, into permanently active mass parties. The trend from notable politicians to career

7. In Berlin voter participation rose from 26.1% to 79.7%, in Hamburg from 28.8% to 71.2%. The national average was 51% in 1871 and 63.4% in 1878 (Ritter and Niehuss, *Wahlgeschichtliches Arbeitsbuch*, pp. 69, 95).

8. For these see Geoff Eley, *Reshaping the German Right. Radical Nationalism and Political Change after Bismarck*, New Hampshire and London, 1980; Roger Chickering, *We Men Who Feel Most German. A Cultural Study of the Pan-German League 1886–1914*, Boston, 1984; Günter Schödl, *Alldeutscher Verband und deutsche Minderheitenpolitik in Ungarn 1890–1914. Zur Geschichte des deutschen 'extremen Nationalismus'*, Frankfurt, 1978; Paul Kennedy and Anthony Nicholls (eds), *Nationalist and Racialist Movements in Britain and Germany before 1914*, London, 1981.

9. Hans-Jürgen Puhle, *Agrarische Interessenpolitik und preußischer Konservatismus im wilhelminischen Reich, 1893–1914. Ein Beitrag zur Analyse des Nationalismus in Deutschland am Beispiel des Bundes der Landwirte und der Deutsch-Konservativen Partei*, 2nd edn, Bonn and Bad Godesberg, 1975; Jan Farr, 'Populism in the Countryside: The Peasant Leagues in Bavaria in the 1890s', in Richard J. Evans (ed.), *Society and Politics in Wilhelmine Germany*, London and New York, 1978, pp. 136–59; Klaus Müller, 'Zentrumspartei und agrarische Bewegung im Rheinland, 1882–1903', in Konrad Repgen and Stephan Skalweit (eds), *Spiegel der Geschichte*, Münster, 1964, pp. 828–57; David Blackbourn, 'Peasants and Politics in Germany 1871–1914', in *European History Quarterly*, vol. 14, 1984, pp. 47–75.

10. Shulamit Volkov, *The Rise of Popular Antimodernism in Germany. The Urban Master Artisans, 1873–1896*, Princeton, NJ, 1978.

11. Robert Gellately, *The Politics of Economic Despair: Shopkeepers and German Politics 1890–1914*, London and Beverly Hills, 1974.

politicians, who often entered politics as representatives of specific interests, also became obvious. Politics became professional.

Simultaneously, the process of adaptation to the existing political system by the bourgeois parties, as was mentioned earlier with the examples of the Catholic Centre Party and the Left Liberals, was persistently advanced through increasing state intervention in economic and social life and the pronounced change towards interest politics connected with it. The abstention from fundamental opposition in matters of national policy and the acceptance of the existing system were the prerequisites which enabled parties to ally with one another and with the government to promote the social and economic interests of their own supporters.

The Regional, Social and Economic Bases of the Major Parties before 1918

The large German parties were closely connected with certain constituent states and regions as well as with certain social and economic interests.

The Centre Party

The Centre Party, which had regularly won roughly one-fourth of the Reichstag seats since 1874, was a party for German catholics, superseding class and social strata. Once the *Kulturkampf* had been terminated, the importance of the denominational clamp diminished, making it increasingly difficult within the party to balance the diverging interests of its socially heterogenous base of support. This consisted of catholic workers, farmers, artisans, shop owners, white-collar employees, civil servants, members of the free professions, entrepreneurs, aristocrats and representatives of the church hierarchy. Unity could only be accomplished in so far as the party adapted its composition and its politics to the differing social structures of the catholic population on the regional and local levels. The over-representation of the farmers and groups of the old middle class and the under-representation of the industrial groups among the catholic population in the large cities, as compared with the total population of the Reich, corresponded with the increasing emphasis put on agricultural and middle-class interests in the party's politics. The party won particularly large electoral successes in the catholic agricultural areas and in small – usually rural – communities. In the Reichstag election of 1912, the last election before the First World War, the Centre Party was able in this way to win nearly one out of every three of the 153 electoral districts in which an absolute or relative majority of the population earned their living from agriculture. The party[12] won only somewhat over an eighth of the 195 electoral districts in which the majority of the population earned their living from industry and trade.[13] Despite the considerable similarities in the social policies of the Centre and Social Democratic Parties and the strong points of agreement in their criticism of the protestant-influenced political and social ruling class of Prussia, these two parties were prevented from co-operating beyond single-issue alliances before 1917. This was due not only to their differing attitudes towards church and religion, but also to the differing economic interests of their supporters.

The Centre Party had an obvious denominational character. In the elections from 1874 to 1887, the party won, on average, two-thirds of all the votes in constituencies with clear catholic majorities, whereas it acquired fewer than 2% of the votes in districts with clear protestant majorities.[14] After the waning of the *Kulturkampf* and the great mobilization of the voters in the direction of interest politics, the trend towards a disintegration of the Centre Party's social basis can be seen beginning in the late 1880s.[15] A catholic majority in the population was still a necessary prerequisite, but decreasingly a sufficient one, for winning a constituency for the party. Especially in the course of industrialization, urbanization and secularization, it became increasingly difficult for the Centre Party to retain the catholic industrial workers, whose support had been massively solicited by the Social Democrats since 1890.

---

12. The two most important recent studies of the Centre Party are Wilfried Loth, *Katholiken im Kaiserreich. Der politische Katholizismus in der Krise des wilhelminischen Deutschlands*, Düsseldorf, 1984, and David Blackbourn, *Class, Religion and Local Politics in Wilhelmine Germany. The Centre Party in Württemberg before 1914*, Wiesbaden, 1980. Neither study, however, discusses the performance of the party in Reichstag elections. For the period up to 1891, the best modern work is the biography of the leader of the party by Margaret Lavinia Anderson: *Windthorst. A Political Biography*, Oxford, 1981.

13. Ritter and Niehuss, *Wahlgeschichtliches Arbeitsbuch*, p. 102.

14. *Statistisches Jahrbuch für das Deutsche Reich*, 1888, pp. 139ff.

15. See Johannes Schauff, *Das Wahlverhalten der deutschen Katholiken im Kaiserreich und der Weimarer Republik. Untersuchungen aus dem Jahre 1928*, edited and with introduction by Rudolf Morsey, Mainz, 1975, p. 100. Schauff, however, overemphasizes the decline of the catholic vote for the Centre Party. His figures are discussed in Ritter, *Die deutschen Parteien 1830–1914*, pp. 57–8.

The Social Democratic Party

The Social Democrats increased their base of support in Reichstag elections from 3% in 1871 to approximately 35% in 1912. However, the percentage of parliamentary seats acquired always remained less than the percentage of votes cast for the Social Democratic Party. This was primarily caused by the fact that the partitioning of electoral districts established at the time of the founding of the German Reich had never been changed. Hence, the population shifts brought about by urbanization and industrialization had not been taken into consideration. As a result, the large cities and industrial areas in which the Social Democrats had their strongholds of support were increasingly disadvantaged to the benefit of the rural agricultural areas. In addition, the Social Democrats, as a radical, left party, could rarely count on help from other parties in the run-off elections, which were occurring more and more often.[16] The party was thereby handicapped in the struggle for seats, especially compared with the parties in the middle of the political spectrum which were equally capable of forming alliances with those to the left or right of them.

In several of the German states, especially in Prussia and in Saxony, the existing voting rights for the state parliaments strongly discriminated against the lower classes and produced even less favourable results for the party. In the 1913 elections for the Prussian Diet, the Social Democrats won only 2% of the seats although they polled nearly 30% of the votes. In contrast, the two conservative parties – the German Conservative Party (Deutschkonservativen) and the Free Conservative Party (Freikonservativen) – together won only 16.75% of the votes cast but obtained 45.6% of the seats.

Therefore, party interest gave rise to the demand for a democratization of voting rights in the constituent German states and for a transition to proportional representation in Reichstag elections. In the light of the Prussian hegemony in the Reich, the demand for reform of the so-called three-class electoral system in Prussia, which was proclaimed by the party in large voting-rights demonstrations during the years immediately preceding 1914, was one of the decisive preconditions, not only for the democratization of Prussia, but also for the hopes of establishing a parliamentary democracy in the Reich itself.

---

16. The number of run-off elections in the 397 constituencies rose from forty-six in 1874 to 147 in 1890 and 190 in 1912. The Social Democrats won in the Reichstag elections between 1871 and 1912 only 186 (27.4%) of the 679 run-off elections in which the party participated. In contrast, the parties of the left liberals were in the same period

Figure 1.1(a). The percentage of votes and parliamentary seats won by the Social Democratic Party in elections for the Reichstag, 1871–1912

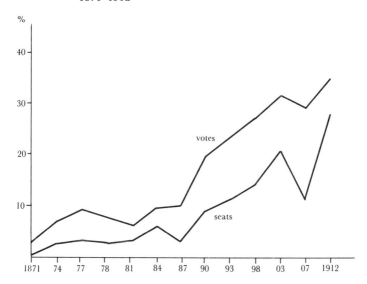

Figure 1.1(b). The percentage of votes and parliamentary seats won by the Centre Party in elections for the Reichstag, 1871–1912

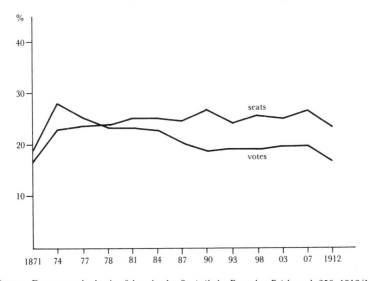

Source: Drawn on the basis of data in the *Statistik des Deutschen Reichs*, vol. 250, 1912/13.

The Social Democratic Party was a class party of urban, industrial workers which did considerably better in protestant areas than in catholic constituencies. As late as 1912, the Social Democratic Party won 106 of its 110 seats in the 195 electoral districts in which the absolute majority of the population gained their living from industry, trade and commerce. Only four seats were won in the remaining 202 electoral districts, where agriculture was more important.[17] Its percentage of the vote was three times as high in the large cities as in small communities, which were usually rural. The party's expansion in the countryside was limited for two reasons. Firstly, it could hardly reach the agricultural workers and farmhands owing to the massive obstacles put in the path of its agitation by the administration and owing to the social control exerted by landowners and farmers over the rural lower classes. Secondly, the farmers opposed political and trade union efforts to emancipate agricultural workers, and their attitudes in favour of tariff protection policy directly contradicted those of the Social Democrats. They were therefore vulnerable to anti-socialist forces, despite the occasional attempts of the Social Democratic Party to win their vote.

The increased political mobilization of master artisans – who had played a significant role in the early history of social democracy – and of the small retailers also resulted in a thrust against the Social Democrats. Even more decisive was the fact that the Social Democrats and their allied Free Trade Unions could not secure any really significant foothold in the rapidly growing group of technical and commercial white-collar employees before 1914. In addition, the lower civil servants of the monarchist state as well as the growing number of state and local authority workers were kept at a distance from the party by the threat of disciplinary measures.

In spite of secularization, industrialization and urbanization, which constantly increased the Social Democratic potential for recruitment before 1914, the party remained in a minority position caused by the social structure of Imperial Germany – a position which could only be overcome by a risky transformation from a class party of workers to a party of the people (*Volkspartei*), covering all major social segments of the population.

---

successful in 430 (79.5%) of 541 run-off elections. (Ritter and Niehuss, *Wahlgeschichtliches Arbeitsbuch*, p. 125).

17. Ritter and Niehuss, *Wahlgeschichtliches Arbeitsbuch*, p. 102. Three of the four mandates were won in the forty-nine constituencies where a relative majority of the population gained their living from industry, trade and commerce; one in the forty-nine constituencies where a relative majority of the population gained their living from agriculture and none in the 104 constituencies in which more than 50% of the population gained their living from agriculture.

The Liberal Parties

In contrast to the Social Democrats, the liberals of all shades had no clear social profile and no strong link with extra-parliamentary forces and institutions. The early broad social basis of the liberals, who had originally won the support of the large industrialists and the petty bourgeoisie, farmers, artisans and workers,[18] progressively disintegrated. The creation of a nation state from above through the power of the Prussian state deprived the liberals of a part of their historical legitimation and led to a breach with regional particularistic forces and those political elements which objected to the exclusion of the German parts of Austria from the German nation state. This also resulted in the political splitting of liberalism between the supporters and the opponents of Bismarck's policies.

Even the mobilization of the catholic voters during the *Kulturkampf* clearly occurred as a reaction against liberalism. Liberalism of all shades nearly became an exclusively protestant movement. Just as decisive as the departure of the catholic voters was the establishment of an independent, political labour movement, which developed very early compared with the rest of Europe. This movement questioned liberal claims to leadership and led to the considerable loss of working-class votes in favour of the Social Democrats.

The conservative turnabout in Bismarckian politics between 1877 and 1879 hit the liberals doubly hard. The National Liberal Party, which until then had been widely considered Bismarck's party and which was supported by the administrative apparatus, lost a portion of its support base with the loss of its position as the most important 'government party' and was permanently weakened by the split successfully orchestrated by Bismarck. At the same time, the tariff protection policy, which had been initiated by this time, had allowed the emergence of economic interest groups, which were well organized in associations and very strongly represented in the liberal parties. This considerably impeded liberal politicians' efforts to balance the differing social and economic interests of their supporters. This was made all the more difficult by the fact that the social and economic contradictions overlapped with and accentuated regional differences.

By consolidating the liberal forces of business into the Hanseatic League (Hansa-Bund), by creating a liberal organization of farmers in

---

18. See the excellent study by James J. Sheehan, *German Liberalism in the Nineteenth Century*, Chicago, 1978, which concentrates on the years up to 1877.

the German Peasants' League (Deutsche Bauern-Bund) and by pushing recruitment of white-collar employees, the liberal parties attempted
in the years immediately preceding 1914 to halt the erosion of their
social basis and to become parties of the old and new middle classes. In
the end, these attempts failed.[19] The social and economic forces which
they addressed had interests which were far too divergent. In addition,
these forces were being strongly wooed by all the other parties.

The political support of the liberals in the Reichstag elections
dropped from just less than half of the votes in 1874 to over a third in
1890 and finally to only a good fifth in 1912 (see Figure 1.2 overleaf).
The liberals' position was especially precarious because they had
hardly any safe constituencies at their disposal. This was different from
that of the Centre Party, which usually had a clear, absolute majority
of the votes, especially in catholic rural districts; the conservatives,
whose strongholds were found in the agricultural regions east of the
Elbe; and the Social Democrats, whose support was concentrated in
the large cities and industrial centres. Therefore, in order to win any
seats, the liberals were more and more dependent on the support of
voters from the other parties in run-off elections. Thus in 1912, all 42
seats won by Left Liberals and 41 out of the 45 won by the National
Liberals were only secured in run-off elections with the support of
voters from other parties.[20]

The Conservative Parties

Social change, industrialization and urbanization hit the
conservative parties even harder than they did the liberals. Their
position was based especially on their close connection with the
socially, economically and politically dominant class of landowners in
the agricultural regions east of the Elbe in Prussia and in Mecklenburg,
as well as on the assistance in elections which they received from the
Prussian administrative apparatus.

In addition, they were closely allied with agricultural interests. From

19. See Dirk Stegmann, *Die Erben Bismarcks. Parteien und Verbände in der Spätphase des
Wilhelminischen Deutschland. Sammlungspolitik 1897–1918*, Cologne and Berlin, 1970, pp.
176ff.; Siegfried Mielke, *Der Hansa-Bund für Gewerbe, Handel und Industrie 1909–1914. Der
gescheiterte Versuch einer antifeudalen Sammlungspolitik*, Göttingen, 1976.
20. Ritter and Niehuss, *Wahlgeschichtliches Arbeitsbuch*, pp. 42, 125. In contrast, the
Centre Party won seventy-nine of ninety-one seats, the German Conservative Party
twenty-seven of forty-three and the Social Democrats sixty-five of its 110 seats in the
initial election. The relatively high number of seats won by the Social Democrats in
run-off elections in contrast to earlier elections was partly due to their electoral alliance
with the left liberals.

the 1890s onwards, they became heavily dependent on the support of the tightly organized Farmers' League, whose apparatus served to a large extent as the party's organization in the countryside. This was especially true for the German Conservative Party, in which, under the influence of the Farmers' League, the pro-government character of the party was weakened and a synthesis of conservative and nationalist populist ideas was introduced. A militant middle-class ideology was developed in order to win the support primarily of artisans and small shopkeepers.[21]

These efforts to extend the social basis of the conservatives, especially in the cities, resulted in little if any success. The one-sided agricultural, rural character of the party, which outside Prussia and Mecklenburg found substantial support only in the Kingdom of Saxony, was strengthened all the more after 1890. In the Reichstag election of 1907, the party's percentage of the votes cast in Prussia east of the Elbe totalled 22.5%, more than ten times greater than in the rest of Prussia and more than six times greater than in the areas of the Reich outside Prussia.

The second conservative party, the Reich Party (Reichspartei) or the Free Conservative Party (Freikonservative Partei) as it called itself in Prussia, was more clearly a government-oriented party of notables which suffered even more than the German Conservative Party in the transition to mass politics. The Free Conservatives counted leading representatives of heavy industry and large landowners among its most influential members. They played an important role in the conservative turnabout of German politics in 1877–9 and especially in the transition to the protective tariff. Bismarck and his successors valued the Reich Party as a bridge between the German Conservative Party and the National Liberal Party, both of which the Reich Party influenced to the government's benefit.

Between 1878 and 1912, the percentage of the vote cast for both conservative parties sank nationwide from more than a fourth to less than an eighth of the vote. Of this, the percentage of the vote they received in primarily small, rural communities – with fewer than 2,000 inhabitants – was more than six times greater than that in cities with a population of over 100,000 in 1912.[22] The actual power base of both conservative parties lay in the Prussian Diet, where they constantly won about 45% of the seats from the mid-1880s onwards. They were thus indispensable in the creation of a parliamentary majority.

21. See Puhle, *Agrarische Interessenpolitik.*
22. *Statistik des Deutschen Reichs*, vol. 250, 1912/13, no. 2, pp. 5ff.; no. 3, pp. 107–25.

Gerhard A. Ritter

Figure 1.2(a). The share of votes of the major German parties in elections
for the Reichstag, 1871–1912

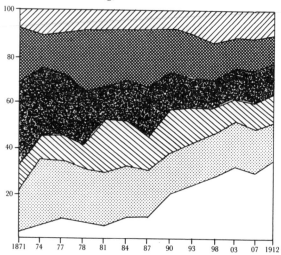

Figure 1.2(b). The share of parliamentary seats of the major German
parties in elections for the Reichstag, 1871–1912

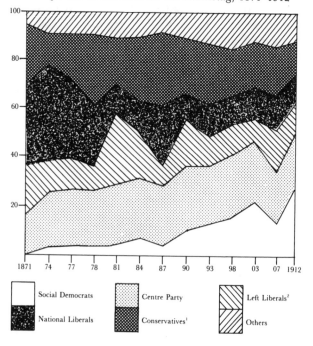

Notes: 1. German Conservatives and German Reich Party (Free Conservatives)
2. 1871–1878, Liberals, German Progressive Party and German People's Party; 1881 Liberal Union (Secessionists), German Progressive Party and German People's Party; 1884–1890 German Liberal Party and German People's Party; 1893–1907 Liberal People's Party (Freisinnige Volkspartei), Liberal Union (*Freisinnige Vereinigung*) and German People's Party; 1912 Progressive People's Party.

Source: Drawn on the basis of data in the *Statistik des Deutschen Reichs*, vol. 250, 1912/13.

Figure 1.3. The share of votes of the German Conservative Party in eastern Prussia, the rest of Prussia and the other states of Germany[1]

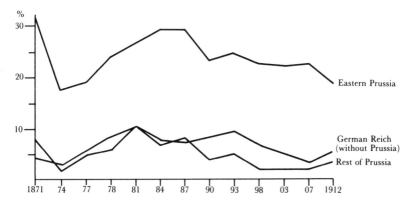

1. Prussia had seven eastern provinces: East Prussia, West Prussia, Brandenburg with Berlin, Pomerania, Posnania, Silesia and the Prussian province of Saxony which included districts east and west of the Elbe. The five further provinces of Prussia in central and western Germany were Sleswick-Holstein, Hanover, Westphalia, Hesse-Nassau and the Rhineland.

Source: Gerhard A. Ritter, *Die deutschen Parteien 1830–1914. Parteien und Gesellschaft im Konstitutionellen Regierungssystem*, Göttingen, 1985, p. 78.

Especially for the German Conservative Party, the major aim increasingly became the protection of their power base in Prussia, which was secured by the undemocratic electoral system there. It therefore used its key position in Prussian politics to prevent any reform of the Prussian three-class voting system until 1918. It also blocked a reorganization of the German financial and taxation system, which might have led to a decline in class conflict and would have strengthened the positions of the Reich and the Reichstag at the expense of Prussia and the Prussian Diet.

The Blockade of Parliamentarization by the Constitution, Government Policy and the Party System

In the dualistic constitutional monarchy system, there did not exist the inducement to reconcile political and social conflicts, which in 'normal' parliamentary systems is presented by the possibility of winning power and office. Federalism and Prussian hegemony secured the special interests of regions and constituent states and reduced the chances of alliances between the large parties at the national level, because the party organizations and parliamentary parties in the constituent states had to be taken into consideration. Government policy actually provoked the organization of the German catholics into the Centre Party by setting off the *Kulturkampf*; and it promoted the development of the Social Democrats into a mass party by making a futile attempt to smash an independent labour movement. Through the transition to a protective tariff policy, it initiated a split among the liberals and, on the whole, it contributed to the segmentation of political will through powerful interest organizations.

The fragmentation of the German party system and the strong influence within the parties relatively narrow, regional, denominational, ethnic won by, social and economic interests were therefore primarily the consequences of the religious split between protestants and catholics, the inclusion of non-German nationalities in the German state and the intensified and altered social and economic conflicts caused by industrialization. The constitutional system and the political tactics of successive German governments only advanced the disintegration of the party system and distracted the parties from their constitutional and political aims. Instead it was easier for them to act as intermediaries on behalf of economic and regional interests.

Next to the reform of the Prussian voting system, the most decisive precondition for a parliamentarization of the Reich would have been the forming of a parliamentary majority able to govern. This would have made it necessary to restructure the party system through stable political alliances between different parties, forming a coalition, and by developing parties into people's parties (*Volksparteien*) by extending their social basis. Some preliminary steps were taken in this direction before 1914. However, they were very tentative and easily blocked by the influence of pressure groups and regional interests, which was exerted from all sides.

The Transition to a Parliamentary System of Government, 1917–1919

A completely new situation evolved during the First World War. The willingness of the Social Democrats to defend the country and to support the war effort[23] offered the possibility of integrating the labour organizations into state and society on the basis of equality and of dismantling the mutually hostile images which the Social Democrats and the non-socialist parties had of one another. A step in this direction was the creation in 1917 of a majority coalition in parliament, built upon the Interparty Parliamentary Committee made up of the Social Democratic Party, the Centre Party and the Progressive People's Party. The effectiveness of the co-ordinating committee, in which even the National Liberals took part for a period, was, however, considerably limited owing to the internal differences both between and within the participating parties. It was also limited in its effectiveness by the isolation of the party leaders on the committee from their party bases, and by a hesitancy to assume political responsibilities. There was also a lack of a clear concept of constitutional political reform and a failure to present a convincing alternative political leadership to the Supreme Army Command and the government.[24] Despite all this, the committee and its personnel lent an element of continuity to the first government of the Weimar coalition.[25] This government was formed in February 1919 by the Social Democratic Party, the Centre Party and the German Democratic Party, based on the results of the election to the National Assembly. It followed the transition government of the Council of People's Representatives (Rat der Volksbeauftragten), set up in the revolution in November 1918 by the then two socialist parties in Germany.

23. For the policy of the Social Democratic Party in the First World War, see Susanne Miller, *Burgfrieden und Klassenkampf. Die deutsche Sozialdemokratie im Ersten Weltkrieg*, Bonn and Bad Godesberg, 1974.

24. For the work of this committee, see the excellent source edition, Erich Matthias with co-operation of Rudolf Morsey, *Der interfraktionelle Ausschuß 1917/18*, Düsseldorf, 1979. See also Udo Bermbach, *Vorformen parlamentarischer Kabinettsbildung in Deutschland. Der Interfraktionelle Ausschuß 1917/18 und die Parlamentarisierung der Reichsregierung*, Cologne and Opladen, 1967.

25. Gerhard A. Ritter, 'Kontinuität und Umformung des deutschen Parteiensystems 1918–1920', in G. A. Ritter, *Arbeiterbewegung, Parteien und Parlamentarismus. Aufsätze zur deutschen Sozial- und Verfassungsgeschichte des 19. und 20. Jahrhunderts*, Göttingen, 1976, pp. 119–21.

The Party System in the Early Weimar Republic: Continuity and Change

The structure of party organization also reveals a strong continuity with Imperial Germany. The liberal parties were unsuccessful in consolidating their political forces by creating a United liberal movement. Instead, they regrouped into two newly constituted parties, the German Democratic Party on the left and the German People's Party on the right.[26] The Centre Party was also unable to develop into an interdenominationally christian mass party, for which some of its leaders had worked.[27] Furthermore, it lost its former stronghold in Bavaria through the organization of its former Bavarian supporters into a separate party, the Bavarian People's Party. On the left, the influence of war and revolution split the Social Democrats at first into three, and later – after the Independent Social Democrats merged with the Communist Party or the Social Democratic Party – into two major parties, thus decisively weakening their effective power.[28] The fractionalization of the right in the Bismarck era ended temporarily with the fusion of the German Conservative Party, the German Reich Party and the populist anti-Semitic groups into the German National People's Party.[29] Later, as new problems and forces appeared, this unity was again dissolved by the splitting away of *völkische* (or racist) groups and by the emergence of the National Socialists.

The shifts of power among the non-socialist parties, which at first led to the strengthening of their left wings, would have most likely continued further had not the election campaign, which started four weeks after the revolution, forced the parties to break off their internal conflicts, at least temporarily, and to fall back for the most part on their old organizations and their former political leaders. The political polarization resulting from the violent conflicts of 1919 and 1920 – when conditions were temporarily similar to a civil war – widened the gulf between the parties of the working classes and the middle classes, a gulf which had been partially closed at the end of the war. This

---

26. Lothar Albertin, *Liberalismus und Demokratie am Anfang der Weimarer Republik. Eine vergleichende Analyse der Deutschen Demokratischen Partei und der Deutschen Volkspartei*, Düsseldorf, 1972.
27. Rudolf Morsey, *Die Deutsche Zentrumspartei 1917–1923*, Düsseldorf, 1966.
28. Heinrich August Winkler, *Von der Revolution zur Stabilisierung, Arbeiter und Arbeiterbewegung in der Weimarer Republik 1918 bis 1924*, 2nd edn, Berlin and Bonn, 1985.
29. J. Striesow, *Die Deutschnationale Volkspartei und die Völkisch-Radikalen 1918–1922*, 2 vols, Frankfurt, 1981.

polarization also caused a considerable portion of the electorate, which originally supported the governing coalition of the middle left, to shift its support to the extremist parties of the right and the left. It also reversed the changes which had appeared at the beginning of 1919 in the programme, the personnel and even to a certain extent in the parties' constituent reservoir of popular support.

The most important changes in the party system and the internal party structure were the direct result of the new system of proportional representation, which ended the discrimination in favour of rural regions which had existed up to that point. Proportional representation also motivated the parties to mobilize voters, even if they were dispersed in hostile areas. It was only at this point that the large bourgeois parties expanded their organizations nationwide.

Especially in the non-socialist parties, the party organization was consolidated and bureaucratized. The transitional process from parties of notables and committees to membership and mass parties, a process which had already begun before 1914, continued at an accelerated speed. The division of labour, as hitherto characteristic of the Centre and the conservative parties, distinguished between an extraparliamentary mass organization – which took over the organization of the masses and the election propaganda – and the party framework, which was loosely grouped around the parliamentary parties in the *Reichstag* and the parliaments of the constituent states. This system was abandoned and all parties attempted to organize as broad a membership as possible, originally with great success. The ties between the parties and certain interest groups, which had existed already before 1914 and were temporarily weakened in 1918/19, now strengthened themselves through the continually increasing importance of state intervention in the economy and society and through the strong influence which the interest associations had in determining the order of candidates on the party lists. In nearly all parties, special, influential organizations representing various occupational and economic interests were formed.

The number of career politicians, like those who had clearly dominated the SPD's parliamentary delegation before 1912, also increased considerably among the elected politicians of the non-socialist parties. The Social Democrats and the Centre Party retained their character as parties which were connected to a relatively closed 'social-moral milieu',[30] although this connection loosened and was more and more

30. This term was first used by M. Rainer Lepsius in his article, 'Parteiensystem und Sozialstruktur. Zum Problem der Demokratisierung der deutschen Gesellschaft', in Wilhelm Abel et al. (eds), *Wirtschaft, Geschichte und Wirtschaftsgeschichte, Festschrift zum 65.*

perceived as a problem in comparison with the period before 1914.

After the state ceased to exert its pressure on the SPD, the party was able to expand its organizations into the agricultural regions and to extend its support among rural labourers, white-collar employees and workers employed by the state and the communities, as well as among the lower- and middle-ranking civil servants. However, the party was faced not only with new competition from the left Socialist and Communist parties among the industrial working classes, but also with the increased attempts by the DNVP (German National People's Party) to win the votes of the workers.

For the Centre Party, the effects of the loosening of religious ties, especially in the large cities, and the impact of severe social and economic conflicts led to a loss of support. Like their predecessors, both the liberal parties, the DDP (German Democratic Party) and the DVP (German People's Party), remained without any strong links to extra-parliamentary mass organizations, and this fact later considerably facilitated the taking over of their voters by the National Socialists.

As the successor party to the earlier conservative parties, the DNVP was faced with a new situation. The earlier electoral support for the conservatives given by the administration largely disappeared and the power of the large landowning class in the east was at least temporarily weakened. Up until the emergence of the broad mass movement of the NSDAP (National Socialist Party), the DNVP tried with considerable success to broaden its social basis by modernizing its organization and its electoral campaign strategies, by presenting itself as a mass party, by expanding into the large cities and by embedding itself into the national milieu of the Weimar Republic.

Geburtstag von Friedrich Lütge, Stuttgart, 1966, pp. 371–93. It was criticized as artificial and not adequate for dealing with the varying conditions on a local level by James J. Sheehan, 'Klasse und Partei im Kaiserreich: Einige Gedanken zur Sozialgeschichte der deutschen Politik', in Otto Pflanze with the co-operation of Elisabeth Müller-Luckner (eds), *Innenpolitische Probleme des Bismarck-Reiches*, Munich and Vienna, 1983, p. 21, and by David Blackbourn, 'Die Zentrumspartei und die deutschen Katholiken während des Kulturkampfes und danach', ibid., pp. 75ff. Gerhard A. Ritter has tried to show that in a modified and developed version, the concept – which in its original form tended to underestimate the dynamics of social, economic and political change, the various points of contact between the different milieus in society at large and the variety of special local and regional forms within a social-moral milieu – might still be a useful instrument in analysing the politics of the Bismarckian Empire and the first ten years of the Weimar Republic. While it is therefore important to keep in mind that this general concept does not always do justice to the several local and regional milieus which stood in contact with the various parties, the concept has not lost its importance in explaining why, in spite of all the political, social and economic changes in Germany, the Social Democratic Party and the Centre Party could maintain their cohesion until 1914 and partly also until the end of the Weimar Republic. See for this the remarks of Ritter on the articles of Blackbourn and Sheehan in Pflanze and Müller-Luckner, *Innenpolitische Probleme*, pp. 292–4 and Ritter, *Die deutschen Parteien 1830–1914*, pp. 49–51, 98–9.

The Electoral Bases of the Parties 1919/20

Between 1912 and 1919/20 the shifts in the parties' electoral support can be revealed by the varying developments in the individual regions and especially by the performance of the parties in communities of various sizes in the elections for the Reichstag in June 1920. Unfortunately, corresponding statistics are missing for the 1919 elections for the constituent National Assembly.[31]

Especially characteristic of the 1919 elections to the National Assembly in Germany was the fact that the socialist parties showed their highest gains by far in the eastern agricultural provinces, as compared with 1912. On the other hand, their percentage in the large cities stagnated or, as in the case of Berlin, actually decreased considerably, despite the high total vote of the two socialist parties. A similar levelling of earlier strongholds also occurred in the case of the Centre Party. The DNVP could at least partially balance out massive left-wing incursions into the electorate of the two conservative parties in the eastern rural regions by an increased expansion into areas west of the Elbe and through gains in the large cities. Among the liberal parties, the Left Liberals – now organized in the DDP – were able to strengthen their position considerably in 1919, as compared with 1912, at the expense of the Right Liberals – now organized in the DVP – which only entered the election campaign late and with an insufficient organization.

However, by 1920, the balance of power within the liberal camp had already totally reversed itself in favour of the German People's Party (DVP). In the course of the political polarization of 1919/20, the DNVP also benefited. Similarly, the USPD (Independent Social Democratic Party), which was to merge with the Communist Party with only about half of its membership in autumn 1920 after a bitter internal struggle,[32] increased its percentage of the vote from barely 8% to nearly 18% at the expense of the majority Social Democrats (SPD).

The push by the right-wing nationalist parties into the cities, and the gains of the socialist parties in rural areas, become especially clear

---

31. An analysis of election results from 1912 to 1920 is given by Gerhard A. Ritter in 'Kontinuität und Umformung' and in 'Die sozialistischen Parteien in Deutschland zwischen Kaiserreich und Republik', in Werner Pöls (ed.), *Staat und Gesellschaft im politischen Wandel. Beiträge zur Geschichte der modernen Welt*, Stuttgart, 1979, pp. 100–55.

32. See R. F. Wheeler, *USPD und Internationale. Sozialistischer Internationalismus in der Zeit der Revolution*, Frankfurt, 1975, and D. W. Morgan, *The Socialist Left and the German Revolution. A History of the German Independent Social Democratic Party, 1917–1922*, Ithaca and London, 1975.

Figure 1.4. The performances of some of the major parties in communities of various sizes, 1912 and 1920/2

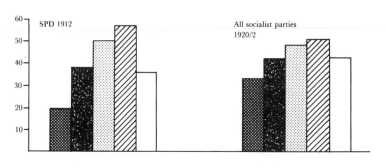

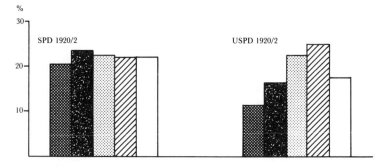

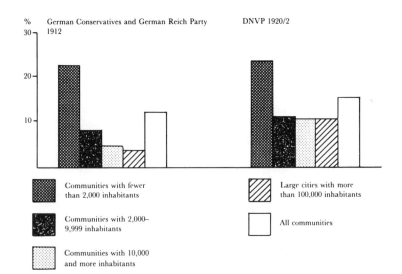

Note: In the three large electoral districts of East Prussia, Oppeln in Upper Silesia and Sleswick-Holstein, there were no elections in 1920 because the results of the plebiscites on the further attachment to Germany, Poland or Denmark of parts of these districts were awaited. Therefore the results of the later elections in East Prussia and Sleswick-Holstein on 20 February 1921 and Oppeln on 22 November 1922 were incorporated in the figures. It has to be kept in mind, however, that a large part of the USPD merged with the Communist Party in December 1920 and that most of the remaining USPD joined the SPD in September 1922.

Source: Draw on the basis of data in: *Statistik des Deutschen Reichs*, vol. 250, 1912/13, no. 2, pp. 5ff. and no. 3, pp. 107–25; *Statistik des Deutschen Reichs*, vol. 291, 1920–3, no. 2, pp. 110ff., no. 3, pp. 17ff. and no. 4, pp. 19ff. The figures for large cities with more than 100,000 inhabitants had to be calculated from results in the individual cities.

when the performances of the parties in 1912 and 1920 are compared in communities of various sizes.

The socialist parties, including the KPD (Communist Party) who, however, only gained 2% of the vote in 1920, were able to increase their percentage in the small communities from roughly one-fifth to one-third of the vote. Simultaneously, they lost nearly an eighth of their vote in the large cities with more than 100,000 inhabitants, despite their high totals in the vote nationwide. The loss in the large cities came primarily at the expense of the SPD, which fell behind the USPD there. Even when the SPD won back a portion of the votes lost to the USPD in the next election of May 1924 – the Communists could not attain the results of the Independent Socialists – the considerable levelling of the results in communities of all sizes shows that the SPD had become less of a class party of industrial labourers than it had been before 1914, as opposed to the USPD and the Communists. Despite the party's concern over further losses of working-class votes to the Communists and the continued, massive defamation by considerable sectors of bourgeois society, the SPD did not, however, complete the move from a class to a people's party with regard to its programme and its politics.

Considerable losses for the socialist parties corresponded with gains for the right-wing parties in the large cities. The 10% of the vote acquired by the DNVP in 1920 represented a tripling of the percentage received by both the conservative parties in 1912. The 23% they received in small communities in 1920 was, however, roughly equivalent to the share of the two conservative parties in these communities in 1912. In 1920, the Right Liberal DVP lost roughly a third of its vote in the small communities, as compared with the National Liberals in 1912; whereas at the same time, it could raise its percentage by more than two-fifths from 11.9% to 16.8% in the large cities. On the other hand, the Left Liberals lost ground especially in the large cities, whereas the Centre Party and the Bavarian People's Party together increased their percentage of the vote slightly in all communities except the small cities.

The shifts in the parties' electorate described here had not gone far enough by 1920 to effect a decisive change in the character of the German parties. Matters were fundamentally altered by the stronger showing of smaller splinter parties after 1924 and by the emergence later of the National Socialist mass movement.[33] The historically determined character of the German parties proved to be a heavy burden on the Weimar Republic, since these parties were more like representatives of mutually exclusive social or occupational groups than politically effective institutions of a 'normal' constitutional system. There was an insufficient adaptation of their political style, which had been shaped by the constitutional system of Imperial Germany, to the conditions of a parliamentary democracy.

Emerging changes in the party system, party organization and party character were primarily consequences of the altered voting system or continuations of the developments which had been started well before 1914. As the split among the Social Democrats and the formation of a strong, radical, nationalist right (which had already started in 1890 and which accelerated after 1918) show, these changes not only failed to improve the development of a functional, democratic parliamentary system capable of mastering the extraordinary burdens of defeat, inflation and depression; they actually hindered it.

33. A summary of election results in the Weimar Republic on the level of the Reich and the individual Länder (the former states) and the correlation of the results of the parties with demographic, confessional, social and economic factors is provided in Jürgen Falter, Thomas Lindenberger and Siegfried Schumann, *Wahlen und Abstimmungen in der Weimarer Republik, Materialien zum Wahlverhalten 1919–1933*, Munich, 1986.

JÜRGEN W. FALTER

The First German Volkspartei: The Social Foundations of the NSDAP

Introduction

The German NSDAP (National Socialist Party) rose within an extremely short time span from a marginal splinter party to a political movement of national prominence. Its share of the vote increased within only fifty months – i.e. within only one 'normal' legislative period of the German Reichstag – from an insignificant 2.6% in May 1928 to 18.3% in September 1930 and then 37.3% in July 1932. It reached its peak only three-quarters of a year later with 43.9% in March 1933, one month after Adolf Hitler had been appointed Reich Chancellor by President von Hindenburg (see Table 2.1).

Ever since then, widely divergent interpretations of the social composition, political background and personal motives of the NSDAP's supporters have been put forward in scientific and journalistic accounts of that period. The existing hypotheses are mainly distinguished by the emphasis they place upon the influx of voters from other political camps. They range from the conviction that it was predominantly the unpolitical, mentally uprooted and socially indistinct 'masses' that flocked to National Socialism[1] to the notion of a clear responsibility of one and only one social stratum – generally the lower middle classes or

1. A mass-theoretical position is proposed, e.g., by Hannah Arendt, *Origins of Totalitarianism*, New York, 1950; Reinhard Bendix, 'Social Stratification and Political Power', *American Political Science Review*, vol. 46, no. 3, pp. 357–75; William S. Kornhauser, *The Politics of Mass Society*, Glencoe, Ill., 1959; Emil Lederer, *State of the Masses*, New York, 1940.

Table 2.1. The political camps in the Weimar Reichstag elections, 1928–33
(% of valid votes)

Reichstag election	1928	1930	1932 (July)	1932 (Nov.)	1933
Turnout	75.6	82.0	84.1	80.6	88.8
KPD + SPD	40.5	37.6	36.1	37.3	30.6
Catholic (Centre Party, BVP)	15.2	14.8	16.2	15.3	13.9
Nationalists (DNVP)	14.2	7.0	6.2	8.9	8.0
Liberals (DDP, DVP)	13.6	8.5	2.2	2.9	2.0
Other	13.9	13.8	2.0	2.6	1.6
NSDAP	**2.6**	**18.3**	**37.4**	**33.1**	**43.9**

Source: Figures calculated by the author on the basis of official voting statistics.

the so-called petty bourgeoisie[2] – for the electoral successes of the NSDAP between 1928 and 1933.

The overall voting results indeed permit widely differing hypotheses. The Nazi electorate swelled between 1928 and 1932 from fewer than a million to more than seventeen million votes. The two liberal groups lost about 5.6 million voters and the various regional and interest-oriented splinter parties lost another 3.6 million votes. The German National People's Party (DNVP) declined by only about a million and the two Marxist parties remained more or less stable. The Catholic Centre Party even managed to win more than three-quarters of a million new votes. The number of non-voters over the same period declined by about 4.8 million (see Table 2.2).

Without further empirical or theoretical evidence, it is simply a matter of persuasion which theory one prefers. With valid empirical evidence not available for quite a few decades, most theoretical conceptions of the electoral successes of the NSDAP rely heavily on partly explicit, partly tacit, but nevertheless rather strong basic assumptions and auxiliary suppositions. I shall first outline the still prevalent public and scientific consensus about Nazism as a typical middle-class phenomenon; then I will give a brief account of a competing hypothesis, which stresses the complexity and heterogeneity of the Nazi electorate, before I concentrate in the main parts of my presentation on the juxtaposition of both these hypotheses with some newly established findings about

2. Proponents of the middle-class view are, among others, Theodor Geiger, 'Panik im Mittelstand', *Die Arbeit*, 1930, pp. 637–54; Seymour Martin Lipset, 'Fascism – Left, Right and Center', pp. 127–79, in S. M. Lipset (ed.), *Political Man. The Social Bases of Politics*, Garden City, 1960.

Table 2.2. The development of the Weimar party vote, 1928–33, in absolute figures (number of votes in thousands)

Pair of elections	1928/30	1930/32 (July)	1932 (July)/ 32 (Nov.)	1932 (Nov.)/33
Non-voters	−4,218	−1,912	+1,412	+3,873
KPD + SPD	+752	−200	−97	−1,203
Catholic (Centre Party, BVP)	+529	+752	−502	+62
Nationalists (DNVP)	−1,923	−181	+855	+5
Liberals (DDP, DVP)	−2,526	−2,173	+190	−233
Other	+472	−4,004	+185	−299
NSDAP	**+5,600**	**+7,369**	**−2,041**	**+5,540**

Sources: Data from Jürgen W. Falter, Siegfried Schumann, Thomas Lindenberger, *Wahlen und Abstimmungen in der Weimarer Republik*, Munich, 1986, p. 41.

the political background and social composition of the voters for National Socialism.[3]

Middle-Class Extremism: A Firmly Established Consensus

The conviction that is was mainly if not exclusively middle-class voters who supported the NSDAP is as old as the first major electoral success of the NSDAP in 1930.[4] The first wave of NSDAP gains after 1928 came for most observers as a big surprise. The enormous increase in the Nazi vote from 2.6% in 1928 to 18.3% of the valid vote in 1930 was – and still is – attributed to the decline of the two liberal parties and to the influx of former (again mainly middle-class) non-voters. Among former DNVP voters the NSDAP is said not to have succeeded particularly. Its further gains in July 1932 again are attributed to the influx of new voters and to the further decline of the liberal and splinter parties. The slight erosion of November 1932 – when the NSDAP lost about two million of its 13.8 million July votes –

3. A more theoretically oriented analysis of two major conflicting conceptions of the Nazi electorate may be found in my earlier article: 'Radicalization of the Middle Classes or Mobilization of the Unpolitical? The Theories of Seymour Martin Lipset and Reinhard Bendix on the Electoral Support of the NSDAP in the Light of Recent Research', *Social Science Information*, vol. 20, no. 2, 1981, pp. 389–430.

4. E.g. Theodor Geiger, *Die soziale Schichtung des deutschen Volkes*, Stuttgart, 1932; Carl Mierendorff, 'Gesicht und Charakter der nationalsozialistischen Bewegung', *Die Gesellschaft*, 1930/1, pp. 489–504; Werner Stephan, 'Zur Soziologie der Nationalsozialistischen Arbeiterpartei', in *Zeitschrift für Politik*, 1931, pp. 793–800.

is generally explained by a temporary abstention of many former non-voters (indeed, turn-out declined from 84% to 80.6%). Finally, the gains of March 1933, when the NSDAP vote rose to 43.9%, are similarly attributed to another surge in turn-out, which now rose to 88.8%, and to a certain influx of former communist voters who now left their politically outcast and prosecuted party.

According to the 'middle-class' view, it is thus agreed that almost all the former voters for the liberal parties and the various bourgeois splinter groups had joined the Nazi electorate. The ultra-conservative German Nationalists (DNVP), in turn, were able to maintain their core electorate. The two catholic groupings, the Centre Party and the Bavarian People's Party, stayed more or less intact, whereas the losses of the SPD (Social Democratic Party) are said to have almost exclusively favoured the ideologically related KPD (Communist Party). It is thus widely agreed that the National Socialists were not able to profit from the SPD's decline. On the other hand, it is said to have benefited from at least some of the KDP losses, owing to a certain totalitarian relationship between the two political extremes.

National Socialism flourished mainly in rural and small town settings where middle-class values and structures prevailed. Among blue-collar workers and under more urbanized conditions it had only limited success. Only the unemployed white- and blue-collar workers, radicalized by the Great Depression, showed a definitely stronger-than-average affinity towards Nazism. It is a widely accepted wisdom that the followers of National Socialism were on the average more strongly affected by the slump than others. This is not only true for the unemployed but also for the heavily indebted farm population of northern and eastern Germany.[5]

The strongest affinity towards National Socialism at the ballot-box could be found, according to this majority view, among the old middle class, i.e. among self-employed artisans, small businessmen, owners of middle-sized farms and their family members. White-collar workers, civil servants and members of the professions are also said to have displayed a much stronger-than-average affinity towards the NSDAP. Among these groups, members of the small middle class – the so-called petty bourgeoisie – are denounced as being by far the strongest followers of the Nazi movement. Upper-class and upper middle-class voters, on the other hand, are generally regarded as being more or less

5. E.g. Rudolf Heberle, *From Democracy to Nazism*, Baton Rouge, 1945; Werner Kaltefleiter, *Wirtschaft und Politik in Deutschland*, Cologne and Opladen 1966; Alfred Milatz, *Wähler und Wahlen in der Weimarer Republik*, Bonn, 1965.

immune to the Nazi contamination. They had predominantly voted, according to many contemporaries and modern historians, for their traditional conservative parties, especially the DNVP.[6]

This consensus is based, as I have shown elsewhere,[7] on rather limited empirical evidence. For more than four decades research into the NSDAP electorate has been regionally restricted, methodologically flawed and statistically over-simplistic. Consequently this consensus represents a kind of historical folklore, i.e. a blend of truth and myth, containing some largely accurate statements, many not completely false but much too undifferentiated, and quite a few completely erroneous statements which have to be partially revised in the light of the empirical evidence now available.

Before turning to that, I shall give a short outline of the opposite viewpoint, which seems to represent a newly emerging consensus on the mass basis of National Socialism. This new consensus, albeit much better empirically grounded than the traditional middle-class conception of National Socialism, is still restricted to the relatively small community of electoral historians dealing with that topic.

The 'Catch-All-Party-of-Protest' Interpretation

During the last fifteen years, a series of dissertations (mostly American), books and articles discerned a somewhat different pattern in the Nazi electorate which may be aptly subsumed under the heading of 'catch-all party of protest'.[8] Among the more noteworthy results of the newer literature on the mass basis of National Socialism is certainly Richard Hamilton's finding that – at least in the protestant metropolises of the Reich – the NSDAP fared best at the polls in the most affluent quarters, where the petty bourgeoisie represented at best a small minority of voters. Other scholars such as Loren K. Waldman, Thomas Childers, Dirk Hänisch and myself found out that the statistical

6. There is general agreement, however, that the two most important factors of immunization were affiliation to the Catholic Church or the socialist workers' milieu.

7. Jürgen W. Falter, 'Wählerbewegungen zum Nationalsozialismus 1924–1933 – Methodische Probleme, empirisch abgesicherte Erkenntnisse, offene Fragen', in Otto Büsch (ed.), *Wählerbewegungen in der europäischen Geschichte*, Berlin, 1980, pp. 159–202. This consensus encompasses, of course, other aspects as well, such as gender, rural background of the Nazi electorate etc.

8. This notion is propagated, for example, by Thomas Childers, 'The Social Bases of the National Socialist Vote', *Journal of Contemporary History*, vol. 3, 1976, pp. 1–30, and in idem, *The Nazi Voter. The Social Foundations of Fascism in Germany, 1919–1933*. Chapel Hill and London, 1983, p. 265.

relationship between blue-collar workers and the Nazi vote is by no means as negative as is generally assumed. The investigations of the American political scientist Theodore Meckstroth as well as my own research revealed that the voter fluctuations to and from the NSDAP were much more complex than was previously thought.[9]

Before I proceed, a word of warning in relation to the concept of catch-all party or *Volkspartei* seems to be necessary. The notion of *Volkspartei* or catch-all party has been established for a number of different purposes. The term itself combines prescriptive and descriptive elements in expressing, on the one hand, the self-definition of a party with regard to its official policy (of speaking for the whole people, that is, not for one segment of the population alone) and the electorate it was aiming at – such as the DNVP (German National People's Party).[10] On the other hand, the term is used to denote the social composition and actual electoral politics of a party. In the following I will restrict the usage of the concept to this latter meaning or, more exactly, to only one fraction of its descriptive dimension: the classification of the social composition of a party's electoral support. I will thus utilize it as a kind of counter-term to the notion of class party (again limited to its mass following). Hence, these two concepts form the opposite poles of a typological continuum which stretches from a strictly class-based party to – in regard to its social basis – a totally undistinct party or movement. Both ends of the continuum represent, of course, so-called ideal types which may only approach reality to a limited degree; thus, a party may turn out to be more of one type than

---

9. T. Childers, *The Nazi Voter*; Richard Hamilton, *Who Voted for Hitler?* Princeton, NJ, 1982; Loren K. Waldman, *Models of Mass Movements: The Case of the Nazis*, Chicago, Ill., 1973 (University of Chicago Ph.D dissertation); Theodore Meckstroth, *Conditions of Partisan Realignments: A Study of Electoral Change*, Minneapolis, 1971 (University of Minnesota, Department of Political Science Ph.D. dissertation); Dirk Hänisch, *Sozialstrukturelle Bestimmungsgründe des Wahlverhaltens in der Weimarer Republik. Eine Aggregatdatenanalyse der Ergebnisse der Reichstagswahlen 1924 bis 1933*, Duisburg, 1983; Jürgen W. Falter, 'Die Wähler der NSDAP 1928–1933. Sozialstruktur und parteipolitische Herkunft', in Wolfgang Michalka (ed.), *Die nationalsozialistische Machtergreifung 1933*, Paderborn, 1984, pp. 47–59; idem, 'Wahlen und Wählerverhalten unter besonderer Berücksichtigung des Aufstiegs der NSDAP nach 1928', in Karl Dietrich Bracher, Manfred Funke and Hans-Adolf Jacobsen (eds), *Die Weimarer Republik 1918–1933. Politik, Wirtschaft, Gesellschaft*. Bonn, 1987, pp. 484–504. Furthermore, the newer membership studies by Michael Kater, *The Nazi Party. A Social Profile of Members and Leaders, 1919–1945*, Cambridge, MA, 1983; J. Paul Madden, *The Social Composition of the Nazi Party, 1919–1930*. Norman, OK, 1976, (University of Oklahoma Ph.D. dissertation).

10. The notion of *Volkspartei* (catch-all party) is discussed, among others, by Richard Stöss, 'Einleitung', in R. Stöss (ed.), *Parteien-Handbuch. Die Parteien der Bundesrepublik Deutschland 1945–1980*, vol. 1, Opladen, 1984; Alf Mintzel, *Die Volkspartei. Typus und Wirklichkeit*, Opladen, 1983; and Otto Kirchheimer, 'Der Wandel des westeuropäischen Parteiensystems', *Politische Vierteljahresschrift*, vol. 6, 1965, pp. 20–41.

another, but there will be no absolute correspondence of a party in reality with the ideal type of 'catch-all' or 'class' party.

Some Methodological Considerations

Before we proceed, some words of warning should be raised with regard to the empirical data available, the statistical problems related to this data and the theoretical relevance of our findings. Starting with the last point, it should be clear that there is no necessary correspondence between the political provenance of the NSDAP voters and their social composition. Even if we were able to prove beyond reasonable doubt that a strong majority of the NSDAP electorate had formerly voted for one of the so-called middle-class parties, this would not automatically imply that they were members of the middle class. As everybody knows today, a 'typical' middle-class party like the British Tories or the West German Christian Democratic Party is able to attract a substantial portion of working-class followers. The reverse is true for such 'typical' working-class parties as the British Labour Party and the West German Social Democrats (blue-collar workers today only represent a minority of Social Democratic voters). Without further evidence the deduction from the former political home of the NSDAP supporters to their social background would be just another instance of begging the question, something quite typical of the folklore nature of the electoral history of the NSDAP sketched out above.

Unfortunately, the electoral historian of the Weimar Republic does not have any survey data on voting behaviour. The only data available to him are election results and a rather large amount of census data, unemployment statistics and fiscal information which were all gathered at the community or county level. Thus he does not have direct information about, say, the political preferences of specific social strata or occupational groups and, as a consequence, he also has no direct knowledge about the social composition of the various party electorates, including that of the NSDAP. The only information available to the electoral historian of the NSDAP is how the different parties fared in communities or counties with a certain percentage of middle-class voters, unemployed, catholics, etc.

From a statistical point of view, it is not legitimate to infer the individual level relationships of any two variables from the covariation of these same variables at an aggregate level without referring to some rather strong (and, in most instances, untestable) assumptions about the statistical properties of the joint distributions of these variables. If we find, for example, a strong positive correlation between the proportion of self-employed and the percentage of NSDAP voters at a certain election, we are not justified in equating this aggregate correlation with the actual voting behaviour of the self-employed. And a negative statistical relationship between, say, the proportion of blue-collar workers and the NSDAP share of the vote does not necessarily imply that the National Socialists did not get any votes from this class. Disregarding the rules of ecological inference may result in some rather serious distortions, the so-called ecological fallacies.

Quite often the interpretation of historical election studies is partially, if not totally, invalidated by the unawareness of this rather common statistical pitfall which again is quite typical of the 'historical folklore' about the NSDAP vote mentioned above. Taking into consideration the simultaneous effect of other potential factors influencing the Nazi vote leads to more adequate statistical models which help to reduce (but unfortunately by no means to eliminate) the risks of ecological fallacies. In the following we will therefore proceed from simple, bivariate analysis to several types of multivariate analysis in order to discern, in the next section, the voter fluctuations to and from the NSDAP and, in the subsequent section, we shall attempt to obtain a somewhat more differentiated view of the social composition of the National Socialist voting body in comparison with that of the other major parties.

Voter Transitions to the NSDAP 1928–1933

In this section I shall try to give an answer to the often raised, but rarely adequately solved, question of the political provenance of the NSDAP voters, and especially to test whether there really is a one-way road from the middle-class parties to the Hitler movement. If one looks at the overall figures at the Reich level, the answer seems to be obvious (see Table 2.1). The NSDAP rise at the polls coincides so closely with the decline of the two liberal parties and the various regional, nationalistic and interest-oriented groups that the middle-class interpretation is almost self-evident.

On the other hand, overall election returns are, as suggested above, a grossly inadequate basis for the analysis of voter transitions between parties because they only represent net figures, i.e. figures in which the wins and losses of the various parties are already summed up. From the perspective of pure arithmetic it is quite possible that a party which in a given election stayed more or less stable underwent a complete transformation in its voting body. In reality voter fluctuations between parties tend to be much smaller; nevertheless they are always two-sided, never one-sided. Even in so-called landslide elections there exists a give-and-take between the winning and the losing party, as is amply demonstrated by modern survey analysis.

The problem is clarified if one takes into account the fact that the election results at the national level are summed up from the 600+ constituency results. These in turn form the net total of community returns which themselves are based on the voting results in some smaller electoral districts which, finally, represent nothing else but the sum of the individual votes in each district. The larger the aggregate, the more comprehensive the net figure representing the outcome of an election and the greater, on the average, the chances of toppling into the pitfalls of ecological fallacy. The smaller the aggregate, the closer we move to the individual voter, and the smaller, on the average, the danger of fallacious inferences from aggregate findings to individual voting behaviour. The following results, therefore, will be either based on the more than 1,000 counties of the Weimar Republic or, in at least some instances, on the 6,000 communities and community units of our data sets.

Bivariate Relationships

In this subsection the change in the NSDAP vote in the 831 county units[11] of the Reich is related to the change in the vote of the other parties. For this purpose the county units for each pair of elections were divided according to the percentage change of the Nazi vote into so-called quintiles, i.e. subdivisions of the whole universe of counties which encompass exactly one-fifth of all cases; thus in the first quintile the 20% of the county units with the lowest percentage change for the NSDAP in a given pair of elections were gathered, in the fifth quintile the 20% with the highest percentage change were gathered etc. For each quintile the mean percentage change figure of the main political parties was calculated. In this manner we are able to assess, for example, for the 1928/30 pair of elections how the voting results of

11. In order to account for various border changes in the course of administrative reforms at the community and county level, the counties of the Weimar Republic (initially more than 1,200) were synthesized into 865 (831) diachronically stable county units.

the other parties developed in the 200-odd counties with the highest or lowest increase for the NSDAP. The resulting relationships fit closely the correlation coefficients reported in the last column of Table 2.3.

Thus we find that between 1928 and 1930 there seems to be no significant relationship between the growth of the NSDAP vote and the increase in turn-out; where the NSDAP share of the vote showed its highest increase, non-voting declined by 6.9% whereas in the quintile with the smallest increase in the National Socialist vote turn-out increased by exactly the same percentage. This is also represented by the extremely low correlation coefficient of −0.03, a figure indicating almost perfect statistical independence in the two variables under consideration. In July 1932 and, particularly, in March 1933 there is a much clearer pattern; the greater the growth of the NSDAP vote, the greater the increase in turn-out. In counties with an above average increase in the NSDAP vote, turn-out figures also tend to rise in a disproportionate manner; in counties with a below average increase in the NSDAP vote the rise in turn-out was also below average. In November 1932, there is again a positive but rather weak correlation between turn-out and the NSDAP vote which, on the other hand, has to be interpreted in a somewhat different manner; the greater the losses of the Hitler movement, the greater the decrease in turn-out. In all three pairs of elections, however, the increase (or decrease) in the NSDAP vote was somewhat greater than the increase (or decrease) in turn-out figures, a phenomenon which should be interpreted as an indicator of an overall swing to and from the NSDAP that cannot be interpreted by turn-out changes alone.[12]

With regard to the so-called middle-class parties, there is a clear linear positive relationship in the 1928/30 pair of elections between the NSDAP surge on the one hand and the decline of the National Liberal DVP (German People's Party) and the arch-conservative DNVP (German National People's Party) on the other. The statistical association between the NSDAP rise and the decline of the Left Liberal DDP (German Democratic Party) is curvilinear in 1930, a fact which is clearly highlighted by the correlation coefficient in the last column of Table 2.3. In July 1932 these relationships seem to be reversed; now there is a curvilinear relation between the Nazi increase and the decline

12. For further detail see Jürgen W. Falter, 'The National-Socialist Mobilisation of New Voters: 1928–1933', in Thomas Childers (ed.), *The Formation of the Nazi Constituency 1919–1933*, London and Sydney, 1986, pp. 202–31. These findings could be regarded as a corroboration of Seymour Martin Lipset's hypothesis about a later influx of the assumedly unpolitical former non-voters into the NSDAP. But, as we shall see below, multivariate analysis somewhat differentiates the picture.

Table 2.3. The development of the NSDAP in relation to the development of the other parties between 1928 and 1933

(a) 1928/30

	Percentage point change of the NSDAP (quintiles)					Aver-age	Pearson's r^1
	1	2	3	4	5		
Nationalists	−1.6	−3.9	−5.1	−6.1	−9.5	−4.9	−50
Other	0.6	1.6	1.1	0.8	0.3	+0.9	−03
DVP	−1.4	−2.4	−3.0	−4.2	−3.7	−2.8	−41
Catholic[2]	2.2	0.5	0.5	0.2	0.3	+0.8	−36
DDP	−0.2	−0.5	−0.7	−0.8	−0.8	−0.6	−17
SPD	−1.7	−2.0	−2.4	−2.3	−2.9	−2.2	−16
KPD	2.7	3.4	2.6	2.6	2.5	+2.8	−10
Non-voters	−6.9	−7.1	−6.4	−6.8	−6.9	−6.8	+03
NSDAP	6.4	10.5	13.5	16.7	20.8	12.9	100

(b) 1930/2 (July)

	Percentage point change of the NSDAP (quintiles)					Aver-age	Pearson's r^1
	1	2	3	4	5		
Nationalists	−0.2	−0.6	−1.1	−1.4	−1.0	−0.8	−11
Other	−6.5	−6.4	−7.4	−10.3	−14.0	−8.8	−63
DVP	−1.6	−2.6	−3.6	−2.8	−2.7	−2.7	−12
Catholic[2]	2.4	1.0	0.5	0.2	0.4	+0.9	−39
DDP	−1.4	−2.5	−2.9	−2.1	−2.1	−2.2	−09
SPD	−0.8	−1.2	−1.5	−3.0	−3.2	−1.9	−33
KPD	2.0	1.5	0.7	1.6	1.3	1.4	−15
Non-voters	0.8	−1.2	−1.1	−2.3	−5.1	−2.1	−46
NSDAP	6.9	12.1	16.2	20.1	26.4	16.2	100

(c) 1932 (July)/1932 (Nov.)

	Percentage point change of the NSDAP (quintiles)					Aver-age	Pearson's r^1
	1	2	3	4	5		
Nationalists	0.9	1.2	1.6	2.2	3.0	+1.8	−61
Other	0.1	0.1	0.1	0.3	0.5	+0.2	−29
DVP	0.2	0.6	0.6	0.6	0.6	+0.5	−28
Catholic[2]	−1.7	−1.4	−1.1	−0.5	−0.4	−1.0	−39
DDP	0.1	0.0	−0.1	−0.2	−0.2	−0.1	+17
SPD	−1.8	−1.8	−1.9	−1.9	−1.4	−1.7	−09

continued on p. 64

Table 2.3. *continued*

(c) 1932 (July)/1932 (Nov.)

	Percentage point change of the NSDAP (quintiles)					Aver-age	Pearson's r^1
	1	2	3	4	5		
KPD	1.4	1.3	1.4	1.6	1.4	+1.4	+01
Non-voters	2.8	3.5	3.8	3.3	4.1	+3.5	−27
NSDAP	−1.9	−3.6	−4.5	−5.5	−7.8	−4.6	100

(d) 1932 (Nov.)/1933

	Percentage point change of the NSDAP (quintiles)					Aver-age	Pearson's r^1
	1	2	3	4	5		
Nationalists	0.7	0.3	0.5	0.1	0.2	+0.4	−11
Other	−0.9	−1.1	−1.4	−1.2	−2.0	−1.3	+18
DVP	−0.4	−0.6	−0.7	−0.5	−0.4	−0.5	+11
Catholic[2]	0.6	0.6	0.4	0.1	−0.4	+0.3	−36
DDP	0.1	0.1	−0.1	−0.1	−0.1	−0.0	−20
SPD	0.1	−0.1	0.2	−1.1	−0.6	−0.2	−18
KPD	−2.6	−2.5	−2.6	−2.8	−2.8	−2.6	−06
Non-voters	−5.2	−6.7	−8.3	−8.5	−12.1	−8.2	−74
NSDAP	**+7.8**	**+10.0**	**+12.0**	**+14.0**	**+18.2**	**+12.2**	**100**

1. The last column shows the correlation coefficient (× 100) of the percentage point change in the NSDAP vote and the change in the vote of the other parties specified.
2. Centre Party plus Bavarian People's Party.
Reading example: In those 20% of the German counties where the NSDAP rise was lowest in 1930 (first quintile), the German Nationalists lost only 1.6% of the vote; in the fifth quintile, where the NSDAP increase was highest (20.8% on average), the mean losses of the DNVP climbed in relation to 1928 to 9.5%. This corresponds to a correlation coefficient of $r = -0.50$ between the NSDAP and the DNVP change in the vote, indicating a medium to strong relationship between the two variables.
Source: Figures computed by the author on the basis of his Weimar elections data set (country level). This data set is distributed by Zentralarchiv für empirische Sozialforschung der Universität zu Köln, Bachemer Str. 40 D–5000 Köln 41.

of the DVP and DNVP, while the relationship for the DDP and, particularly, the splinter parties is quite strong. This can also be seen by the correlation coefficients.

In November 1932 the NSDAP vote and turn-out declined considerably while the DNVP and DVP share of the vote increased to some extent. Both the decline in turn-out and the increase in the DNVP and DVP vote display a positive relationship with the NSDAP losses; i.e. the greater the decrease in the Nazi vote, the greater the average decline in turn-out and the increase in the DNVP and DVP vote. The DDP stayed about the same, as did the various splinter parties. In 1933, finally, the last, at least half-free, election of the Weimar Republic, there was not much change in the already decimated middle-class parties, and so there could be no significant relationship between their electoral development and the further rise of the NSDAP.

With regard to the other parties, i.e. the two catholic groups and the two socialist parties, there is a near zero relationship between the gains and losses of the communists and the development of the NSDAP, while the gains of the NSDAP – with the exception of March 1933 – seem to have negatively affected the moderate increase of the two catholic parties. For the first two pairs of elections, however, there is a small but nevertheless quite remarkable statistical association between the development of the SPD vote and the NSDAP surge, a relationship which is also clearly present in the correlation coefficients. Where the SPD lost significantly the NSDAP gains were above average; where the NSDAP rise was disproportionately low, the SPD losses fell below average or even turned into growth.

In sum, on the bivariate level the evidence is somewhat mixed. On the one hand, there is a clear relationship between the losses of most middle-class parties (with the noteworthy exception of the Left Liberal DDP) and the NSDAP gains; on the other hand, there seems to be some statistical association between the rise of the Nazi vote and the relative decline of the Social Democrats as well. And, quite unexpectedly, there seems to be no relationship between the considerable increase in turn-out and the surge of the NSDAP in the 1928/30 pair of elections.

Multivariate Relationships

As emphasized above, such bivariate relationhips at the aggregate level should not be interpreted as individual voter switches. The use of multivariate statistical models, which take into account the developments of the other parties, gives somewhat better indicators of the true voter fluctuations. In the following section I shall look at the results of a multiple regression analysis. The dependent (or target) variable is the change in the NSDAP vote; independent variables are turn-out change and the fluctuations of the two (combined) liberal

Table 2.4(a). Multiple regression analysis of the impact of the gains and losses of selected parties on the NSDAP vote

| Target variable: % NSDAP | Predictor variables | | | | |
	% Turn-out	% Nationalists	% Liberals	% Other	R^2 (%)
1928/30	0.184	−0.512	−0.487	–	49
1930/2 (July)	0.392	−0.492	−0.421	−0.797	81
1932 (July)/					
1932 (Nov.)	0.469	−0.687	−0.122	−0.094	59
1932 (Nov.)/					
1933	0.785	−0.170	−0.021	−0.061	59
R^2 − Change (%)					
1928/30	0.1	26	23	–	
1930/2 (July)	21	2	6	52	
1932 (July)/					
1932 (Nov.)	7	50	2	1	
(Nov.)/1933	55	4	0	0.3	

Note: The table shows a hierarchical regression analysis of so-called change variables for 831 German county units. For 1928–30, 'Other' has been left out of the equation in order to minimize multicollinearity. Standardized regression coefficients.
Source: As Table 2.3.

parties, the Nationalists and the various splinter parties. The splinter parties were left out of the 1930 prediction equation in order to minimize multicollinearity (see Table 2.4).[13]

With the exception of 1930, the multivariate analysis confirms the results of the correlation and percentage change analysis. In 1930 there seems to be in addition to the correlational findings a positive but very small effect of turn-out change on the NSDAP increase. By far the most important effects, however, are exerted at this election by the DNVP losses and the combined liberal losses. Part of the 1930 DNVP losses seem to have reached the NSDAP via intermediate hosts such as the splinter parties, which indeed were in part split off from the German nationalists. In July 1932 the losses of these splinter parties account for more than 60% of the total explained variance of the regression model. The DNVP losses and the decrease of the liberals at that election are of minor importance. In November 1932 the DNVP gains

13. This seems to be legitimate since the intercorrelation between this variable and the Nazi surge is extremely low in 1930, while the relationship with the DNVP change is rather strong. The latter may be regarded as an indicator of some voter exchange between the splinter parties and the DNVP after 1928.

Table 2.4(b). Multiple regression analysis of the gains and losses of the major parties (standardized regression coefficients)

Predictor variables	Target variable: NSDAP change (%)							
	1928/30		1930/2 (July)		1932 (July)/ 1932 (Nov.)		1932 (Nov.)/ 1933	
Non-voters	−0.52	3	−0.62	21	−0.90	20	−0.90	55
Nationalists	−0.45	24	−0.16	2	−0.65	35	−0.17	3
DVP	−0.37	17	−0.18	2	−0.22	5	−0.11	1
Catholics	−0.30	3	−0.29	22	−0.61	13	−0.41	19
DDP	−0.25	5	−0.15	2	−0.08	1	−0.09	1
SPD	−0.37	6	−0.48	7	−0.60	5	−0.36	9
KPD	−0.40	2	−0.33	10	−0.55	15	−0.28	5
R^2 (%)	61		65		95		92	

Note: The table shows a step-wise regression analysis of percentage change variables for 831 county units. 'Other' has been left ouf of the equation in order to minimize multicollinearity (in a differently specified regression model they account for more than 50% of the explained variance in the 1930/1932 (July) pair of elections; see Jürgen W. Falter, 'The National-Socialist Mobilisation of New Voters: 1928–1933', in Thomas Childers (ed.), *The Formation of the Nazi Constituency 1919–1933*, London and Sydney, 1986, p. 216). The first column of each pair of elections gives standardized regression coefficients; the second column gives R^2 – change. Predictors are ordered politically from 'right' to 'left'.
Source: As Table 2.3.

are of primary importance and the decrease in turn-out of secondary importance in the NSDAP losses. In 1933, finally, the change in turn-out accounts for about 95% of the total explained variance.

With the exception of the 1930 and July 1932 pair of elections, the regression model shown in Table 2.4a does not explain more than 50% to 60% of the variance of the dependent variable, i.e. the change in the NSDAP vote. This may be attributed to the fact that the percentage change of the catholic and socialist parties was deliberately left out of the regression model in order to minimize multicollinearity, i.e. the biasing intercorrelation of predictors. In my next step, in which I shall try to figure out by means of multiple ecological regression analysis the 'real' voter fluctuations towards and from the NSDAP, I shall include these parties in both the statistical models and the interpretations.

Even in the multivariate model, standardized regression coefficients do not provide percentages. Even behind strongly negative regression or correlation coefficients there may be hidden substantial numbers of voters fluctuating into the opposite direction, as indicated by the sign of the coefficient. The statistical instrument of ecological regression analysis as developed by the German statistician F. Bernstein in 1932 and reinvented by Leo Goodman in 1953 tries to overcome these deficiencies of correlation and standardized regression coefficients.

There is no room to explain in greater detail the statistical intricacies of ecological regression analysis. Basically it is the use of unstandardized regression coefficients which are treated in a specific way. Let us assume that we are interested in the voting behaviour of the various religious denominations in the country without having access to opinion surveys. Let us further assume for the moment that there are only catholics and protestants, who live in strictly separated regions, as was the case in parts of the Continent for quite a long time. In this situation it would be very easy to find out about the party preferences of catholic and protestant voters. Their propensity to vote for a given party would equal the percentage of that party in the catholic or protestant constituencies. Now let us imagine that there also exist confessionally mixed counties. If we have reason to believe that all voters of the same denomination display roughly the same voting behaviour irrespective of the denominational context they are living in, we are able by means of (unstandardized) regression analysis to estimate their propensity to vote for a given party by simple intrapolation or extrapolation (or, more technically speaking, by using the slope and the intercept of the regression line as indicators of voter transitions between parties).[14]

Table 2.5 represents the findings of such an ecological regression analysis. They are correct estimates of the political provenance of the NSDAP electorate if the underlying assumptions of ecological regression analysis are met by the data.[15] Since the results of various regression models at the county and community level do coincide, we may put some trust in the reliability of these findings. The overall

14. See Fritz Bernstein, 'Über eine Methode, die soziologische und bevölkerungsstatistische Gliederung von Abstimmungen bei geheimen Wahlverfahren statistisch zu ermitteln', *Allgemeines Statistisches Archiv*, vol. 22, 1932, pp. 253–6; Leo A. Goodman, 'Ecological Regression and Behavior of Individuals', *American Sociological Review*, vol. 43, 1953, pp. 557–72; and Jan-Bernd Lohmöller and Jürgen W. Falter, 'Some Further Aspects of Ecological Regression Analysis', *Quality and Quantity*, 1986, pp. 109–25. For an extension of ecological regression analysis where potentially 'disturbing' factors are controlled, see Jan-Bernd Lohmöller, Jürgen W. Falter, Andreas Link and Johann de Rijke, 'Unemployment and the Rise of National Socialism. Contradicting Results from Different Regional Aggregations', in Peter Nijkamp (ed.), *Measuring the Unmeasurable*, Dordrecht, Boston and Lancaster, 1985, pp. 357–70.

15. Some of these underlying assumptions are simply the normal assumptions of regression analysis which are listed in every statistical primer; others, such as non-contextuality, are special to ecological regression analysis. Unfortunately it is not possible to test all these assumptions – and especially the non-contextuality assumption – by means of the information available. If the assumptions are not met ecological inference is inadequate.

Table 2.5. Where did the NSDAP voters come from?

Reichstag election	KPD	SPD	Catholics	Liberals	Nationalists	Other	NSDAP	Non-voters
1930	3	14	8	18	22	8	5	24
1932 (July)	2	10	4	8	6	18	40	12
1932 (Nov.)	2	4	3	0	0	1	89	1
1933	3	2	1	6	1	2	63	22

Note: The table shows transition probabilities won by ecological regression analysis with religious denomination and urbanization as moderator variables. Computations based on 831 county units, cases weighted by population figures. Negative estimates are smoothed by proportional fitting. For further technical details, see Jan-Bernd Lohmöller, Jürgen W. Falter, Andreas Link and Johann de Rijke, 'Unemployment and the Rise of National Socialism. Contradicting Results from Different Regional Aggregations', in Peter Nijkamp (ed.), *Measuring the Unmeasurable*, Dordrecht, Boston and Lancaster, 1985. For row percentages the basis is NSDAP voters.
Reading example: 24% of the 1930 NSDAP voters had not voted in 1928, 18% had voted Liberal in 1928, 14% SPD, 22% DNVP etc.

impression is that of a rather unexpected complexity and heterogeneity in the political origin of the NSDAP voters. It is true that about 50% of the NSDAP electorate of 1930 had originally voted for one of the so-called middle-class parties (including the Nationalists, which are, however, generally regarded by partisans of the middle-class hypothesis as being predominantly upper class). The greatest single source of the National Socialist rise in the 1930 Reichstag election, however, seems to have been the former non-voters and the newly eligible voters. It may be a surprise to note the number of socialist voters (mainly former SPD supporters) switching to the NSDAP. This number is as large as that of the former liberal followers who joined the NSDAP electorate in September 1930.

The July 1932 election shows roughly the same pattern of complexity and heterogeneity as the 1930 election. Among the new joiners of the NSDAP again the already seriously diminished so-called middle-class parties prevail, and again former liberal and nationalist voters represent about the same percentage of joiners. The greatest single source now are previous voters for the various regional and interest-oriented splinter parties. Every fifth new Nazi voter came from the socialist camp or had abstained from voting in 1930. Finally, in March 1933 the bulk of the NSDAP growth has to be attributed to the mobilization of more-or-less habitual non-voters.

These figures do not represent a definite repudiation of the middle-class folklore. Nevertheless, they suggest an extensive differentiation and partial reformulation of the notion of the political provenance of the NSDAP electorate. Only two party electorates proved to be relatively immune against the Nazi contamination: the catholics and the communists. All other political groups, including not only the Nationalists but also the Social Democrats, lost a substantial part of their followers to the Hitler movement. Compared with the other political parties, the NSDAP proved to be politically much more mixed, comprising neither exclusively former middle-class voters nor exclusively unpolitical newly eligible and former non-voters, as stipulated by the theory of middle-class extremism on the one hand and the mass-society hypothesis on the other. As pointed out above, the political provenance of the NSDAP voters does at best offer some rather indirect evidence of the social foundation of the Nazi support. It cannot substitute for direct indicators of the social composition of the National Socialist electorate and the affinity of the various social classes, strata, groups and categories towards the NSDAP. In the following section I shall concentrate on this latter aspect in order to consider the question of whether the NSDAP really represented the first catch-all party in German history in somewhat more detail.

The Social Composition of the Nazi Electorate

Correlates of the NSDAP Share of the Vote

From the perspective of the middle-class hypothesis, one could expect that the NSDAP share of the vote in middle-class strongholds would be considerably above average while it should be substantially below average in working-class districts. In other words, the statistical association between the percentage of Nazi voters and middle-class indicators should be positive in sign and rather strong, whereas the correlation with working-class attributes of our territorial units of analysis should be strongly negative. The catch-all party position, on the other hand, implies no such strong – or at least significantly lower – correlations with the middle-class and the working-class areas.

Some of the earlier studies of the Nazi electorate indeed discerned the predicted middle-class pattern. Unfortunately they were territorially restricted and methodologically rather flawed and misinterpreted, as I have described elsewhere.[16] Correlation and regression

---

16. See, for example, Falter, 'Wählerbewegungen zum Nationalsozialismus'; Jürgen W. Falter and Wolf D. Gruner, 'Minor and Major Flaws of a Widely Used Data-Set: The

studies with a complete data set comprising all counties of the Weimar Republic, with meaningfully defined variables and cases weighted by population figures or the number of eligible voters, show that at least the initial electoral successes of the NSDAP did not follow the pattern predicted by the pure middle-class hypothesis. Only after the 1930 election did the NSDAP eventually become a socially more distinct (but by no means uniform) party, at least with regard to its territorially defined social correlates, as can be seen in Table 2.6.

By far the most important correlate of the Nazi vote is the religious denomination of the counties. The strong negative correlation between the percentage of catholics and the NSDAP share of the vote indicates that the National Socialist vote tends to be lower in a county with a higher percentage of catholics or, in other words, that in strongly protestant regions the NSDAP vote usually rose strongly to above average while in predominantly catholic regions it fell significantly below average. The influence of the other social characteristics on the NSDAP vote ranges from small to insignificant, or even zero. Neither the percentage of blue-collar workers (as might be expected) nor the percentage of self-employed nor the degree of urbanization nor any of the other variables displays a stronger statistical association with the NSDAP vote before March 1933, i.e. before Hitler came into power.

With the exception of the ultra-conservative, already greatly decimated DNVP, there is no other Weimar party with such a low (territorially defined) social profile. This is clearly demonstrated by the catch-all party index reported in Table 2.7, which represents the mean quadratic deviation from zero of the most important social correlates of each party under consideration. The index ranges from a theoretical maximum of 100 to a theoretical minimum of 0. The higher the index number, the more evenly distributed the party; the lower the number, the more extreme its social profile at the county level. The index shows that the NSDAP in 1928 was not only extremely small but also a socially indistinct splinter group. When its electorate increased it eventually gained a somewhat more distinct social profile without, however, becoming the class-based movement portrayed so vividly by the middle-class hypothesis. As mentioned above, the notion of *Volkspartei* embraces more than the social dimension. If one centres only on this aspect, however, the NSDAP may be properly characterized as a

ICPSR "German Weimar Republik Data 1919–1933" Under Scrutiny', *Historical Social Research* 1981, pp. 4–26.

Table 2.6. Social correlates of the Weimar parties (Pearson's $r \times 100$)

	1928	1930	1932 (July)	1932 (Nov.)	1933
NSDAP %					
Catholic	−9	−53	−71	−66	−55
Urban	−2	−4	−20	−21	−29
Agrarian	−7	−2	20	21	43
Blue collar	−10	0	−7	−8	−24
White collar	4	2	−22	−23	−39
Civil servant	16	15	−4	−6	−15
Self-employed	8	−4	16	18	37
Unemployed	−	13	−9	−13	−38
DNVP %					
Catholic	−43	−36	−47	−53	−55
Urban	−14	−15	−14	−8	−11
Agrarian	26	18	11	5	4
Blue collar	−9	−3	−6	−7	−1
White collar	−12	−2	3	11	8
Civil servant	−2	7	12	21	17
Self-employed	1	−10	−8	−12	−12
Unemployed	−	1	6	−1	−3
DVP %					
Catholic	−50	−40	−28	−31	−32
Urban	25	33	22	28	31
Agrarian	−48	−47	−37	−44	−46
Blue collar	19	18	2	5	9
White collar	45	46	38	47	49
Civil servant	37	34	34	37	34
Self-employed	−38	−40	−20	−25	−28
Unemployed	−	38	32	35	39
Z/BVP %					
Catholic	92	92	93	92	93
Urban	−10	−11	−9	−9	−8
Agrarian	25	27	25	25	21
Blue collar	−29	−31	−30	−30	−27
White collar	−24	−25	−23	−23	−21
Civil servant	−15	−16	−15	−15	−14
Self-employed	29	31	29	29	26
Unemployed	−	−28	−32	−30	−23
DDP %					
Catholic	−47	−32	−35	−31	−34
Urban	25	18	29	31	31
Agrarian	−42	−31	−26	−28	−39

Table 2.6. *continued*

Blue collar	−1	−8	−5	−6	−3
White collar	54	42	39	41	55
Civil servant	38	32	23	24	32
Self-employed	−21	−8	−8	−7	−17
Unemployed	−	5	12	15	27
SPD %					
Catholic	−66	−66	−66	−66	−62
Urban	17	14	19	15	20
Agrarian	−41	−38	−44	−40	−48
Blue collar	41	36	36	35	39
White collar	29	28	36	31	37
Civil servant	21	22	27	24	27
Self-employed	−46	−40	−45	−42	−45
Unemployed	−	37	45	40	42
KPD %					
Catholic	−25	−21	−17	−22	−26
Urban	35	37	40	41	41
Agrarian	−59	−63	−64	−67	−69
Blue collar	62	68	72	72	71
White collar	49	49	47	51	53
Civil servant	12	12	10	11	13
Self-employed	−65	−69	−71	−71	−70
Unemployed	−	45	65	70	73

movement which, at least at the territorial level, more than any other major party of the Weimar Republic matched the ideal type of *Volkspartei* or catch-all party of protest.

The Social Composition of the Nazi Constituency

Let us remain for a moment at the county level and take a closer look at the territorial provenance of the NSDAP voters. I shall now proceed from a bivariate to a multivariate perspective, a step which is justified by the fact that there are no one- or two-dimensional property spaces in reality. Each person is not only catholic or protestant, but lives in a rural or urban environment, is a member of the working or the middle class, earns his or her money in one of the three economic sectors, etc. The same is true for counties, communities and constituencies. They can all be characterized by a multitude of social attributes which may influence the electoral success of a party in an interactive or additive manner.

Table 2.7. The social profile of the major Weimar parties according to the
catch-all party index[1]

Party	1928	1930	1932 (July)	1932 (Nov.)	1933
NSDAP	93	83	76	77	68
DNVP	83	84	81	77	78
DVP	61	61	70	66	65
Z/BVP	68	67	67	68	69
DDP	62	72	74	74	65
SPD	64	67	62	65	62
KPD	54	53	51	50	50

1. Catch-all party index = 100 − squared mean of the correlation coefficients of selected
social variables $(100 - \sqrt{\Sigma(r.100)^2/n})$. The higher the index (upper limit = 100), the
less socially distinct is the party under consideration; the lower the index (lower limit
= 0), the more distinct is the social profile of the party. The above index is based on
sixteen different social characteristics (eight of them reported in Table 2.6). For
further detail, see Jürgen W. Falter and Dirk Hänisch, 'Die Anfälligkeit von Arbeitern
gegenüber der NSDAP bei den Reichstagswahlen 1928–1933', *Archiv für Sozialgeschichte*, vol. 26, 1986, p. 208.
Source: Jürgen W. Falter et al., *Wahlen und Abstimmungen in der Weimarer Republik*, Munich,
1986, pp. 163–70.

One method of displaying the joint effects of various social characteristics of the county units upon the vote is to use a form of tree
analysis. The 831 county units of the Weimar Republic are divided in a
consecutive sequence of steps into subclasses which are distinguished
by the (relative or absolute) presence or absence of a particular social
attribute. In the first step, the county units are divided into two
subclasses according to their degree of urbanization: into 592 predominantly rural counties where more than 50% of the population live in
villages with under 5,000 inhabitants and 239 urbanized counties. In
the next step these two subclasses are again divided, according to the predominating religious denomination. We thus obtain 213 rural counties
and forty-six urban counties with more than 67% catholics; about 100
(partly rural, partly urban) counties with a confessionally mixed
population; and 468 predominantly protestant counties (with less than
one-third of the population catholic), 312 of them mainly rural and 156
more urbanized. These six subgroups are then, in the third and final
step, split up into twelve categories according to the share of blue-collar
workers. We thus get a group of counties which are rural, predominantly catholic, and with an above or below average percentage of
blue-collar workers, etc.

For each of these county classes, on the one hand, the average share of the NSDAP vote has been calculated and, on the other, the percentage of Nazi voters coming from each group of counties. The results are displayed in Table 2.8, with the first four numbers representing the share of the NSDAP vote in each county group and the next four numbers showing the percentage of NSDAP voters coming from the particular county subclass. There is not enough room to discuss the results of this tree comparison (or, more precisely, of these two tree comparisons) in greater detail. We do, however, find out that there are theoretically significant differences with regard to the variables of religious denomination (with the NSDAP ranging far below average in catholic regions) and, to a lesser extent, urbanization (with above average NSDAP results in the rural parts of Germany, especially the protestant rural counties). But once again, the blue-collar factor does not exert a comparable influence to that of the confessional and urbanization variables, as would be expected if the middle-class hypothesis were adequate. If we change the perspective and look at the distribution of the National Socialist electorate within the various branches of our tree, we easily discover that despite the reported differing affinities of the various county classes towards National Socialism, NSDAP support is present in all branches of the tree. Again this may be regarded as an anomaly of the middle-class hypotheses.

We may conclude at this point in the analysis that the empirical basis of the middle-class conception is not only more or less disintegrating, but that there is in addition some positive evidence in favour of the catch-all hypothesis. On the other hand, we are still dealing with aggregate level relationships while the middle-class, as well as the catch-all, notion of National Socialism is expressed in individual level terms. It should be stressed that the findings concerning the social basis of the NSDAP support are based on county and community level relationships which should not be generalized down to the level of individual voters. It is clear that such aggregate findings do not necessarily imply a refutation of the predominating middle-class view. Below I shall therefore concentrate on the results of a series of ecological regression analyses of the affinity towards and the social composition of the Nazi constituency. These analyses follow the same logic (and suffer from the same restrictions) as explained above in connection with the ecological regression analysis of the voter fluctuations.

Table 2.8. A 'tree' comparison of the National Socialist electorate

Reichstag election	Percentage of electorate
1930	15
1932 (July)	31
1932 (Nov.)	26
1933	39
1930	100
1932 (July)	100
1932 (Nov.)	100
1933	100

Urbanization	
Rural	Urban
15	15
34	28
29	24
42	35
50	50
54	46
55	45
56	44
(49)	(51)

Religious denomination					
Catholic	Mixed	Protestant	Catholic	Mixed	Protestant
8	15	18	12	13	16
18	33	41	20	25	32
15	29	35	16	21	27
31	40	48	30	32	37
8	6	37	6	10	35
7	7	41	5	10	32
7	7	41	5	10	33
12	6	38	5	10	32
(13)	(6)	(30)	(7)	(12)	(32)

Table 2.8. *continued*

					Blue collar						
−	+	+	−	+	−	−	+	−	+	−	+
8	9	14	18	19	16	15	10	17	12	17	15
18	17	33	32	45	37	22	18	32	22	32	31
15	14	29	29	39	32	18	15	28	19	27	27
32	28	41	39	53	44	32	28	39	29	38	37
7	1	2	4	19	18	3	3	4	6	14	20
6	1	2	5	21	20	2	3	4	6	14	18
6	1	2	5	21	20	2	3	4	6	14	19
10	2	2	4	18	20	2	3	4	6	14	18
(11)	(2)	(4)	(2)	(14)	(16)	(3)	(4)	(4)	(8)	(13)	(19)

Source: As Table 2.3.

Some Results of Ecological Regression Analysis

The individual dispositions, which again were estimated by means of ecological regression analysis, indicate with regard to the social background of the NSDAP voters a much less distinct composition of the Nazi electorate than is implied by most varieties of the middle-class hypothesis. Only in regard to religious denomination are there some really clear-cut differences of affinity towards the NSDAP. Thus in July 1932 only one out of seven eligible catholic voters opted for National Socialism, while almost 40% of the non-catholic voting body seem to have voted NSDAP. During the last half-free election, of March 1933, this catholic resistance started to wither away. But even then the relative affinity of non-catholics towards National Socialism was almost double that of the catholics. If we look at the number of votes cast by the Catholic Centre Party, there is great overall stability. Only its Bavarian counterpart, the Bavarian People's Party, in comparison with 1930 and 1932, lost a few hundred thousand votes. Furthermore, if we consider that the social characteristic 'catholic' encompasses both believers and non-believers and church-going and non-practising members of the Catholic Church, we get a somewhat better idea of the immunization function exerted by political catholicism. This does not necessarily imply that Centre Party voters were more democratic or less authoritarian than the bulk of the National Socialist supporters (the same is certainly true with regard to the similarly 'immune' partisans of the Communist Party). Nevertheless it is utterly improbable that Hitler would have come to power in January 1933 with only 16% of the electorate behind him (this is the share of the vote he might have got in 1932 had all of Germany been catholic and the patterns of voting behaviour the same overall).

With respect to community size, the NSDAP appears to be one of the most evenly spread parties of the Weimar Republic. In 1928 and 1930 there were only insignificant differences in the voting propensities of village dwellers, small-town residents and inhabitants of the larger cities with regard to the NSDAP. After 1930, however, the NSDAP managed to expand more rapidly in the rural parts of Germany, especially in the protestant regions. Because of the total share of the electorate living in the countryside, the NSDAP's support thus came mainly from a rural or small-town background (see Table 2.9). But even in 1933 the percentage difference between the NSDAP vote of villagers and residents of large cities was much smaller than that between catholics and non-catholics, and the difference was much smaller, as we have shown elsewhere, than that of most other parties.

As pointed out above, the middle-class hypothesis claims a strong disparity of voting preferences towards Nazism between working-class and middle-class voters. Our ecological regression estimates indeed show a somewhat smaller affinity of working-class voters to the NSDAP. But the differences between the social strata displayed in Table 2.10 are much smaller than would be expected from the perspective of the middle-class hypothesis. In 1932 and 1933, according to our findings, not only blue-collar but also white-collar workers showed a below average sympathy for National Socialism at the polls, and the difference between these social categories is far from overwhelming. The only social layer with a strong (upward) deviation from the average NSDAP vote seems to have been the old middle class, i.e. the independent businessmen, artisans and farmers. At least in respect to this group Lipset seems to have been correct. Taken together, the two middle strata embrace about 60% of the Nazi constituency, a proportion which remains remarkably stable over the course of the five years under consideration. Working-class voters, on the other hand, consistently represent 40% of the NSDAP electorate (see Table 2.9).

Hence, even if we take into consideration the fact that the blue-collar category of the German census not only includes industrial workers but also farm labourers, craftsmen and workers in small shops, to name but a few, this margin appears much too high to speak any longer of the NSDAP as a pure or at least clearly predominant middle-class

Table 2.9. The social composition of the NSDAP electorate (reconstructed from Table 2.10)[1]

	1928	1930	1932 (July)	1932 (Nov.)	1933
Religious denomination					
Catholic	30	20	17	17	24
Other	70	80	83	83	76
Community size[2]					
0–5,000	39	41	(45)	(47)	47
5,000–20,000	14	13	(13)	(12)	12
20,000–100,000	16	15	(13)	(13)	13
More than 100,000	31	31	(28)	(27)	28
Social stratum					
Working class	40	40	39	39	40
New middle class	22	21	19	19	18
Old middle class	37	39	42	41	42
All	2	15	31	27	39

1. Entries show the percentage of NSDAP voters belonging to each category.
2. See note 2 for Table 2.10.
Source: As Table 2.3.

movement.[17] Again, our figures seem to support quite forcefully a catch-all conception of Nazism, a notion which accidentally is reflected both in the election propaganda of that party[18] and in the self-interpretation of some of its leaders, including Joseph Goebbels and even Adolf Hitler himself.[19]

Concluding Remarks

Having considered all things, the results of our findings show the NSDAP emerging as a party which drew support from

17. The same result is discerned by the newer membership analyses in Madden, *The Social Composition*, and Kater, *The Nazi Party*. For a comparison between membership figures and the NSDAP electorate, see Jürgen W. Falter, 'Warum die deutschen Arbeiter während des 3. Reiches zu Hitler standen', *Geschichte und Gesellschaft 1986–87*, pp. 217–31.
18. An attempt at reconstructing the Nazi campaigns of 1928–33 is made in Childers, *The Nazi Voter*.
19. Ample evidence in this regard may be found in the newly released Goebbels diaries (see Elke Fröhlich (ed.), *Die Tagebücher von Joseph Goebbels. Sämtliche Fragmente, Teil I: Aufzeichnungen 1924–1941*, 4 vols, Munich 1987); and Rainer Zitelmann, *Hitler. Selbstverständnis eines Revolutionärs*, Stuttgart, 1987.

Table 2.10. An ecological regression analysis of the affinity of voters from differing social backgrounds towards the NSDAP[1]

	1928	1930	1932 (July)	1932 (Nov.)	1933
Religious denomination					
Catholic	2	9	16	14	28
Other	2	18	38	33	44
Community size[2]					
0–5,000	1.8	14.6	(34)	(31)	43.9
5,000–20,000	2.0	15.8	(32)	(26)	37.3
20,000–100,000	2.3	15.7	(29)	(25)	36.6
More than 100,000	2.0	14.4	(28)	(23)	33.3
Social stratum					
Working class	2	12	25	21	31
New middle class	2	16	29	25	35
Old middle class	2	18	42	36	53
All	2	15	31	27	39

1. Entries show the percentage for the NSDAP of eligible voters of each category (estimated by means of ecological regression analysis).
2. Community figures for 1928, 1930 and 1933 represent 'real' percentages calculated on the basis of a recently established Weimar community data set (see Jürgen Falter, Thomas Lindenberger and Siegfried Schumann, *Wahlen und Abstimmungen in der Weimar Republik, Materialien zum Wahlverhalten 1919–1933*, Munich, 1986, p. 174). Numbers in brackets represent ecological regression estimates which were calculated on the basis of this community data set (for further detail see Jürgen W. Falter, 'Die Wähler der NSDAP 1928–1933. Sozialstruktur und parteipolitische Herkunft', in Wolfgang Michalka (ed.), *Die nationalsozialistische Machtergreifung 1933*, Paderborn, 1984, p. 51)
Source: As Table 2.3.

different social strata, and was – with two notable exceptions, religious denomination and the industrial proletariat – more equally distributed among the different social and demographic categories than any other major party of the Weimar Republic.[20] The same holds true with regard to the social composition of its voters and members. Thomas Childers therefore seems to be right to characterize the NSDAP as a catch-all party of protest which united – clearly visible differences of affinity notwithstanding – citizens of all regions, beliefs and social

20. Results for parties other than the NSDAP are given in Jürgen W. Falter, 'Die Stärke und Persistenz politischer Teilkulturen in der Weimar Republik', in Klaus Megerle and Detlef Lehnert (eds), *Politische Gedenktage als Indikatoren politischer Kultur in der Weimarer Republik*, Opladen, 1989, pp. 281–305, which is based in part on Jürgen W. Falter and Reinhard Zintl, 'The Economic Crisis of the 1930s and the Nazi Vote', in *Journal of Interdisciplinary History*, 1989, pp. 55–85.

backgrounds. The NSDAP thus emerges as a party which managed to a surprising extent, even before its seizure of power and the establishment of the Third Reich, to mould its socially fragmented followers into a *Volksgemeinschaft*-type of movement, an achievement which certainly did not make the appointment of Adolf Hitler as Reich Chancellor inevitable but at least made it conceivable. It should be clear by now that simple explanations of the electoral rise of the NSDAP such as the common variants of the middle-class hypothesis are thoroughly inadequate to grasp this phenomenon in all its complexity.

According to our findings, we may regard the surge of the NSDAP at the polls as a combination of middle-class formation (or extremism, to use Lipset's terminology) and working-class protest.[21] This mixture was amalgamated by many different factors; some more or less unique to German history, such as an extraordinarily fragmented political culture, a particularly splintered party system and the absence of a democratic consensus among political elites; and by others common to most Western nations at the time, such as the impact of the Great Depression, the effects of unemployment and the agrarian crisis of the 1920s. These factors, plus the organizational and propagandistic ability of Adolf Hitler and Joseph Goebbels, brought the Weimar Republic to an end and paved the way for a most inhuman totalitarian regime. Historical electoral analysis helps us to understand these processes – but only if its reconstruction of past voting behaviour is adequate and not over-simplified, as is the case with both the standard middle-class hypothesis and the mass-theoretical explanation.

21. For further detail with regard to terminology and theoretical background, and for some more detailed empirical evidence see Falter and Zintl, 'The Economic Crisis'.

MERITH NIEHUSS

Party Configurations in State and Municipal Elections in Southern Germany, 1871–1914

Politics in southern Germany has always differed from the politics of the German Reich as a whole. In particular, the function of the SPD (Social Democratic Party) within south-western parliaments diverged substantially from that in Prussia and in most middle and north German state parliaments. Thus, for example, according to August Bebel, the first time that a member of the government ever addressed a word to him in his almost forty-year parliamentary career was when Chancellor Bethmann Hollweg inquired as to the state of his health in 1913 (shortly before Bebel's death).[1] In the three south-western states of Bavaria, Baden and Württemberg, on the other hand, contacts between bourgeois and Social Democratic parliamentarians were not unusual at all.[2]

The manifestly greater integration of the south German Social Democrats into bourgeois society can be ascribed to their far less class-conscious attitude. They focused less on the final goal of socialist reorganization and more on step-by-step improvements, particularly in the realm of social policy: 'We must keep the future in mind but at the same time we must not forget the present, the imminent and that which is most urgent.'[3] The particular economic situation of the south German

This paper was translated by Catherine Stodolsky.
1. Gustav Mayer, *Erinnerungen*, Munich, 1949, p. 179.
2. See for further examples Reinhard Jansen, *Georg von Vollmar. Eine politische Biographie*, Düsseldorf, 1958, and Wilhelm Keil, *Erlebnisse eines Sozialdemokraten*, vol. 1, Stuttgart, 1947.
3. Georg von Vollmar, *Reden und Schriften zur Reformpolitik*, selected and introduced by

states was certainly an important factor in accounting for this pragmatic Social Democratic line. In Bavaria, Baden and Württemberg, in contrast with the Reich or Prussia, more inhabitants lived and worked in the agricultural sector and fewer in the bigger cities; industrialization was not as advanced as in most of the German Reich. Likewise the agrarian sector differed substantially in Bavaria and in Prussia; in the south of Germany, small peasant holdings dominated the farm economy; giant agricultural estates, such as those found in east Prussia, were practically non-existent.[4] Where large industrial settlements did exist, as for example in the areas around the major cities of Munich, Nuremberg, Stuttgart and Mannheim, they were strongly diversified; unskilled labourers, common in the heavily industrialized areas of the Rhineland and Silesia, were not present there. Even in the so-called 'industrial agglomerations', in the big cities, the working classes were generally less well represented than was the case in the German Reich as a whole.[5]

Social Democratic electoral potential was relatively low in all three states, on the assumption that industrial workers constituted the major proportion of the SPD's potential voters. Yet in the southern German states, social democracy attracted a large proportion of its voters from among the bourgeois classes. A contemporary analysis of the Reichstag elections of 1893 and 1898 even tried to prove that at least a quarter of Social Democratic voters came from the bourgeoisie and that in the large cities this percentage constituted as much as a third to one-half of the Social Democratic vote.[6]

This meant that, on the one hand, in the less industrialized states of the south-west, the Social Democrats sought to increase their representation among this bourgeois electoral potential, composed mostly of members of the petty bourgeoisie and including many employees and to a certain extent also including the self-employed. On the other hand, the party tried to make inroads into the heavily agricultural areas and among the stratum of small farmers.

Willy Albrecht, Berlin, Bonn and Bad Godesberg, 1977, p. 140 (from speech in 1891).

4. See figures in Gerhard A. Ritter and Merith Niehuss, *Wahlgeschichtliches Arbeitsbuch. Materialien zur Statistik des Kaiserreichs, 1871–1918*, Munich, 1980, p. 43; and *Bayerns Entwicklung nach den Ergebnissen der amtlichen Statistik seit 1840*, Munich, 1915, p. 19.

5. The percentage of workers in Munich out of the total number of employed in 1895 was 47.6%, while in the Reich at that time the average was already 52.8%, including all agricultural areas; summarized in *Statistik des Deutschen Reichs*, vol. 107, *Berufsstatistik der deutschen Großstädte*, 1895, pp. 268, 284.

6. Robert Blank, 'Die soziale Zusammensetzung der sozialdemokratischen Wählerschaft Deutschlands', *Archiv für Sozialwissenschaft*, vol. 20, Tübingen, 1905, pp. 507–50; figures on pp. 520, 527. However, this calculation does not seem to be correct in every detail. For a critique see Gerhard A. Ritter, *Die Arbeiterbewegung im wilhelminischen Reich. Die Sozialdemokratische Partei und die Freien Gewerkschaften 1890–1900*, Berlin, 1963, p. 77ff.

The discord between the southern German party and the national party came to the fore in the 'agrarian question' and even more so in the quarrel over the sanctioning of state-parliamentary budgets. According to Social Democratic tradition, approval for government budgetary proposals was unthinkable – and yet it was often practised in the southern German Diets (Landtage). This example and also the example of the suffrage issue (*Wahlrechtsfrage*) illustrate the policy of step-by-step reform (*Politik der kleinen Schritte*). Though this tactic was strongly attacked and condemned by the party as a whole, the southern German party organizations became unquestionably the most successful state organizations of social democracy at the turn of the century.

The extent to which the SPD could gain influence in the Landtage depended upon the size of its parliamentary faction. This in turn depended largely on the nature of the electoral system in each state. These differed widely and were compared in their results with the franchise in the German Reichstag. It is thus necessary briefly to discuss three important aspects of the Reichstag electoral law.

(1) Election to the Reichstag was by absolute direct majority vote, e.g. a representative who received more than 50% of all votes in an electoral district was directly elected. In the event of no clear majority, a second ballot would be held. These second-ballot elections, the so-called run-off elections, gained major importance towards the end of the imperial period because they took place in almost every electoral district of the Reich. A party which had not reached the second ballot had to decide whether to advise its supporters to abstain or whether to ask them to give their votes to one of the two rival parties' candidates. The strategy adopted in these run-off elections, and especially the parties' ability to form political alliances, were decisive factors in determining the strength of the respective party factions. On the whole, the Social Democrats were in a weak position, since the bourgeois parties generally united against them. For example, in 1903, the SPD won only twenty-four out of 117 run-off elections in which they had placed a candidate; the others were won by bourgeois opposition candidates. The left liberal Liberal People's Party (Freisinnige Volkspartei), by contrast, won twenty-one out of the twenty-four second-ballot races in which they participated.[7]

(2) The second central aspect of the Reichstag electoral law was its liberality regarding the right to vote. Every German male over 25 years

---

7. Ritter and Niehuss, *Wahlgeschichtliches Arbeitsbuch*, p. 125.

of age who resided in one of the German states was entitled to vote. There were relatively few exceptions – they were primarily active military personnel and persons who received poor relief. The franchise in the Reich was thus 'universal' and also 'equal' (one man, one vote), in contrast with most state franchises; and, in addition, in great contrast to the Prussian electoral system, it was secret. One can therefore assume that the distribution of votes for each party in the Reichstag was an accurate reflection of the attitudes of the population of the German Reich towards these parties – more accurate in any case than most European electoral systems of the period would have allowed. On the basis of the workings of this electoral system, the Social Democratic Party was able to gain a fairly exact picture of its strength in each regional area. Normally one of the most prominent figures of the party, such as August Bebel, would be run as a candidate in many electoral districts at the same time in order to assure the largest possible number of voters.[8] In the same way the catholic Centre Party, despite the fact that it only made sense for it to place candidates in those electoral districts with a high percentage of catholics, would nevertheless put up candidates in districts in which their chances of victory were slim. The object was to get some of their candidates into the run-off elections and use them for bargaining with other parties.[9]

(3) The third factor which significantly influenced electoral procedure in the Reichstag elections was the apportionment of electoral districts. Although the law of 1869 provided that district boundaries could be changed in accord with population movements in order to secure approximately 100,000 inhabitants per district, this was never in fact put into effect.[10] This meant that the enormous demographic displacements from the countryside to the cities or industrial conglomerations – from east to west – which were taking place at this time, were not being taken into account. Thus, for example, in a district near Berlin, it took nearly 340,000 voters to elect one representative, while in a country district (Schaumburg-Lippe) only 10,700 were required to elect one representative. Those who profited from this system were the parties whose electoral potential came from the countryside, i.e. the

---

8. If one of these candidates (*Zählkandidaten*) had won in several districts, he was obliged to choose one of them. In all other districts new elections (*Nachwahlen*) would have to take place.

9. Wolfgang Schulte, *Struktur und Entwicklung des Parteisystems im Königreich Württemberg. Versuche zu einer quantitativen Analyse der Wahlergebnisse*, Mannheim, 1970 (dissertation), pp. 118, 120.

10. For an introduction to the Reichstag electoral laws and also for the data following see Ritter and Niehuss, *Wahlgeschichtliches Arbeitsbuch*.

Prussian Conservative Party and, in the catholic areas, the Centre Party. Those significantly disadvantaged were the Social Democrats, whose electoral base was in densely populated areas, in industrial centres and in the large cities. In the Reichstag election of 1907 the SPD received nearly 30% of the vote but only 11% of the seats.

The negative consequences of this situation for the SPD came not only from unfavourable delineation of electoral boundaries, but also from the fact that in the run-off elections, bourgeois parties were far more likely to form a coalition against the SPD than the SPD was likely to form a coalition with one bourgeois party against another.[11] Despite these disadvantages, the positive outweighed the negative in the view of contemporary Social Democrats, who compared this with other electoral systems. This was because under this system, first of all, the potential SPD constituency, the workers, were fully enfranchised (unless they were among the relatively small percentage of voters who were on poor relief). In the Kaiserreich the increase in the number of industrial workers as well as the workers' growing consciousness of their inferior social position had led to a considerable increase in the electoral potential of the SPD.

Secondly, in those electoral districts in which industrial workers dominated and constituted a majority, a socialist representative could be elected. The party won five out of six Berlin electoral districts in 1912, nineteen out of twenty-three districts in Saxony and continuously dominated all three Hamburg electoral districts from 1890 onwards. These were impressive successes for a party which was under great political and social persecution.

The position of the bourgeois parties, i.e. all the other parties in the Reichstag, on the suffrage issue was significantly influenced by the performance of the SPD, whose meteoric rise in the Reichstag was regarded as a severe threat. And although proposals to restrict the vote were put forward, they proved politically and socially unacceptable. Once the right to vote had been granted, it could not be taken away. On the other hand, the SPD's demand to reorganize the electoral districts was equally unacceptable to the bourgeois parties loyal to the government, despite the fact that the liberal parties also stood to gain from a redrawing of electoral boundaries.

The liberality of the Reichstag suffrage could be measured in terms of

11. For a description of election campaigns, see Jürgen Bertram, *Die Wahlen zum deutschen Reichstag vom Jahre 1912. Parteien und Verbände in der Innenpolitik des wilhelminischen Reiches*, Düsseldorf, 1964.

the performance of the parties in the state elections (*Landtagswahlen*).[12] None of the state suffrage systems was nearly as 'general' or 'equal' as the Reichstag franchise; indeed, the Prussian elections were not even secret. A suffrage system which severely restricted the franchise, the three-class electoral system, had been introduced in Prussia and Saxony. In Saxony, although the Social Democrats received almost 50% of the votes in the 1903 Landtag election, they did not win a single seat in the state parliament. In the same year they sent twenty-two out of twenty-three Saxon representatives to the Reichstag. Before 1898, out of protest against this discriminatory suffrage system, the Social Democrats in Prussia, the largest of the German states, refused to participate in the Landtag elections. In 1903 the Prussian Social Democrats did not win a single seat in the Landtag, whereas in the Reichstag election of the same year they were able to seat thirty-four representatives – i.e. 14% of all the representatives from Prussia – with a voter participation of 29%. The situation in southern Germany was different: although here state electoral laws were also balanced against the interests of the lower classes, they nevertheless more closely resembled the Reichstag suffrage system.

Landtag Elections in Bavaria

Until the electoral reform in 1906, the Bavarian franchise meant much greater restriction of voter rights than the Reichstag franchise did.[13] Excluded from the right to vote were all those who had not paid direct taxes for at least six months in the year before the election (i.e. mostly those citizens whose incomes lay under the taxable minimum); those who had received poor relief within the previous twelve months; those placed under legal disability or those whose estate was in bankruptcy and, lastly, active military personnel (law of 1881). Altogether about one-third of adult male Bavarians were thus excluded from the vote, most of them coming from the lower social strata. The second essential curtailment of the franchise in Bavaria, the

---

12. For an overview see Ritter and Niehuss, *Wahlgeschichtliches Arbeitsbuch*.
13. For the development of the Bavarian electoral laws, see Ludwig Hubbauer, *Die geschichtliche Entwicklung des bayerischen Landtagswahlrechts, mit Beschränkung auf die Kammer der Abgeordneten*, Borna and Leipzig, 1908 (Ph.D. dissertation); Robert Theilhaber, *1808–1908. Hundert Jahre bayerische Wahlrechtsentwicklung. Ein Beitrag zur wissenschaftlichen Politik*, Munich, 1908; Dietrich Thränhardt, *Wahlen und politische Strukturen in Bayern 1848–1953. Historisch-soziologische Untersuchungen zur Entstehung und Neuerrichtung eines Parteiensystems*, Düsseldorf, 1973.

largest of the south German states, was the indirect vote. At first, so-called *Urwähler* or electors elected delegates (*Wahlmänner*) for the parties under absolute majority vote. These delegates in turn elected one or more representatives (*Abgeordnete*) to the Landtag, once again under absolute majority rule. This meant that there could be run-off elections on two levels. First of all, the parties could build coalitions for the run-off election as early as at the *Urwähler* level, if and when the delegates had not achieved the necessary majority. On the second level – certainly a procedure which the parties found it easier to control – coalitions could be formed on the delegate level, in a situation when the delegates were unable to elect a candidate for parliament with an absolute majority.

Bavaria, unlike Prussia, reorganized its electoral districts often. In practice, however, this led to clear manipulation by the Liberal government in favour of the Liberal Party minority.[14] Nor did such a redistribution change the over-population in the individual districts. This so-called 'electoral geometry', which at first was primarily directed against the Centre Party, ended up in the 1880s by favouring it, since it had in the meantime gained support among the peasantry. Now the Social Democrats, who were most active in the inner-city electoral districts, were placed at a disadvantage. Even before the Landtag election of 1905, right before the electoral law reform was to take place, the government – which was still dominated by the liberals – tried to redistribute once again. 'The idea was to take two or three seats from the SPD and one from the Peasant League', wrote a contemporary observer, 'so that the Centre Party would be somewhat compensated and thus stop complaining about unfair districting and, further, so that the Liberals could continue to enjoy the benefits of the previous redistribution.'[15]

In the course of the 1890s the Centre Party and the Social Democrats together gradually developed a common strategy for a new electoral district reform. Election coalitions were officially established by the respective party leaders; in the 1880s, when the *Sozialistengesetz* was still in effect, the socialists had been unable to form coalitions. Here and there isolated alliances (for example in 1884, with the liberals against the rule of the Centre Party in the two Munich districts) had been formed, but they were kept secret at the time.[16] The first official election

---

14. These examples are from Thränhardt, *Wahlen und politische Strukturen*, p. 115.
15. Adolf Braun, 'Die bayerische Wahlkreisgeometrie', *Die Neue Gesellschaft*, vol. 1, pp. 137–9.
16. Thränhardt, *Wahlen und politische Strukturen*, p. 119.

agreements between the Centre Party and the Social Democrats in 1899 doubled the Social Democratic representation in the Landtag (from five to eleven representatives) and brought the Centre Party an absolute majority. This new position of power brought the possibility of electoral reform in the Landtag in sight. The fact of a Centre Party majority in the Landtag guaranteed that Centre Party interests would be taken into account when a new electoral law was framed. After several setbacks in the legislative sessions after 1899, the two parties finally succeeded in getting the representatives who had been elected in 1905 to discuss the new electoral law, to dissolve the Landtag and to set up new elections for 1907, when the new law would be in effect.[17]

   The electoral demands of the Social Democrats were indirectly but substantially influenced by the 1899 electoral agreement. The mere willingness to co-operate with supposed opponents appeared to some members as leading to a weakening of 'combative class consciousness',[18] thus casting a shadow over the joy produced by the doubling of the number of seats. Some Social Democrat members were dismayed at the ease with which their own people were able to enter into this opportunistic electoral co-operation with the Centre Party.[19] At the same time, the overwhelming Centre Party majority in 1899 also influenced the discussion concerning the new electoral law. First of all, however, the two most important demands of the Social Democrats had now been fulfilled. These were the introduction of direct elections for the representatives, and a reorganization of electoral districts. However, simultaneously, the suffrage was restricted because the minimum age for voters was raised from 21 to 25 and the minimum length of residence (including paying direct taxes) required for voters in Bavaria was now increased from six months to one year. This meant an average reduction of voters in Bavaria by about 1%; in Munich it meant a reduction in the percentage of qualified voters from 19.6% of the inhabitants in 1905 to 17.9% in 1907.

   Despite these reductions, the Social Democrats voted in favour of the new electoral law. This decision met with general sympathy among Social Democrats in south-west Germany. The Augsburg Social Democratic Party Congress of 1904 expressly approved the electoral coalition and unanimously voted for a resolution that the party should push energetically to secure a two-thirds majority for the electoral reform.[20]

17. For a detailed description, see Jansen, *Georg von Vollmar*, pp. 63ff.
18. Ibid., p. 69.
19. Heinrich Hirschfelder, *Die bayerische Sozialdemokratie 1864–1914*, 2 vols, Erlangen, 1979, quotation from Ehrhart, socialist leader in the Palatinate.
20. Ibid., p. 479.

Table 3.1. Elected representatives in Bavaria
(a) Reichstag elections

Year of election	Number of representatives	Centre Party	National Liberals	Liberals	Left liberals[1]	Conservatives	Peasant League[2]	People's Party	Social Democratic Party	Other
1871	48	18	10	14	6	–	–	–	–	–
1874	48	32	10	1	5	–	–	–	–	–
1877	48	31	10	2	3	2[3]	–	–	–	–
1878	48	31	10	3	1	3[3]	–	–	–	–
1881	48	32	8	4	2	–	–	1	1	–
1884	48	33	9	–	2	–	–	2	2	–
1887	48	33	13	–	1	–	–	–	1	–
1890	48	33	9	–	2	1	–	–	3	–
1893	48	30	8	–	1	1	2	1	3	2
1898	48	29	6	–	–	1	6	1	4	1
1903	48	30	6	–	2	1	5	–	4	–
1907	48	34	4	–	2	2	3	–	3	–
1912	48	29	3	–	1	2	4	–	9	–

(b) Bavarian Landtag

Year of election	Number of representatives	Centre Party[4]	Liberals[5]	Peasant League[2]	Conservatives	Middle-class Party	People's Party	Social democrats	Belonging to no party
May 1869	154	78	59	–	–	16	1	–	–
Nov. 1869	154	80	63	–	–	11	–	–	–
1875	156	79	77	–	–	–	–	–	–
1881	159	70	89	–	–	–	–	–	–
1887	158	81	71	–	5	–	1	–	–
1893	159	74	67	9	3	–	1	5	–
1899	159	83	44	13	5	–	1	11	2
1905	157	102	22	15	4	–	2	12	–
1907	163	98	25	13	6	–	–	20	1
1912	163	87	30	8	7	–	–	30	1

1. Until 1881 German Progressive Party (Deutsche Fortschrittspartei); 1884–90 , Liberal Party (German Independent Party/Deutsche Freisinnige Partei); 1893–1907 Liberal People's Party (Freisinnige Volkspartei); 1912 Progressive People's Party (Fortschrittliche Volkspartei).
2. German Peasant League (Deutscher Bauernbund), Bavarian Peasant League (Bayerischer Bauernbund), League of Farmers (Bund der Landwirte).
3. German Reich Party (Deutsche Reichspartei).
4. Until 1887, Bavarian Party of Patriots.
5. The Liberal faction consists of National Liberals and left liberals.
Source: Gerhard A. Ritter and Merith Niehuss, *Wahlgeschichtliches Arbeitsbuch. Materialien zur Statistik des Kaiserreichs, 1871–1918*, Munich, 1980, pp. 88, 155.

In the first elections under the new electoral law, no agreement concerning coalitions was made. Despite the reduction in the number of eligible voters, the Social Democrats ended up with a substantial victory; they now had twenty instead of their previous twelve representatives in the Landtag. The Centre Party also got something out of their agreement with the Social Democrats, and merely lost four seats. With ninety-eight out of 163 seats in the Landtag they still held the absolute majority. The Liberals won twenty-five seats.

As early as 1906 this predominance of the Centre Party in the Landtag – and it is worth noting that the Social Democrats had adopted no common policy stand with the Centre Party except for the electoral reform – pushed the Social Democrats towards a *rapprochement* with the left wing of the Liberal Party. (In Bavarian Landtag elections left-wing and National Liberals united.) They hoped that with the Liberals they could strive for co-operation especially in the areas of school and university policy. Until 1907 the politics of the Liberals had blocked a closer tie, but by 1912, comparable to the big block policy (*Großblockpolitik*) in the Reich, the ground in Bavaria had been prepared for concerted action in the electoral campaign, but this time with the aim of breaking the Centre Party majority. In addition, a substantial dispute had broken out between the Centre Party and the SPD concerning union representation of Bavarian railway workers. None the less, the Social Democrats did receive Centre Party support once more for a new community (*Gemeinde*) electoral law in 1908.

Landtag Elections in Württemberg

The franchise for the Württemberg Landtag was traditionally the most liberal of all the south-western German states. It was general, equal and direct, and was valid for every male citizen over 25 years of age. The right to vote in Württemberg was not distorted by restrictions concerning the amount of taxes paid nor were there any requirements of minimum residency. Even the paragraph in the law code denying the vote to those who had received poor relief in the previous year was substantially weakened by various exceptions.[21] Care was taken to ensure secrecy of the ballot – envelopes were available in the polling booth – and the polling-stations were held

---

21. For the Württemberg electoral law, see Carl Große and Carl Raith, *Beiträge zur Geschichte und Statistik der Reichstags- und Landtagswahlen in Württemberg seit 1871*, Stuttgart, 1912.

open as long as possible – from 10 a.m. until 7 p.m. – so that all those working could take part in the vote. Elections, however, continued to be held on work days, despite socialist demands that elections be held on Sundays.

Nevertheless, there were substantial restrictions on the democratic character of the state parliaments in Württemberg thus elected. In addition to the seventy elected parliamentary representatives, there were twenty-three so-called 'privileged ones'; these included thirteen members of the knighted aristocracy, six members of the state Protestant Church and three members of the Catholic Church as well as the Chancellor of the state university. Elements of the upper chamber, which existed in all German states and which generally were reserved for the aristocracy and special dignitaries, were clearly being incorporated into the people's chamber. It was the aim of almost all parties to shift this privileged group from the lower chamber into the upper house. This idea found support even within the upper house, whose members barely got through their tasks since many of the aristocrats were continually absent, leaving the law-making job to those few who remained, and incidentally making the adoption of resolutions nearly impossible.[22]

The fact that it took twenty years for an electoral reform – despite agreement on it in principle, as we have seen earlier – is explained by the opposition mounted against it by the Centre Party, particularly in the final phase, around 1906.

The Centre Party was founded in Württemberg only at the beginning of the 1890s as a state association. Württemberg was traditionally liberal in its religious policies, and allowed for equal rights for both churches. There was no *Kulturkampf* in Württemberg and the catholic parliamentary representatives in the catholic southern parts of Württemberg either regarded themselves as part of a weakly organized, conservative-leaning catholic state party, or voted with the democratic left. When in 1894 a state association of the Centre Party came into existence, it moved into the so-called 'Halbmondsaal', or Landtag with a powerful block of eighteen representatives. The transfer of the twenty-three 'privileged' of whom only three were catholic, to the upper chamber meant the loss of the catholic majority in the upper chamber which had hitherto existed, thanks to the presence of the nobles. The catholic faction in the lower chamber fearfully regarded every possible idea of electoral reform as an attempt to worsen their

22. Walter Grube, *Der Stuttgarter Landtag 1457–1957*, Stuttgart, 1957, p. 547.

position. In particular, they feared the powerful Left Liberal People's Party, which vehemently demanded, along with the two new Social Democratic representatives, that proportional representation should be introduced, and that the districts were to be redrawn. The Centre Party, like the Conservative Party, profited substantially from the totally outdated electoral boundaries, which dated back to 1819.

According to the antiquated system, sixty-three *Oberämter* (districts) had one representative each and the seven 'good cities' of the state also each had one representative.[23] Even by 1871, population shifts in the cities and in the *Oberämter* had altered the balance most unequally so that it took nearly 13,000 voters to elect one representative in Stuttgart while in the country districts it took only 3,000 to 5,000; in 1906 51,000 voters in Stuttgart were required to elect one representative, whereas in the country districts it was only 5,000 to 8,000. The six 'good cities' did not follow Stuttgart's pattern and the number of their inhabitants remained at the same level as the *Oberämter*.[24]

Since the subsequent Landtag elections of 1900 produced only unimportant changes in individual party factions, compromises were desired by all those involved. The final draft thus left intact the boundaries of the *Oberämter* and also those of the 'good cities'. Stuttgart, exceptionally, was assigned six rather than the one representative it had previously had. By retaining the absolute majority principle in the *Oberämter* and in the six 'good cities' in a modified form – whereby in a run-off election all the representatives would stand for election a second time, but for this second ballot they would be elected by a simple majority – the Conservatives were guaranteed most of the protestant *Oberämter* and the Centre Party most of the catholic south. Despite the fact that Stuttgart was not included, extreme inequalities in the size of the electoral districts remained. In 1906 the ratio was one member of parliament for 4,700 inhabitants in the city of Ellwangen and one for 58,000 inhabitants in Eßlingen.

To replace the twenty-three 'privileged', who had moved to the upper chamber, the six representatives from Stuttgart, as well as seventeen more representatives (i.e. twenty-three altogether), were still to be elected in two *Landeswahlkreisen* (Land constituencies) according to proportional representation. In the future, it was decided, elections on this level would be scheduled only after the results of the

---

23. The exceptional position of these cities (Stuttgart, Tübingen, Ludwigsburg, Ellwangen, Ulm, Heilbronn and Reutlingen) called 'our good cities' was established in 1810. See Große and Raith, *Beiträge zur Geschichte*, p. 8.
24. Data from ibid., pp. 37–41.

elections according to the majority principle had been announced.

Those who profited most from the new electoral law were the Social Democrats, who were able to triple the number of their representatives in 1906 over those gained in 1900 and come into the Landtag with fifteen representatives. The Centre Party also picked up strength, as did the Conservatives. While the National Liberal Party could maintain the number of its seats, the People's Party lost three seats as well as its position as the second strongest faction after the Centre Party in the Landtag. In the subsequent election of 1912, the People's Party lost seats once again, the Social Democrats and the Centre Party each won several seats and the Conservatives moved into the Landtag substantially strengthened, with twenty seats instead of their previous fifteen.

The example of Württemberg clearly illustrates the emergence of parliamentary factions. Before 1895 most parliamentary representatives were not able to give a specific party affiliation. Many of the dignitaries (*Honoratioren*) who went under the label 'catholic', 'liberal' or 'democratic' had been representing their electoral districts for decades. In the elections of 1876, 1882 and 1889, in one-half of all electoral districts only one candidate was nominated, so that 'One can hardly call it an election.'[25]

In 1894, the founding of the Centre Party faction in the Landtag and the election of two Social Democrats initiated a period of explosive politicizing of the factions. In 1895 the Württemberg State Party (Landespartei), to which the acting prime minister (*Minister präsident*) belonged, was no longer one of the parties in the Landtag. It was not until after the 1906 election that the representatives decided to change the seating arrangement, which was according to age, and to base a new one on party affiliation.[26]

Despite this general democratization, the still very reserved attitude of the government towards the Social Democrats is illustrated best by the case of a protestant pastor who was elected as a parliamentary representative for the Social Democrats in 1900, but who was obliged to give up his status and rank of pastor of the church of Württemberg.[27] Another example is the case of one of the mayors in a municipality, a member of one of the bourgeois parties, who warmly applauded a speech by the Social Democrat Wilhelm Keil and was promptly

25. Schulte, *Struktur und Entwicklung*, p. 73.
26. Grube, *Der Stuttgarter Landtag*, p. 554.
27. See the priest's self-defence in Maja Christ-Gmelin, 'Die württembergische Sozialdemokratie 1890–1914', in Jörg Schadt and Wolfgang Schmierer (eds), *Die SPD in Baden-Württemberg und ihre Geschichte. Von den Anfängen der Arbeiterbewegung bis heute*, Stuttgart, Berlin and Cologne, 1979, pp. 107–31.

removed from office. Only the personal intervention of the Lord Mayor made it possible to commute his punishment to a fine.[28]

Even the adoption of the proportional vote revealed the bias characteristic of the age. The proportional electoral procedure in state elections was first introduced in Württemberg (if Hamburg, a city state, is not considered) but was restricted, as was common in quite a few communities at the time, to specific regions, in particular to those in which it was feared the Social Democrats were gaining too much ground. Thus in Württemberg the party with the most votes, the SPD, did not win enough seats to constitute the strongest parliamentary faction.

It is interesting that the proportional electoral procedure came to be adopted in its most difficult form, with the use of open lists. The voter was even allowed to 'accumulate' votes and select candidates from other lists. It is obvious that the parties often had difficulty in convincing their voters of the validity of their electoral lists.[29]

Despite the above examples, Württemberg certainly ranks as the state in which social democracy was least exposed to coercive measures. In 1898, SPD members were allowed to organize a First of May parade. This was the first in the German Reich. In 1907 the International Socialist Congress took place in Stuttgart because the participants regarded Württemberg as the only state in Germany in which they would be granted freedom of speech.

Landtag Elections in Baden

In contrast to the situation in peaceful neighbouring Württemberg, fierce disputes over the *Kulturkampf* raged in Baden for even longer than they had in Prussia. And just as the storm had begun to calm, it started anew in the wake of the politically motivated assassination of a catholic clergyman in 1888. Unlike other German states, where the Conservative Party represented most of the protestant agrarian constituency, in Baden it was the National Liberals who were most identified with protestantism. The Catholic People's Party and the National Liberals were opposed to each other as irreconcilable blocks, even though they were, at least at first, very unequal in size.

---

28. Ibid., p. 115.
29. Heinz Striebich, *Konfession und Partei. Ein Beitrag zur Entwicklung der politischen Willensbildung im alten Lande Baden*, Heidelberg, 1955 (dissertation), p. 49; Karl Bachem, *Vorgeschichte, Geschichte und Politik der deutschen Zentrumspartei*, vol. 8, Cologne, 1931, p. 100.

Table 3.2. Elected representatives in Württemberg
(a) Reichstag elections

Year of election	Number of representatives	Centre Party	National Liberals	Left liberals[1]	People's Party	German Reich Party	Social Democratic Party	Peasant League[3]	Other
1871	17	1	12	–	–	3	–	–	1
1874	17	3	9	1	–	4	–	–	–
1877	17	3	3	1	2	8	–	–	–
1878	17	3	2	1	1	10	–	–	–
1881	17	4	–	1	6	6	–	–	–
1884	17	4	4	1	4	4	–	–	–
1887	17	4	8	–	–	5	–	–	–
1890	17	4	3	–	9	1	–	–	–
1893	17	4	2	–	10	1	–	–	–
1898	17	4	3	–	7	2[2]	1	–	–
1903	17	4	1	–	5	–	4	3	–
1907	17	4	2	1	6	–	1	3	–
1912	17	4	2	6	–	–	3	2	–

(b) Württemberg Landtag

Year of election	Number of representatives	Centre Party	National Liberals	Conservatives[4]	People's Party	Social Democratic Party
1895	70 (+23)	18	14	5	31	2
1900	70 (+23)	18	13	7	27	5
1906	92	25	13	15	24	15
1912	92	26	10	20	19	17

1. As note 1 of Table 3.1
2. One Conservative.
3. German Peasant League (Deutscher Bauernbund) and League of Farmers (Bund der Landwirte).
4. Several Conservative groups.
Sources: Gerhard A. Ritter and Merith Niehuss, *Wahlgeschichtliches Arbeitsbuch. Materialien zur Statistik des Kaiserreichs, 1871–1918*, Munich, 1980, p. 89; Carl Große and Carl Raith, *Beiträge zur Geschichte und Statistik der Reichstags- und Landtagswahlen in Württemberg seit 1871*, Stuttgart, 1912, pp. 51–8, 2*–69*.

Whereas the National Liberal Party had achieved an early majority, the power of the Catholic People's Party dwindled at every election after 1883, moving from nineteen to fourteen seats, and finally ending up at seven seats in 1887. This was the consequence of an inner split within the party, the struggle of the hawks against the doves.[30] 'The situation was irreparable.'[31] Even the organizational tie between the Catholic People's Party and the Centre Party in 1888/9 and the change

30. Striebich, *Konfession und Partei*, p. 48.
31. Bachem, *Vorgeschichte, Geschichte und Politik*, p. 99.

of name to the Baden Centre Party did nothing to calm things down. The Baden Centre Party, by this time under the dictatorial leadership of Theodor Wacker, was not always in agreement with the politics of the national Centre Party. Its main aim was to try to wear down the powerful National Liberal/protestant opponent, which itself was under the influence of its radical wing. Since the National Liberals in Baden held the majority and composed the government, the Centre Party sought to build an alliance with the opposition, primarily, at least in the 1890s, with the left.

The franchise for the Landtag in Baden at this time was based upon an absolute majority system with indirect elections. This offered the parties the possibility of forming coalitions or even obliged them to do so either on the elector level or on the delegate level. This indirect electoral system, as well as the setting up of electoral districts which obtained, worked to the considerable benefit of the National Liberals. All opposition parties therefore advocated a reform of the electoral laws and were prepared to enter into coalitions for this purpose.

Under this system the Social Democratic Party's chances of gaining seats in the Landtag were very slim. They therefore boycotted the Landtag elections until 1891, when they finally did run and came into the Landtag with two seats.[32] The existence of a clear-cut opposition block of all the different parties opposed to the National Liberals, a block determined to put through a new electoral law, encouraged the Social Democrats, as early as the Reichstag elections of 1890, to enter into run-off election coalitions with all the bourgeois parties. By the beginning of the 1890s, the Social Democrats had already set up negotiations with the Centre Party, the Left Liberals and the Democrats on the issue of the Landtag elections. In order to unite in working for direct elections and a change in electoral districts, the party decided to abandon its own demand for the introduction of proportional representation.[33] In the subsequent Landtag elections the Social Democrats – and this was a totally new strategy – ran no candidates in those districts in which their following was weak, and instead advised their voters to vote for the bourgeois opposition parties. In those districts in which their chances were better, they joined official run-off election coalitions with the Democrats or the Left Liberals. Co-operation with the Centre Party, whose educational policy the Social Democrats opposed, was more difficult. In the Landtag elections which preceded

---

32. Jörg Schadt, *Die sozialdemokratische Partei in Baden. Von den Anfängen bis zur Jahrhundertwende (1868–1900)*, Hanover, 1971, p. 172.
33. Ibid., p. 178 (see also for secondary election tactics of the SPD).

the 1904 electoral reform, the party thus put up candidates in some districts against the Democrats and the Left Liberals; in others, on the other hand, they allied with Democrats and/or the Centre Party against the National Liberals. The situation became uncomfortable when the SPD paper, the *Volksfreund*, published a call for electoral support for the Democratic candidate in Karlsruhe and on the next page printed a sharp attack by the Social Democratic candidate from Offenbach against his Democratic Party opponent there. Some of the rank-and-file Social Democrats simply no longer wanted to go along with this tactic.[34] Co-operation with the Democratic Party carried more political implications than co-operation with the other parties. In Karlsruhe the two parties were even able to organize and finance a common election campaign.

The struggle over the new electoral law of 1904 ended with a pyrrhic victory for all the opposition parties. Further compromise had finally succeeded in bringing in direct voting as well as the reapportionment of the electoral districts. But this victory was achieved at the cost of a substantial restriction of the suffrage. The National Liberals, who were responsible for this, were able this last time to assert their power in spite of a decline in seats.[35] Henceforth, only those who had lived in Baden for two years, who were citizens of Baden and who had no outstanding tax debts for the year before the election were entitled to vote. Further, the influence of the primarily aristocratic upper chamber was augmented. All this moved the Social Democrats ultimately to refuse to vote for the new electoral law. Yet the remaining opposition parties did approve it and thus succeeded in passing it through both houses.[36]

The unyielding confessional line pursued by the Centre Party, which had previously hindered co-operation between the parties opposed to the National Liberals, was one reason for the collapse of this tactical coalition. Even in this modified form, the National Liberals, however, could see only disadvantages in the new electoral law. Under the franchise in the Reichstag, which was similar to this new, modified version, the National Liberals had not won a single seat in the elections of 1890 in Baden. They now felt it necessary to join in coalitions with the left Liberals and the upcoming SPD. The preponderance of the

---

34. Ibid., p. 181.
35. In public, they expressed their opinion that they were not going to saw the branch they sat on; quoted by Bachem, *Vorgeschichte, Geschichte und Politik*, p. 128.
36. Emil Eichhorn, 'Aus einem Kleinstaatenparlament', *Die neue Zeit*, vol. 22, 1904, p. 555.

Table 3.3. Elected representatives in Baden
(a) Reichstag elections

Year of election	Number of representatives	Centre Party	Conservatives	National Liberals	Left Liberals[1]	People's Party	Peasant League[2]	Social Democratic Party
1871	14	2	1[3]	10	1	–	–	–
1874	14	2	1[3]	11	–	–	–	–
1877	14	2	1	11	–	–	–	–
1878	14	3	2	8	–	1	–	–
1881	14	4	1	7	1	1	–	–
1884	14	4	3	5	1	1	–	–
1887	14	2	3	9	–	–	–	–
1890	14	8	3	–	1	1	–	1
1893	14	7	2	4	1	–	–	–
1898	14	7	–	3	–	–	1	3
1903	14	7	–	4	–	–	–	3
1907	14	8	–	2	–	–	1	3
1912	14	6	1	4	2	–	–	1

(b) Baden Landtag

Year of election	Number of representatives	Centre Party	Conservatives	National Liberals	Left Liberals[4]	Democrats	Social Democratic Party
1903	63	23	1	25	2	6	6
1905	73	28	4	23	1	5	12
1909	73	26	3	17	7		20
1913	73	29	5	20	6		13

1. See note 1 of Table 3.1.
2. League of Farmers (Bund der Landwirte).
3. German Reich Party (Deutsche Reichspartei).
4. Liberal Party (Freisinnige Partei).
Sources: Gerhard A. Ritter and Merith Niehuss, _Wahlgeschichtliches Arbeitsbuch. Materialien zur Statistik des Kaiserreichs, 1871–1918_, Munich, 1980, p. 90; Karl Bachem, _Vorgeschichte, Geschichte und Politik der deutschen Zentrumspartei_, vol. 8, Cologne, 1931, pp. 144–55.

Centre Party became apparent in the first election after the new law had been adopted, in 1905, when the National Liberals were able to gain only half as many seats as the Centre Party. Coalitions formed for the run-off elections between National Liberals, Democrats and the SPD led to the result that out of the twenty-three run-off elections in 1905, the Centre Party came out without a single victory. By means of their agreement with the National Liberals, in Baden the Social Democratic Party had finally become part of a working majority (they became _regierungsfähig_).[37]

37. Hannelore Schlemmer, _Die Rolle der Sozialdemokratie in den Landtagen Badens und_

Party Representation in Local Government

The slow decline of the liberals, which first became evident in the elections to the Reichstag, continued in the Landtag elections. However, around the turn of the century there still existed important bastions – the cities – in which liberal power was unbroken. The running of the city administrations was traditionally the domain of bourgeois dignitaries. Their financial independence, their intellectual potential and, above all, their self-image as responsible taxpayers, predestined this group for positions of power within their bourgeois world. 'In comparison to their condition in the Reichstag and in most state parliaments, liberals in the cities showed a marked staying power.'[38] Of course, the label 'liberal' in this context was seldom used in a political sense; on the contrary, almost all municipal self-government bodies consciously tried to exclude party politics from city government. 'The ideal mayor in the late imperial period, therefore, was a man like Franz Adickes of Frankfurt, who was vaguely liberal in his sympathies but resolutely avoided any relationship to a political party.'[39] Above all, the early municipal and community elections in the 1870s were almost exclusively personality contests. In the city of Ludwigshaven on the Rhine in the Bavarian Palatinate, the municipal councillors were made up of 10% of the eligible voters, so that one could say that the voters knew their elected representatives well.[40] On the other hand, this also shows that the number of those entitled to vote was very low. Legal decisions at that time were made by the *Bürgergemeinde*.[41] The right to vote was directly linked to the elector's civic rights, granted either by birth or attainable by means of a series of precisely fixed regulations: a definite length of residence, a definite minimum income and/or the ownership of property and the payment of a so-called citizenship fee (*Bürgerrechtsgebühr*), the amount being generally set by the communities themselves.[42] This fee was particularly high in Bavaria, and in Munich it went up to about half of the average

Württembergs und ihr Einfluß auf die Entwicklung der Gesamtpartei zwischen 1890 und 1914, Freiburg, 1953 (dissertation).

38. James Sheehan, 'Liberalism and the City in Nineteenth-Century Germany', *Past and Present*, vol. 51, 1971, pp. 116–37 (quotation on p. 131).

39. Ibid., p. 126.

40. Rolf Weidner, *Wahlen und soziale Strukturen in Ludwigshafen am Rhein 1871–1914. Unter besonderer Berücksichtigung der Reichstagswahlen*, Ludwigshaven, 1984, p. 257.

41. Compare for southern Germany the description of the communal constitution in *Kommunalpolitische Blätter*, vol. 2, no. 9, 1911, 'Bavarian series', pp. 264ff.

42. See for more detailed information about communal electoral laws; Paul Hirsch and Hugo Lindemann, *Das kommunale Wahlrecht*, Berlin, 1905.

monthly wage of a worker at the turn of the century.[43] In Württemberg this fee was about equal to two days' wages and the same was true for Baden.[44] Apart from proof of property ownership ranging between 1,000 and 3,000 marks, and assets worth 300 marks if he was married, an aspirant for the *Bürgerrecht* in Baden, for example, also had to prove that he was neither a poor householder nor a drunkard, and that he did not lead a dissolute or disorderly life.[45] But, most important, the high fees and multiple secondary regulations also served to assure that the number of those entitled to vote remained small and that the lower classes would be represented in extremely small numbers. In the city of Munich, for example, the number of those entitled to vote for the Reichstag was 107,000, for the Landtag 56,000 and for the municipal election only 19,000 in the years 1907/8,[46] so that fewer than one-fifth of those entitled to vote for the Reichstag elections were also entitled to vote in the community elections. In addition, in Baden there was also a class suffrage system, reason enough for the Social Democrats to call Baden 'the most Prussian of all the south German states'. Under this system, an average of three-quarters of all those entitled to vote, namely those who were taxed the least, were placed in the third class, which elected one-third of the community councillors in the local elections; similarly the group of those who paid the most taxes, one-twelfth of those entitled to vote, were placed in the first class and were also able to elect one-third of the community councillors in the local elections.[47]

With incredible energy the Social Democrats of the three south German states had managed repeatedly to place their own members – despite discriminating electoral laws – in the self-governing bodies of the cities. It is illustrative of the value which the party organization attached to municipal politics[48] that although the SPD party organiz-

43. *Die Sozialdemokratie im Münchner Rathaus. Ein Handbuch für Gemeindewähler*, Munich, 1914, pp. 136ff. Before 1896 one had to pay double the amount for the citizenship fee.
44. Christ-Gmelin, 'Die württembergische Sozialdemokratie', p. 109.
45. Hirsch and Lindemann, *Das kommunale Wahlrecht*, p. 44.
46. Merith Niehuss, 'Parteien, Wahlen und Arbeiterbewegung in München 1890–1910', in Friedrich Prinz and Marita Krauss (eds), *München – Musenstadt mit Hinterhöfen. Die Prinzregentenzeit 1886–1912*, Munich, 1988, pp. 44–53. As the district boundaries of Munich for Reichstag, Landtag and community elections were not quite the same, the numbers given only show the broad differences.
47. Hirsch and Lindemann, *Das kommunale Wahlrecht*, p. 46. The percentages varied according to the size of the cities. See also Schadt, *Die sozialdemokratische Partei*, p. 173, and Fritz Dürr, *Die geschichtliche Entwicklung der Gemeindevertretung in Baden*, Heidelberg, 1931 (dissertation).
48. For a detailed description of Social Democratic communal policy, see Adelheid von Saldern, 'Die Gemeinde in Theorie und Praxis der deutschen Arbeiterorganisation 1863–1920. Ein Überblick', *Internationale wissenschaftliche Korrespondenz zur Geschichte der Arbeiterbewegung*, vol. 12, 1976, pp. 295–352. For an overview see also G. Fülberth,

ation in Baden boycotted the Landtag elections, it participated with verve in the local elections, even though the latter provided a much less favourable franchise.[49] Statistics for Baden show 1,266 Social Democratic members of committees of citizens (*Bürgerausschußmitglieder*), sixty-eight local councillors (*Gemeinderäte*) and two mayors in the year 1910.[50]

The presence of the Social Democrats in the city halls led to increased politicization, reflected in the formation of factions among the hitherto non-party local dignitaries. Demands concerning social policy as well as the fight for a new municipal electoral law sharpened the electoral battles. Without forming coalitions with the bourgeois parties, it was rarely possible for the Social Democrats to get their candidates elected to the city halls. Electoral coalitions on this lowest political level were formed more spontaneously and adopted far more recklessly than they were on the state or Reich level. The coalitions also generally involved the same bourgeois parties with which pacts in the Landtag elections had been made. Exceptions were of course possible, and some are documented.[51] In opposition to a resolution passed by the Social Democratic Party in Baden at their annual congress, socialist candidates were even run on bourgeois electoral lists in many cities in the 1890s.[52] The Social Democrats' integration in local government made them often the butt of jokes by the bourgeois parties as well as a cause for fierce criticism in the party as a whole. Thus the Munich Centre Party newspaper made disparaging remarks about a Social Democratic local government representative who had been drawn into a conversation during a gala dinner by the Emperor and Empress.[53] And in Stuttgart, the radical left wing of the party inveighed against members of their party being sworn into office by the King of Württemberg with an oath on the constitution: 'It all begins with pressing the flesh of the king.'[54] In Baden the local party organization of the SPD sometimes requested a written pledge to the party programme from their candidate – they were the wiser for having had bad experiences.[55]

Konzeption und Praxis sozialdemokratischer Kommunalpolitik 1918–1933. Ein Anfang, Marburg, 1984.

49. Schadt, *Die sozialdemokratische Partei*, p. 172. On the other hand, in Nuremberg Social Democrats refused to take part in municipal elections because of the discriminating 'election tax', i.e. the rates for citizenship, until the end of the century. The Nuremberg Social Democrats were very successful in Landtag and Reichstag elections. See Hugo Eckert, *Liberal- oder Sozialdemokratie. Frühgeschichte der Nürnberger Arbeiterbewegung*, Stuttgart, 1968, p. 47.

50. Schadt, *Die sozialdemokratische Partei*, p. 170.

51. Ibid., p. 173.

52. Ibid.

53. *Die Sozialdemokratie im Münchner Rathaus*, p. 100.

54. Christ-Gmelin, 'Die württembergische Sozialdemokratie', p. 121.

55. Schadt, *Die sozialdemokratische Partei*, p. 174.

In southern Germany the same parties which tackled and successfully pushed through the new versions of the discriminatory Landtag electoral laws acted directly afterwards to reform municipal franchise laws. In all three states the Social Democrats and the Centre Party linked up together against liberal predominance in the cities. In Bavaria the Landtag electoral amendment of 1906 was followed by the community electoral reform of 1908. In Baden the Landtag electoral law was reformed in 1904; a communal electoral franchise reform followed in 1910, although in this case it had been undergoing continuous improvement since 1890 – simplifying the procedure of becoming a citizen.[56] In Württemberg a change in the franchise took place during the period of the Anti-Socialist Laws (*Sozialistengesetze*) in 1885, restricting the franchise, which previously had been almost identical to the Reichstag election law, to the citizens of the community.

The proportional voting system was introduced in cities with a specific minimum number of inhabitants, in Württemberg and Bavaria in 1906, and in Baden in 1910.[57] The proportional vote was – and remained – a basic Social Democratic demand. It was, however, endorsed by the bourgeois parties, primarily in order to limit the SPD in the larger cities of the state. In return, so to speak, for this concession to the Social Democrats, restrictions on the franchise remained in all three states.

The proportional vote was practised with closed lists in Baden, and in Württemberg and Bavaria with open lists, i.e. the voters did not have to keep to the suggestions offered by their own party and could choose candidates from other parties or even add the name of their own candidate to the list. From this it is quite easy to measure the level of voter satisfaction with the party-suggested lists. The municipal election in Munich in 1908 revealed that of the Social Democratic voters only 3% altered the electoral choices offered by their party; among Centre Party voters, it was 21% and among voters from the Liberal Party 59%.[58] Apparently the Social Democratic voters approved of the pragmatic reform course of their 'royal Bavarian Social Democracy'.

This is also clear from a municipal election in Stuttgart where a strong radical wing around Clara Zetkin managed to put their own candidates in the top positions of the list. By contrast, the reformist and

---

56. Hirsch and Lindemann, *Das kommunale Wahlrecht*, pp. 40ff.
57. In Bavaria, in cities with more than 4,000 inhabitants; in Baden and Württemberg, in cities with more than 10,000 inhabitants. See also Ernst Cahn, *Das Verhältniswahlrecht in den modernen Kulturstaaten. Eine staatsrechtlich-politische Abhandlung*, Berlin, 1909.
58. *Die Sozialdemokratie im Münchner Rathaus*, p. 100.

extremely popular expert on municipal politics, Hugo Lindemann, was placed seventh on the list. The voters went against the list and advanced Lindemann by a significant margin to the top of the list.[59] In 1911 Lindemann was ultimately – after great hesitation on the part of party leaders – made a candidate for the position of Lord Mayor of the city of Stuttgart. He came in just behind the coalition candidate for the bourgeois coalition parties.[60]

In southern Germany, primarily at the municipal level, social democracy appeared to have succeeded in striking deep social and political roots; this success was gained – it would seem – almost at the price of losing its political identity.

The Social Democrats had shown by their reform tactics and their willingness to enter second-ballot coalitions that they were willing to make concessions. The means chosen differed, depending upon the states; in Württemberg the run-off electoral coalitions with the People's Party seemed also to bring a general political *rapprochement* between the two parties.[61] In Bavaria the party entered into changing single-issue coalitions, first with the Centre Party and after 1908 with the liberals. The Social Democrats in Baden went through the most extreme changes and were also the ones for whom breaking faith with their own programme was most likely.

The party was forced to learn from others where the bounds of its power lay. It seems that the bourgeois parties had not really lost the battle over the franchise. This was especially apparent with regard to the proportional voting system. The proportional vote had become dogma[62] for Social Democrats, although it was always used in practice to prevent a possible socialist majority.

Finally, it is to be noted that as we have shown above with the example of the electoral system reforms, the far-reaching successes of social democracy were only possible in those areas where – for structural reasons – the Social Democrats presented no real threat. Thus electoral reforms on this scale were only possible where social democracy was numerically weak – i.e. in the less industrialized catholic, south German states – and not, for instance, in Prussia or Saxony.

59. Christ-Gmelin, 'Die württembergische Sozialdemokratie', p. 125.
60. Ibid., p. 126.
61. James Clark Hunt, *The People's Party in Württemberg and Southern Germany, 1890–1914. The Possibilities of Democratic Politics*, Stuttgart, 1975.
62. Axel Misch, *Das Wahlsystem zwischen Theorie und Taktik. Zur Frage von Mehrheitswahl und Verhältniswahl in der Programmatik der Sozialdemokratie bis 1933*, Berlin, 1974, p. 129.

KARL ROHE

Political Alignments and Re-alignments in the Ruhr 1867–1987: Continuity and Change of Political Traditions in an Industrial Region

Some years ago, after the Bundestag election of 1976, the West German weekly *Der Spiegel* tried to analyse the election results of the Ruhr by employing two popular regional cartoon figures, Anton and Cervinsky, invented by the late Ruhr journalist and writer, Wilhelm Herbert Koch. Cervinsky's analysis reads as follows: 'What my grandpa was, he went to Schalke [the home of a once famous German soccer team] and he voted for the SPD. My father, too, went to Schalke and voted for the Social Democrats as well. And I went to Schalke, too, Anton; you can imagine what I have voted for.'[1]

This is a remarkable example of inventing a tradition. It does not stand up to any analysis. Cervinsky's grandfather, apparently of Polish origin, would probably have voted for the catholic Centre Party in the 1890s, a decade later for the Polish Nationalist Party; his father during the Weimar Republic would probably have voted for the communists. Statistically it seems rather unlikely, especially in the northern parts of the Ruhr where Schalke is situated, that his father and grandfather would ever have voted for the Social Democrats before 1945.

Cervinsky's analysis reveals, however, that even journalists living in

---

1. *Der Spiegel*, no. 42, 11 October 1976, p. 131.

the Ruhr today are so accustomed to a Social Democratic political hegemony and consider it such a natural phenomenon that they subconsciously assume it must always have been like this. So there arise two main questions. Firstly, why is it that this region – with the highest degree of industrialization and proletarization in Germany – was for most of the Kaiserreich and the Weimar Republic an electoral desert for the SPD? And secondly, why is it that the SPD did so well in the Ruhr after the Second World War and has apparently had no problems until recently in maintaining its hegemonial position, in marked contrast to some regions with a stronger and older socialist tradition?[2] Next to the CSU (Christian Social Union) in Bavaria the Ruhr SPD has proved to be regionally the most successful political party in the Federal Republic.

By trying to answer these two questions, which are in any case closely interrelated, it is hoped that some general insights can be gained into the history of political alignments, de-alignments and re-alignments in Germany. True, in many aspects the Ruhr is a very special case. But at the same time it is a kind of political laboratory which contains nearly all the social material German political society is made of: catholics and protestants, working and middle classes, Germans and non-Germans, towns and villages. So an analysis of political society in the Ruhr, especially if explanations of this special case are sought at a more global level,[3] should reveal some general characteristics of the German party system's development.

The Rise and Decline of Socialism, 1867–1877

It was in the decade between 1867 and 1877 that a stable political cleavage structure emerged in the Ruhr, which by that time was already the largest industrial area within Germany. This grouped itself along denominational lines and not along class lines. True, at the beginning there loomed the prospect of a socialist hegemony, but this did not in fact materialize. In a by-election to the North German Reichstag in the Duisburg constituency, Lassallean Socialists even succeeded in winning the seat, and in Essen, too, they were highly

2. Amt für Statistik und Stadtforschung Duisburg (ed.), *Politische Wahlen in 65 Großstädten und in Bundesländern 1949–1987*, Duisburg, 1987.
3. Harry Eckstein, 'Case Study and Theory in Political Science', in Fred J. Greenstein, and Nelson W. Polsby, (eds), *Handbook of Political Science*, vol. 7 Reading, MA, 1975, pp. 79–137.

Figure 4.1. The SPD in the Ruhr and the German Reich/FRG, 1871–1987

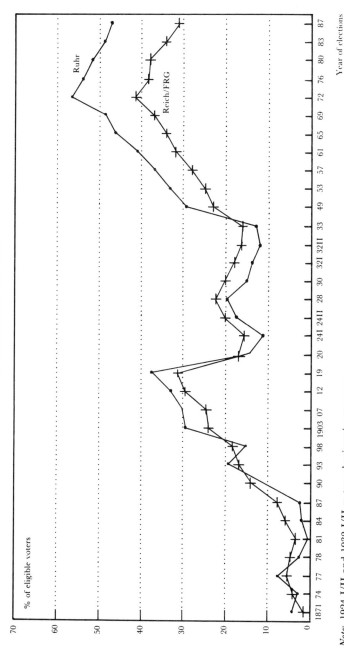

Note: 1924 I/II and 1932 I/II = two elections in one year.
Source: Own computations based on the *Statistik des Deutschen Reichs* and the *Statistik der Bundesrepublik Deutschland*.

successful. But they experienced a set-back in the early 1870s, and the main cause of this was the rise of political catholicism in the Ruhr.[4]

To be sure, repressive legislation known as the *Sozialistengesetz*, which was passed in 1878 and was not dropped until 1890, played a part in making the Ruhr a 'belated socialist region'. One might well speculate about the character of regional political development without any political suppression. The *Sozialistengesetz* confronted a socialist working-class movement in the Ruhr which was still in a state of infancy and had not yet really taken off. With few local exceptions, at that time the SPD (Social Democratic Party) was a party without firm roots in local mining or working-class communities. Therefore the party only managed to survive in some villages and towns. The overwhelming majority of the constituencies in which the SPD had done fairly well in the early 1870s started to support bourgeois parties. The turn-out was always relatively high, despite the existence of the *Sozialistengesetz*. This may indicate that, except for some villages and districts, neither a socialist milieu[5] nor an independent working-class culture existed in the Ruhr in the 1870s.

Political oppression and internal strife within the socialist camp, mainly between Lassalle's workers' association (Allgemeiner Deutscher Arbeiterverein) on the one hand and the Social Democratic Workers' Party (Sozialdemokratische Arbeiterpartei) under the leadership of Bebel and Liebknecht on the other, weakened the early socialist movement in the Ruhr. Historians have rightly stressed these aspects, but they have often missed the more decisive point, namely the catholic factor.[6] To put it another way: before the socialists in the Ruhr had

4. Karl Rohe, *Vom Revier zum Ruhrgebiet. Wahlen – Parteien – Politische Kultur*, Essen, 1986; Karl Rohe, Wolfgang Jäger and Uwe Dorow, 'Politische Gesellschaft und politische Kultur im Ruhrgebiet 1848–1987', in Dietmar Petzina et al. (eds), *Das Ruhrgebiet im Industriezeitalter*, vol. 2, Düsseldorf, 1990; Klaus Tenfelde, *Sozialgeschichte der Bergarbeiterschaft an der Ruhr im 19. Jahrhundert*, 2nd edn, Bonn, 1981; Paul Möllers, *Die politischen Strömungen im Reichstagswahlkreis Essen zur Zeit der Reichsgründung und des Kulturkampfes* (1867–1878), Bonn, 1955, (Ph.D. dissertation); Ludger Heid, *Von der Zunft- zur Arbeiterpartei. Die Sozialdemokratie in Duisburg 1848–1878*, Duisburg, 1983; Jonathan Sperber, *Popular Catholicism in 19th-Century Germany*, Princeton, NJ, 1984.
5. Karl Rohe, 'Wahlanalyse im historischen Kontext. Zu Kontinuität und Wandel von Wahlverhalten', *Historische Zeitschrift*, vol. 234, 1982, pp. 337–57; Karl Heinz Naßmacher, 'Kontinuität und Wandel eines regionalen Parteiensystems. Zur politischen Entwicklung Oldenburgs im 20. Jahrhundert', in Wolfgang Günther (ed.), *Sozialer und politischer Wandel in Oldenburg. Studien zur Regionalgeschichte, vom 17. bis 20. Jahrhundert*, Oldenburg, 1981, pp. 221–51.
6. Arno Herzig, 'Die Entwicklung der Sozialdemokratie in Westfalen bis 1894', *Westfälische Zeitschrift*, vol. 121, 1971, pp. 97–172, esp. pp. 151ff.; Horst Lademacher, 'Wirtschaft, Arbeiterschaft und Arbeiterorganisation in der Rheinprovinz am Vorabend des Sozialistengesetzes 1878', *Archiv für Sozialgeschichte*, vol. 15, 1975, pp. 111–43, esp. p. 142.

Table 4.1. Decline of socialist votes in the western Ruhr, 1867–78

Elections	Duisburg constituency			Essen constitutency		
	Valid votes	Socialist total	%	Valid votes	Socialist total	%
First election 12 Feb. 1867	9,731	1,734	17.8	9,072	–	–
First election 31 Aug. 1867	5,826	1,207	20.7	6,392	1,733	27.1
Second election 7 Sep. 1867	–			7,471	3,419	45.8
By-election 21 Sept. 1867	6,198	440	7.1	–	–	–
By-election 27 Mar. 1868	–	–	–	4,797	2,089	43.6
Second election 7 April 1968	–	–	–	6,765	3,280	48.5
By-election 25 Jan. 1869	11,826	6,801	57.5	–	–	–
First election 3 Mar. 1871	16,840	2,392	14.2	13,772	1,425	10.3
First election 10 Jan. 1874	24,060	1,217	5.1	19,914	1,234	6.2
First election 10 Jan. 1877	24,414	3,474	14.2	24,222	3,062	12.6
First election 30 July 1878	24,960	470	1.9	28,829	381	1.3

Source: 1867–9: Hans-Werner Tiedtke, '*Die Reichstagswahlen und die Reichstagswahlkämpfe im südlichen Teil des Ruhrgebiets von der Gründung des Norddeutschen Bundes bis zum Beginn des Ersten Weltkriegs*', Bochum, 1976 (unpublished thesis). 1871–8: *Statistik des Deutschen Reichs.*

become a victim of the *Sozialistengesetz* they had already succumbed to political catholicism.

The Emergence of a Stable Voting Structure Divided along Confessional and Cultural Lines

Why was the Centre Party able to attract so many workers and deny the socialists a stronger say? For what reason did political catholicism become such a force in the Ruhr basin, given that, in 1848/9, it did not exist in the area at all, which was different from the situation in parts of the Rhineland and Westphalia?[7] Some explanation can be sought in the two decades after the 1848/9 Revolution, during which there emerged what later became known as the Ruhr, that is the largest interconnected industrial region in Central Europe. During that formative period, the number of catholics in the Ruhr increased from about 38% in 1849 to 47.8% in 1871. But catholicism also experienced a religious revival which led to new forms of religious practice and

7. Konrad Repgen, *Märzbewegung und Maiwahlen des Revolutionsjahres 1848 im Rheinland*, Bonn, 1955, pp. 102ff.; Ute Schmidt, *Zentrum oder CDU. Politischer Katholizismus zwischen Tradition und Anpassung*, Opladen, 1987, pp. 28ff.

associational life.[8] A predominantly lower-class immigrant population, mainly from the rural areas of the nearby provinces of Rhineland and Westphalia, was successfully integrated into catholic parish communities. Thus it was not simply the influx of traditionally minded catholic immigrants, but their integration into a specific catholic culture – which had adapted itself to life in an industrial society – which preceded the sudden rise of political catholicism in the early 1870s and must be seen as an essential explanation for its success.

Additionally, in the late 1860s a predominantly catholic workers' movement had spread in the western parts of the Ruhr, led by so-called 'red chaplains', that is to say, by younger members of the catholic clergy. This Christian Social Movement was not always easy to integrate into the Centre Party. In the 1877 Reichstag elections there appeared two catholic candidates in the Essen constituency, an official candidate, supported by the bourgeois wing of the Centre Party, and an unofficial one, the candidate of the Christian Social Movement (Christlich-Soziale). And the unofficial candidate, the catholic worker Gerhard Stötzel, succeeded in the run-off elections. The regional Centre Party, however, had learned its lesson and was flexible enough to avoid a split within the catholic camp along class lines. One year later Gerhard Stötzel had become the official Centre Party candidate.

Despite these internal tensions, the very existence of a powerful catholic workers' movement and the emergence of social catholicism made political life difficult for the socialists in the Ruhr. Socialist activists could only envy the forces and equipment the catholics were able to rely upon and most of which they lacked: a rich network of catholic associations and organizations; an interpretation of political and social reality with which religiously minded workers could identify themselves; and a popular clergy sharing the same rural background as the catholic immigrants, and which was prepared to articulate their grievances. And, after all, in a parochial culture it is not only what is said that matters but also who says it. To sum up, when the era of mass politics and of 'original political accumulation' began, political catholicism in the Ruhr had advantages as compared with socialism, not only at the level of political potential – that is to say, at the level of the

8. Sperber, *Popular Catholicism*, pp. 39ff.; idem, 'The Shaping of Political Catholicism in the Ruhr Basin 1848–1881', *Central European History*, vol. 16, 1983, pp. 347–67, esp. p. 351; idem, 'Roman Catholic Religious Identity in Rhineland-Westphalia 1800–70. Quantitative Examples and Some Political Implications', *Social History*, vol. 7, 1982, pp. 305–18; idem, 'The Transformation of Catholic Associations in the Northern Rhineland and Westphalia 1830–1870, *Journal of Social History*, vol. 15, 1981, pp. 253–63.

workers' mentality and way of life – but also at the level of what might be called intervening political mechanisms, which ranged from media and associations to local elites.

Seen from this perspective, it is not the rise of political catholicism in the early 1870s which is so surprising, but the 'socialist spring' in the late 1860s. Indeed, it must primarily be seen not as a reflection of genuine socialist strength in the Ruhr, but of a temporary weakness of their political opponents. Other than in the Dortmund area, the Progressive Party (Fortschrittspartei) had failed to create a popular basis in the Essen and Duisburg areas; in addition between 1866 and 1870 political catholicism was in difficulties; indeed it had more or less faded away. Catholic elites were unsure about how to react and how to cope with the new political constellation created by Bismarck in 1866. Some local activists in the Essen constituency supported a separate catholic candidate in 1867, but others were against this move. Characteristically, however, the catholic candidate did not even get into the run-off elections. Four years later, the same catholic candidate in the same constituency scored 70.3% of the votes. By that time catholic elites had regained their confidence and successfully launched the foundation of the Centre Party.

So it was the rise of political catholicism which caused the restructuring of the voting system in the Ruhr, and it was the socialists who suffered most, whereas the National Liberals reaped all the advantages from this confrontation. The old political dividing line of 1848/9 between moderates and democrats had been gradually transformed, as reflected in the election results to the Prussian diet, into a political conflict between liberal candidates on the one hand – who, since the early 1860s, were mostly allied in the newly founded Progressive Party – and conservative, or 'governmental' candidates on the other. This conflict still dominated the 1867 elections, the first elections based on an equal and direct male suffrage, the liberal candidates having their strongholds in the cities and the 'governmental' ones – as a rule, Prussian civil servants – primarily among farmers and workers living in the countryside. And at least in some parts of the Ruhr, especially in the Essen area, the conservatives were highly successful. As the Essen Landrat and successful conservative candidate Devens wrote, the Conservatives were supported by all elementary school teachers and by the protestant clergy as well as by most members of the catholic clergy.[9]

9. Möllers, *Die politischen Strömungen*, pp. 58ff.

Four years later, a completely new voting structure had emerged. In all Ruhr constituencies, liberal candidates were no longer facing conservative candidates but catholic or 'clerical' ones, as the regional liberal press used to call them. And this in turn changed the 'meaning' of a liberal vote considerably, regardless of whether liberal candidates belonged to the National Liberal Party – as in Duisburg and Essen – or to the Progressive Party – as was the case in the eastern constituencies of Dortmund and Bochum during the early 1870s. Accordingly, there was only a slight similarity between the liberal strongholds of 1867 and those of 1871. Basically all liberal candidates stood for the same cause and represented the same camp, namely the *Nationale Lager* or the *Reichstreue Lager*, as it was often called, including not only former liberals and their more secular traditions but the former conservative and protestant traditions as well. And in all parts of the Ruhr, the National Liberals were soon to become the main political expression of this camp, notwithstanding the fact that in the predominantly catholic Essen constituency the *Nationale Lager* was sometimes represented by Conservative candidates. This only underlines the basic fact that what really mattered was not the political party but the political camp.

There were a few political coalitions which crossed camp lines; for example, those between catholics and the declining Left Liberals in the eastern part of the Ruhr in the 1880s. In principle, however, election politics can best be understood against the background of an existing two-camp system: a catholic one which in the 1890s could still mobilize about 90% of the catholic voters and a protestant-based one, which also included small numbers of catholics without special attachment to their church. This camp was primarily kept together by the fact that all its components, ranging from heavy industry and protestant middle classes to protestant workers and national-minded parts of the working classes, took a pro-Bismarckian stance and were fiercely opposed to political catholicism and all it was supposed to stand for: ultramontanism, anti-modernism and, as far as the industrialists were concerned, social demagogy and crypto-socialism. Some of the industrialists were indeed at first more frightened by catholicism than by socialism. After all, one of the first great strikes in the Ruhr was called the Jesuit strike. And during the 1870s and 1880s catholic leaders and journalists not infrequently used rather radical language in attacking industrialists and capitalism. Compared with that, as the Social Democrats later maliciously remarked, socialist agitation had always been moderate.[10]

---

10. *Die Arbeiterbewegung im Ruhrgebiet. Eine Gabe an den Parteitag 1907 vom Sozialdemokrat-*

Transformation of the Traditional Two-Camp System into a Three-Camp System between 1890 and 1914

So, in many ways it was a multifaceted conflict system, including religious, national, cultural and social dimensions, which developed in the Ruhr on the original basis of the sectarian split between catholics and protestants. This, no doubt, contributed to its stability and long-term impact, and made political life for the Social Democrats so difficult in the Ruhr. Why, then, did they get in at all? Leaving aside all factors concerning the improvement of socialist agitation and organization which took place after the dropping of the anti-socialist law in 1890, two main causes can be distinguished. The first one is closely connected with the great miners' strike of 1889, the second one with mass immigration at the turn of the century. On a more general level, the first one can perhaps best be understood as a spiritual breakdown of 'patriarchalism' in large parts of the Ruhr, especially in the coal industry. This process started with the great miners' strike in 1889; a further stage was the 'Krupp scandal' in 1902.[11] It finally led to a political delegitimization of the ruling protestant elites; as a result, the protestant-based camp, beginning with the Reichstag election of 1890, split along class lines. It must, however, not be overlooked that parts of the protestant working class, especially in wards where metal workers were living and in denominationally mixed villages,[12] still continued to vote for the National Liberals. But in 1890 some protestant miners' villages in the eastern parts of the Ruhr virtually turned socialist overnight. This occurred, for example, in (Witten) Rüdinghausen, where in 1887 more than 90% of the votes had gone to liberal parties, 71.1% to the National Liberals and 21% to the left Liberals.[13]

So in the 1890s the Ruhr SPD, at least as far as its voters were concerned, was a protestant-based party. Its ideal type constituency was a small protestant miners' village. At this time, the catholic camp,

ischen Verein Kreis Essen, Dortmund, 1907; new edition by Walter Wehner, Essen, 1981, p. 11.

11. Alex Hall, *Scandal, Sensation and Social Democracy*, Cambridge, 1977, pp. 176ff.; Frank Bajohr, *Zwischen Krupp und Kommune. Sozialdemokratie, Arbeiterschaft und Stadtverwaltung in Essen vor dem Ersten Weltkrieg*, Essen, 1988, pp. 73ff.

12. Rainer Maria Buhr, *Industriegesellschaft und organisierter politischer Liberalismus. Eine Untersuchung zu den sozialstrukturellen Voraussetzungen liberaler Wahlerfolge im Ruhrgebiet zur Zeit des Kaiserreiches*, Essen, 1987 (Ph.D. dissertation).

13. Rohe et al., 'Politische Gesellschaft und politische Kultur'; Wilhelm Nettmann, 'Witten in den Reichstagswahlen des Deutschen Reiches 1871–1918', in *Jahrbuch des Vereins für Orts- u. Heimatkunde in der Grafschaft Mark*, vol. 70, 1972, pp. 77ff.

except for a few villages and towns, was virtually unaffected by the new political split along class lines. It was still able to mobilize its catholic potential to an amazingly high degree.

This was partly owing to its traditional location within the regional cleavage structure, but partly also owing to a highly skilful adaptation to the new conditions emerging since the 1890s. So, for example, the catholic association, Volksverein für das Katholische Deutschland kept highly effective so-called *Volksbüros* in several cities of the Ruhr, which gave practical advice in all matters of social life to people who could not help themselves. In addition christian trade unions were founded in the 1890s, the most important among them being the Christian Miners' Union.[14] This again caused quarrels within the catholic camp; but the important fact is that they got off the ground and completed an organizational network on which catholicism in the Ruhr could rely.

These institutional innovations, however, could not prevent the set-back the Centre Party had to face in the first decade of the twentieth century. In some towns and villages the set-back had already begun at the 1898 Reichstag elections. Firstly, there occurred a split along ethnic lines: the majority of the Polish immigrants now voted for the Polish Nationalist Party; and, secondly, the Social Democrats for the first time achieved a significant share of the catholic vote. The main cause for this was no doubt mass immigration from the eastern provinces of the German Reich which occurred at the turn of the century and which doubled or even tripled the electorate in some villages in less than a decade. If one takes a closer look, it soon becomes obvious that local catholicism – especially in the northern parts of the Ruhr, where it still had a primarily agrarian basis and lacked much of the associational and organizational network characteristic of other parts of the region – was no longer able or willing to integrate the new immigrants. Local societies, even if they were basically catholic, now became divided between natives and immigrants, between those who lived in the centre of the town or the village and those who often lived in so-called miners' colonies.[15] And this split was reflected in voting patterns, the SPD and the Polish votes being much stronger in these 'colonies'.

---

14. Michael Schneider, *Die christlichen Gewerkschaften 1894–1933*, Bonn, 1982.
15. Helmuth Croon and Kurt Utermann, *Zeche und Gemeinde. Untersuchungen über den Strukturwandel einer Zechengemeinde im nördlichen Ruhrgebiet*, Tübingen, 1958; S.HF. Hickey, *Workers in Imperial Germany. The Miners of the Ruhr*, Oxford, 1985, pp. 56ff.

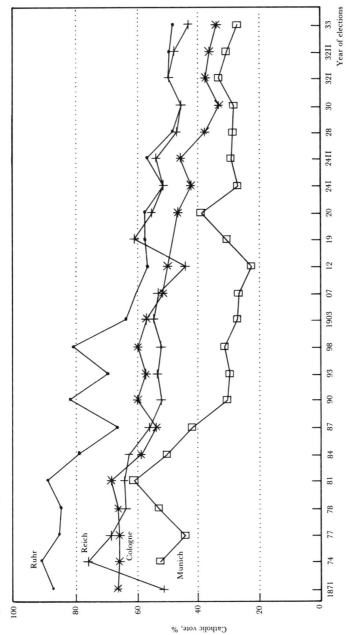

Figure 4.2. Centre Party (Bavarian People's Party) vote as related to catholic voters in different regions, 1871–1933

Note: See note on fig. 4.1
Source: Own computation based on the *Statistik des Deutschen Reichs.*

Milieupartei and *Sammlungsbewegung*: Type and Character of the Centre Party and the National Liberal Party in the Ruhr

These political changes and their geographical and sectarian patterns reveal something about the social and cultural foundations of the Centre Party and the SPD in the Ruhr. The Centre Party remained what it had always been in the Ruhr since its very beginning, a *Milieupartei par excellence*, the political expression of the catholic social milieu – that is to say, of those catholics who belonged to a catholic parish community, the social and political importance of which can hardly be over-estimated. Catholic workers' associations and christian trade unions, which provided opportunities for workers to express their material and nonmaterial interests, no doubt played a considerable part in keeping catholic workers within the confines of the catholic camp. But it must not be overlooked that only those catholic workers who already belonged to the catholic milieu joined christian trade unions. Christian trade unions and the social democratic free trade unions were not really competing for members in a free market. So, it was the catholic parish community and the associational life around it which was the key unit not only for integrating the catholic population but also for mobilizing them at elections. Those who belonged to a parish community could also be firmly relied on politically, those who did not could not be assumed to be Centre Party voters. This, at least, was the pattern in the Ruhr; it was not necessarily so in all other parts of Germany, where it was, it seems, not impossible to attend Mass and also to vote for the SPD.[16] In the Ruhr, however, cultural and political divisions were more or less identical. So, there are good reasons to assume that the share of Centre Party votes reflects quite accurately the strength of the catholic milieu in the Ruhr.[17]

Habitual voting or even affirmative voting[18] of this type does not

16. Merith Niehuss, 'Zur Schichtungsanalyse der SPD-Wähler in Bayern 1890–1900, in Peter Steinbach (ed.), *Probleme politischer Partizipation im Modernisierungsprozeß*, Stuttgart, 1982, pp. 217–30.

17. For the importance of the religious divisions in German society and politics see Gerhard Schmidtchen, 'Protestanten und Katholiken. Zusammenhänge zwischen Konfession, Sozialverhalten und gesellschaftlicher Entwicklung, in Hans-Georg Wehling (ed.), *Konfession – eine Nebensache? Politische, soziale und kulturelle Ausprägungen religiöser Unterschiede in Deutschland*, Stuttgart, 1984, pp. 11–20; Karl Schmitt, 'Inwieweit bestimmt auch heute noch die Konfession das Wahlverhalten? Konfession, Parteien und politisches Verhalten in der Bundesrepublik', in Wehling, *Konfession – eine Nebensache?*, pp. 21–57.

18. Stanley Suval, *Electoral Politics in Wilhelmine Germany*, Chapel Hill and London, 1985, pp. 55ff.

imply that voting behaviour was irrational. Devoted catholic workers still had a lot of good reasons for voting for the Centre Party in order to defend their way of life, the more because political catholicism allowed them to articulate and pursue their own material interests. Rational people, after all, not only defend their material interests but also their way of life.[19] And catholicism, like socialism, must not only be understood as a political party or a political creed but as a distinctive way of life, despite internal differences which even allow us to speak of sub-milieus within an overall catholic milieu.[20]

The close relationship between catholic milieu and Centre Party was a source of both strength and weakness. The weakness became apparent when, at the turn of the century, the catholic milieu had to face a relative decline. It was still expanding, as the growth of Centre Party votes in absolute numbers indicates, but, contrary to the situation in the nineteenth century, it did not grow in relation to the growth of the electorate. The reason was not, except for the case of the Poles, political de-alignment but political non-alignment; catholicism was no longer able to integrate the bulk of the new catholic immigrants, and had lost some of its former capacity to reproduce the catholic milieu in the next generation. Frequent complaints by catholic activists that the younger generation was no longer willing to join catholic associations point in that direction.

Secularization, and to some extent even mass immigration, created fewer problems for the nationalist camp than for the catholic one. The nationalist camp from its very beginnings had included devoted protestants and secular-minded people. To some extent it recovered from the heavy blow suffered at the 1890 Reichstag elections when it had lost the confidence of the protestant workers, especially that of the miners, and had fallen in absolute numbers from 105,374 votes in 1887 to 74,877 votes in 1890. It is true that there was a relative decline, but it should not be overlooked that the nationalist camp was able to increase its overall vote in the Ruhr from 74,877 in 1890 to 135,055 in 1912. And in the Duisburg constituency it even succeeded in remaining the strongest political camp until the end of the Kaiserreich.

19. Aaron Wildavsky, 'Choosing Preferences by Constructing Institutions: A Cultural Theory of Preference Formation', *American Political Science Review*, vol. 81, 1987, pp. 3–22.
20. David Blackbourn, 'Die Zentrumspartei und die deutschen Katholiken während des Kulturkampfs und danach', in Otto Pflanze and Elisabeth Müller-Luckner (eds), *Innenpolitische Probleme des Bismarck-Reiches*, Munich and Vienna, 1983, pp. 73–94; Wilfried Loth, *Katholiken im Kaiserreich. Der politische Katholizismus in der Krise des wilhelminischen Deutschland*, Düsseldorf, 1984.

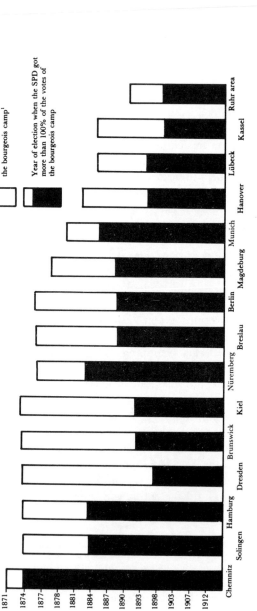

Figure 4.3. Votes for the bourgeois camp and the Social Democrats, regional comparisons

Year of election

☐ Year of election when the SPD got more than 50% of the votes of the bourgeois camp[1]

◼ Year of election when the SPD got more than 100% of the votes of the bourgeois camp

Chemnitz · Solingen · Hamburg · Dresden · Brunswick · Kiel · Nüremberg · Breslau · Berlin · Magdeburg · Munich · Hanover · Lübeck · Kassel · Ruhr area

1871 · 1874 · 1877 · 1878 · 1881 · 1884 · 1887 · 1890 · 1893 · 1898 · 1903 · 1907 · 1912

1. Bourgeois camp: addition of the votes for Conservatives, National Liberals, Left Liberals and Anti-Semites. The election results are calculated for the following constituencies:

Chemnitz: Saxony 16 and 19
Solingen: Düsseldorf 3
Hamburg: Hamburg 1–3, Sleswik, Altona

Dresden: Saxony 4 and 5
Brünswick: Brünswick 1
Kiel: Sleswik 7
Nüremberg: Central-Franconia 1

Breslau: Breslau 6 and 7
Berlin: Berlin 1–6
Magdeburg: Magdeburg 4
Munich: Upper Bavaria 1 and 2

Hanover: Hanover 8
Lübeck: Lübeck
Kassel: Kassel 2
Ruhr area:
Arnsberg 5 and 6
Düsseldorf 5 and 6.

Source: My own computations based on the *Statistik des Deutschen Reichs.*

There are several factors which help to explain its relative stability. Firstly, it managed to establish stable political relationships with some of the immigrant groups, notably with the Masuren from East Prussia, who spoke a Polish dialect but were protestants. Secondly, it profited from the efforts of large firms in the early twentieth century to build up employers' unions, the so-called *Gelbe Gewerkschaften*, which in some firms outnumbered the trade unions, and from the conscious attempts of industrialists like Krupp to create a *politische Stammarbeiterschaft*, that is to say, a workforce characterized not by special qualifications but by political loyalty.[21] And, thirdly, it could still rely on the political loyalty of the national sector of the working class and on most protestant workers connected with the Protestant Workers' Associations (*Evangelische Arbeitervereine*),[22] although some tensions arose because of the support given by employers to the *Gelbe Gewerkschaften*.[23] Fourthly, the nationalist camp to some extent gave way to workers' social and political aspirations at a symbolic level; as early as 1890 it presented a miner as its candidate in the Essen constituency and figured as National Workers' Party (Nationale Arbeiterspartei). And in 1912 a National Liberal miner indeed won the Reichstag seat in the Bochum constituency in a run-off election.

The national camp had never been as integrated as the catholic one, and the National Liberal Party, its main political exponent, was not a *Milieupartei* like the Centre Party. It can best be understood as a *nationale Sammlungsbewegung* collecting different milieus with different levels of attachment to the dominant culture and, in addition, a growing number of voters not belonging to a particular milieu at all. Some of the potential voters of the national camp were habitual non-voters who only went to the polls when elections could be presented as a kind of national referendum – like the Reichstag elections of 1878, 1887 and 1907. And there were astonishing signs of volatility across camp lines as far as the socialists and the national camp were concerned. In certain circumstances social democratic voters were quite prepared to vote for the candidate of the national camp, as was

21. Bajohr, *Zwischen Krupp und Kommune*, pp. 79ff.

22. Günter Brakelmann, 'Die Anfänge der evangelischen Arbeitervereinsbewegung in Gelsenkirchen 1882–1890', in Kurt Düwell and Wolfgang Köllmann (eds), *Rheinland-Westfalen im Industriezeitalter*, vol. 2: *Von der Reichsgründung bis zur Weimarer Republik*, Wuppertal, 1984, pp. 40–55; Harri Petras, *100 Jahre Evangelische Arbeiterbewegung in Hattingen 1886–1986. Ein Beitrag zur Kirchen- und Sozialgeschichte*, Hattingen, 1988; Bajohr, *Zwischen Krupp und Kommune*, pp. 110ff.; Klaus Martin Hofmann, *Die Evangelische Arbeitervereinsbewegung 1882 bis 1914*, Bielefeld, 1988.

23. Klaus Mattheier, *Die Gelben. Nationale Arbeiter zwischen Wirtschaftsfrieden und Streik*, Düsseldorf, 1973.

the case with Krupp at Essen in 1893, and vice versa. The SPD in the Essen constituency, for example, took it more or less for granted that they would receive the bulk of the national workers' votes in run-off elections if the choice was between a catholic and a socialist candidate.

Cultural Foundations of the Ruhr SPD in the Kaiserreich

In more than one respect, the SPD in the Ruhr had more structural similarities with the National Liberal Party than with the Centre Party. The SPD, too, was primarily a *Sammlungsbewegung* and not a *Milieupartei*. But unlike the National Liberals, it was a protest movement collecting those groups and elements in the Ruhr which for one reason or another were dissatisfied with the prevailing conditions. It is, without doubt, difficult to make general judgements about the Social Democratic voter. But if one considers the sudden rise of the SPD to a political mass movement – which can only be understood against the background of mass immigration from rural districts at the turn of the century – it seems almost certain that the average SPD voter in the pre-war Ruhr had only a slight similarity with that secular-minded and culturally aspiring industrial worker we normally envisage when we speak of socialist culture.[24]

That is not to say that a socialist culture did not exist at all in the Ruhr. There were a few towns and villages where the SPD had survived during the period of the anti-socialist laws. And in the Ruhr, too, there developed the typical network of ancillary organizations ranging from leisure time associations to more practical organizations. But at the same time it must be said that places with an uninterrupted socialist tradition were exceptions and that the network of socialist associations in the Ruhr was rather weak, not only in comparison with other German regions,[25] but also in comparison with associations connected with the two churches, especially with the Catholic Church. As the Social Democratic delegate Becker from Dortmund had to admit at the Bremen national party meeting in 1904, 'Our fight against the blue [protestant] and black [catholic] clergy is difficult, especially

24. Vernon L. Lidtke, *The Alternative Culture. Socialist Labour in Imperial Germany*, New York and Oxford, 1985; Richard J. Evans, 'Social Democracy and the Working Class in Imperial Germany', *European History Quarterly*, vol. 18, 1988, pp. 77–90.
25. Stefan Goch, *Sozialdemokratischer Arbeiterkultur und Politik im Ruhrgebiet. Eine sozial-wissenschaftlich-sozialhistorische Untersuchung am Beispiel des Raumes Gelsenkirchen*, Bochum, 1987 (Ph.D. dissertation).

against the Catholic Church with its numerous organizations. We have nothing similar to put against them.'[26]

So the most influential cultural forces shaping society in the Ruhr were the churches and not the socialist working-class movement. As Brepohl once put it, social and political life in the Ruhr did not start 'with class struggle but rather with the support and development of traditionalism and the spheres of church and religion'.[27] Not only associations, but also social service institutions such as infirmaries and cultural institutions like schools were in one way or another connected with the two churches; of the two the most lasting and powerful influence, without doubt, was exercised by the Catholic Church.

The cultural impact of socialism, which, like the churches, proudly considered itself a civilizing influence on the German working class, admittedly was stronger in some parts of the Ruhr, especially in the Dortmund/Witten area.[28] But one has to be extremely cautious in using voting turn-outs as indicators of a socialist milieu, which means a culture as a distinct way of life. This can be done in the catholic case, but not in the socialist one. If one looks at the pattern of political change in some miners' villages which all of a sudden turned socialist in 1890, one receives the impression that political change was not necessarily accompanied by cultural change. What happened is that at a certain stage the protestant miners' milieu built a new 'political coalition' with the SPD when the old alliance with the National Liberals had lost its legitimacy after the great miners' strike in 1889. So, a distinction should be made between a socialist working-class movement milieu in its proper sense and a miners' milieu which was politically 'occupied' by the SPD, but which stuck to its own values and its own traditional way of life.

The relative weakness of the socialist milieu in the Ruhr is also revealed by the ratio of SPD members to SPD voters. In 1912, even in the Dortmund constituency, the Social Democratic stronghold in the Ruhr area, the figure (19.1%) was below the national average of 22.8%. The figures for the other Ruhr constituencies read as follows: Duisburg 13.4%, Essen 12.3% and Bochum 11.9%. In some other German industrial towns the ratio of members to voters approximated nearly 50%.

26. *Protokoll SPD-Parteitag*, 1904, p. 162.
27. Wilhelm Brepohl, *Industrievolk im Wandel von der agraren zur industriellen Daseinsform dargestellt am Ruhrgebiet*, Tübingen, 1957, p. 287.
28. David F. Crew, 'Steel, Sabotage and Socialism. The Strike at the Dortmund "Union" Steel Works in 1911', in: Richard J. Evans (ed.), *The German Working Class 1888–1933. The Politics of Everyday Life*, London, 1982, pp. 108–41, esp. pp. 121–2.

Basically the same picture emerges if one takes the results of the Prussian Landtag elections, which required open voting, as cultural indicators and compares them with the Reichstag election results. What emerges is that the ratio of 'open socialists' to 'anonymous socialists' was much lower in the Ruhr than in most other industrial regions.[29] To sum up, the sudden rise of the SPD to electoral strength in the Ruhr in the decade before 1914 was not matched by a corresponding cultural strength.

Social Democratic ascendancy in the Ruhr before the First World War, then, lacked a broad cultural foundation. And this fact is closely connected with the type of radicalism which emerged in this industrial area shaped by coal mining, heavy industry and mass immigration. There never existed a broad cultural basis for 'political radicalism' of the Remscheid type. Typical of the Ruhr was 'social radicalism' of the Hamborn type.[30] But a basis for socialist 'reformism' existed as well, especially in the predominantly protestant areas of the eastern parts of the Ruhr as was, for example, reflected in the 'radicalism' of the Essen SPD versus the 'reformism' of the Dortmund SPD. Later on, during the Weimar Republic, this was also reflected , in communist strength in catholic areas of the Ruhr and Social Democratic strength in the predominantly protestant one of the Witten Dortmund area. The obvious, but often overlooked reason which helps to explain this behavioural pattern is that in catholic areas those 'settled elements' within the working class, which were the backbone of 'reformism' within the SPD, did not belong to the socialist working-class movement at all but were linked with political catholicism. So, if one really wants to understand the pattern of 'radicalism' and 'reformism' in the Ruhr, one has to look beyond the narrow confines of the socialist labour movement.

'Reformism' in a wider sense includes not only socialist 'reformism' but catholic 'reformism' and, to some extent, protestant 'reformism' as well. At least, the Naumann wing within the Protestant Workers' Associations comes close to that. Seen from this perspective, it must be said that regional society in the Ruhr provided a fairly large potential for reformism, but only a restricted one for socialist reformism.

---

29. Karl Rohe, 'Die Ruhrgebietssozialdemokratie im wilhelminischen Kaiserreich und ihr politischer und kultureller Kontext', in Gerhard A. Ritter (ed.), *Der Aufstieg der sozialistischen Arbeiterorganisationen zur Massenbewegung im deutschen Kaiserreich*, Munich, 1990.

30. Erhard Lucas, *Zwei Formen von Radikalismus in der deutschen Arbeiterbewegung*, Frankfurt, 1976; Klaus Tenfelde, *Proletarische Provinz. Radikalisierung und Widerstand in Penzberg/Oberbayern 1900–1945*, Munich and Vienna, 1982, p. 5.

Table 4.2. Reichstag election results (RTE) as compared with Prussian Landtag election (LTE) results in Prussia and in the Ruhr, 1907/8 and 1912/13

	Eligible voters	Turnout	SPD	Centre Party	Votes cast at LTE in % of the preceding RTE	
					SPD	Centre Party
RTE 1907 in Prussia	8,168,592	6,905,220 (84.5%)	1,816,950 (22.2%)	1,274,224 (15.6%)		
RTE 1907 in the Ruhr	462,759	406,853 (87.9%)	138,307 (29.9%)	123,107 (26.6%)		
LTE 1908 in Prussia	7,682,721	2,522,656 (32.8%)	598,522 (7.8%)	499,343 (6.5%)	32.9	39.2
LTE 1908 in the Ruhr	450,930	234,695 (52%)	41,885 (9.3%)	94,782 (21%)	30.3	77.0
RTE 1912 in Prussia	8,890,149	7,515,170 (84.5%)	2,407,318 (27.1%)	1,249,536 (14.1%)		
RTE 1912 in the Ruhr	540,026	479,874 (88.9%)	176,861 (32.8%)	137,749 (25.5%)		
LTE 1913 in Prussia	8,400,114	2,750,086 (32.7%)	775,171 (9.2%)	451,511 (5.4%)	32.2	36.1
LTE 1913 in the Ruhr	537,621	234,513 (43.6%)	40,733 (7.6%)	86,109 (16%)	23.0	62.5

Source: Own calculations based on the *Statistik des Deutschen Reichs* and *Preußischer Statistik.*

Whereas 'reformism' reflects a workers' milieu which never completely cut its traditional ties with local society, notably with the churches, and/or which had been – by whatever means – reintegrated into local or national society, 'social radicalism' can best be understood as an *Extraditionalismus-Phänomen*.[31] It was primarily the political expression of industrial workers and miners whose traditional social and cultural bonds had faded away but who had not yet found a new and proper place in existing industrial society or had not yet developed a long term cultural perspective beyond the confines of capitalist society which gave their lives a new stability and meaning.

From Kaiserreich to Weimar: Continuity and Change of Political Alignments

Before the First World War, these mentalities and social realities found their main political expression in the Social Democratic Party, and to a lesser extent in the Polish Nationalist Party[32] and the small syndicalist movement. After the war it was the Communist Party which, at least in the long run, was able to collect the pre-war protest votes, including the former Polish votes, and to appeal to the 'new social radicalism' of former 'traditionalists' such as, for example, the Masuren and pre-war members of the Yellow Trade Unions.[33] In addition one has good reason to assume that members of the catholic working class, when they fell out of the catholic milieu, as a rule turned communist.[34]

'Social radicalism' was not merely a floating vote, but could provide a fairly solid basis for a political party as long as the social conditions in which it was rooted remained basically the same. Nevertheless it sometimes displayed a somewhat strange voting behaviour which gave

31. Karl Rohe, 'Vom alten Revier zum heutigen Ruhrgebiet. Die Entwicklung einer regionalen politischen Gesellschaft im Spiegel der Wahlen', in Karl Rohe and Herbert Kühr (eds), *Politik und Gesellschaft im Ruhrgebiet. Beiträge zur regionalen Politikforschung*, Königstein 1979, pp. 21–73, esp. pp. 49ff.

32. Christoph Kleßmann, *Polnische Bergarbeiter im Ruhrgebiet 1870–1945. Soziale Integration und nationale Subkultur einer Minderheit in der deutschen Industriegesellschaft*, Göttingen, 1978.

33. Dick Geary, 'Identifying Militancy. The Assessment of Working-Class Attitudes towards State and Society', in Evans, *The German Working Class*, pp. 220–46, esp. p. 232; compare the election results in Essen after 1918, in Eric D. Weitz, *Conflict in the Ruhr. Workers and Socialist Politics in Essen 1910–1925*, Boston University, 1983, pp. 292ff. (dissertation).

34. Johannes Schauff, *Die deutschen Katholiken und die Zentrumspartei. Eine politisch-statistische Untersuchung der Reichstagswahlen seit 1871*, Cologne, 1928, pp. 108ff.

proof of its weak cultural foundations. At the presidential elections in 1925, for example, Hindenburg did extremely well in some communist strongholds. So KPD (Communist Party) strength in the Ruhr during the Weimar Republic does not reflect a long and continuous tradition of left voting, as has been suggested by André Siegfried[35] for some French *départements*, but quite the reverse. It cannot be said, however, that 'social radicalism' in principle could not be gradually transformed into some kind of culturally based 'political radicalism'. That is precisely what did happen in the long run in some KPD areas, provided they were not based on Polish radicalism; one example is Bottrop-Eigen which even today is a communist stronghold. But this was not a political development which was bound to happen.

Whereas the KPD in a sense was a continuation of the pre-war Social Democratic protest vote and was typically strong in those places where the SPD had been successful comparatively late, the Social Democratic Party became heir to pre-war 'reformism' and had its strongholds in the south-eastern part of the Ruhr. And again, as in the 1890s, the SPD became a strongly protestant-based party. This is not only a merely statistical relationship. There are hints that, as far as the voters were concerned, the SPD had some features of a protestant 'little man's party' in some districts.[36] In Bochum, for example, the Social Democratic *Volksblatt* regularly announced protestant Sunday services. And it is highly illuminating that the 1929-founded Christian People's Service (*Christlich-Sozialer Volksdienst*), which attracted moderate protestants with close attachment to the Protestant Church and was often led by protestant clergymen, was to some extent competing with the SPD for the same voters. As representative statistics in Bottrop at the ward level seem to indicate, the SPD lost votes to the Christian People's Service, especially among female voters.

In the Ruhr, KPD and SPD votes taken together amount nearly to the pre-war strength of the old socialist camp, which left the Kaiserreich with a share of 32.8% of the electorate and gained a total share of 31.1% at the end of the Weimar Republic. True, there were ups and downs in between; but the overall political stability is nevertheless quite amazing given the fact that the political regime, the party system and the electoral system had changed dramatically, and that, mainly owing to the new women's suffrage and the lowering of the voting age,

---

35. André Siegfried, *Tableau des partis en France*, Paris, 1930, pp. 169–70.
36. Horst Nöcker, *Der preußische Reichstagswähler in Kaiserreich und Republik 1912 und 1924. Analyse, Interpretation, Dokumentation. Ein historisch-statistischer Beitrag zum Kontinuitätsproblem eines epochenübergreifenden Wählerverhaltens*, Berlin, 1987, pp. 71ff.

Table 4.3. Political camps in the Ruhr, 1871–1912

Year of election	Population[1] Total	Catholics %	Employed Population[2] Total	Industry %	Eligible voters	Turn-out	Valid votes
1871					94,628	57.6	54,187
1874	558,356	47.8			148,179	60.9	89,972
1877	696,658				154,639	67.2	103,615
1878					157,595	77.2	121,383
1881	769,346	48.1	256,130	75.1	166,507	61.1	101,255
1884					187,298	70.9	132,360
1887	904,190	48.1			190,878	85.5	162,142
1890					219,773	75.4	165,368
1893	1,085,107	48.3	426,829	75.5	255,546	78.4	200,214
1898	1,311,656	48.5			326,182	78.7	252,084
1903	1,766,023	49.4			406,518	84.6	343,367
1907	2,121,797	50.2	773,293	76.2	462,759	87.9	405,800
1912	2,515,136	51.0			540,026	88.9	478,245

1. According to census 1871–1910.
2. According to occupational census 1882, 1895 and 1907.
3. Addition of the votes for Conservatives, National Liberals, Left Liberals and Anti-Semites.
Source: Own computations based on the *Statistik des Deutschen Reichs*.

National camp[3] in % 1. El. vot.		Centre Party in % 1. El. vot.		Poles in % 1. El. vot.		SPD in % 1. El. vot.	
Total	2. Val. vot.	Total	2. Val. vot.	Total	2. Val. vot.	Total	2. Val. vot.
27,588	29.2	22,654	23.9			3,902	4.1
	50.9		41.8				7.2
46,678	31.5	39,221	26.5			4,077	2.8
	51.9		43.6				4.5
49,499	32.0	42,301	27.4			11,747	7.6
	47.8		40.8				11.3
68,429	43.4	49,140	31.2			3,748	2.4
	56.4		40.5				3.1
56,696	34.1	43,506	26.1			890	0.5
	56.0		43.0				0.9
78,199	41.8	50,345	26.9			3,667	2.0
	59.1		38.0				2.8
105,374	55.2	51,795	27.1			4,859	2.5
	65.0		31.9				3.0
74,877	34.1	65,296	29.7			25,105	11.4
	45.3		39.5				15.2
84,087	32.9	67,294	26.3			48,744	19.1
	42.0		33.6				24.3
103,395	31.7	98,550	30.2			50,047	15.3
	41.0		39.1				19.9
103,543	25.5	107,783	26.5	13,421	3.3	118,497	29.1
	30.2		31.4		3.9		34.5
121,951	26.4	123,107	26.6	21,765	4.7	138,307	29.9
	30.1		30.3		5.4		34.1
135,055	25.0	137,749	25.5	28,522	5.3	176,861	32.8
	28.2		28.8		6.0		37.0

the electorate in the Ruhr more than tripled between 1912 and 1920.

One might well question whether it still makes sense to speak of political camps, especially if one looks at the changed party system of the Weimar Republic and the changed political relationships between political parties at the parliamentary level. After all, terms like 'camp', 'milieu' etc. are analytical tools, the usefulness of which may vary according to time and place. Some qualifications, no doubt, have to be made, if one applies these concepts to Weimar. The spread of mass culture and of politically neutral sports[37] diminished the political importance of the traditional cultures. Milieus, too, were no longer what they had been in the past. Families were politically less homogeneous than in pre-war times, the father, for example, sometimes being a communist and his wife a devoted catholic, or the father being a member of the Centre Party and the son voting for the Communists.[38] But far more widespread was radicalization within camp lines, that is a Social Democratic father with a son who voted for the Communists or a Conservative father with a son who voted for the Nazis. So, if one looks at the social and cultural bases of politics it still makes sense to speak of three major political camps.

Beneath the surface, however, some de-alignment and re-alignment processes must have taken place. This comes to the fore the more one accounts for the fact that political camps were able to profit differently from the newly introduced women's suffrage. Representative statistics which are available for some towns in the Westphalian part of the Ruhr show that in a town like Bottrop the Centre Party in the Reichstag elections of May 1924 got 40.9% of the female votes but only 23.6% of the male votes; and in the Reichstag elections of 1928, 35.2% of the female votes as against 18.6% of the male votes. If one looks only at the male votes, the Centre Party fell in Bottrop from 52.7% in 1912 to 18.2% in 1928. That is to say, it lost nearly two-thirds of its male votes.

As representative statistics are available only for some towns, it is difficult to generalize. The capacity of the Centre Party to utilize its catholic potential differed greatly within the Ruhr area. But despite huge local differences, the general picture which emerges is that the decline of the traditional catholic milieu in the Ruhr was much more

---

37. Siegfried Gehrmann, *Fußball – Vereine – Politik. Zur Sportgeschichte des Reviers 1900–1940*, Essen, 1988.

38. Alexander von Plato, '"Ich bin mit allen gut ausgekommen". Oder: war die Ruhrarbeiterschaft vor 1933 in politische Lager zerspalten?', in Lutz Niethammer (ed.), *'Die Jahre weiß man nicht, wo man die heute hinsetzen soll'. Faschismuserfahrungen im Ruhrgebiet. Lebensgeschichte und Sozialkultur im Ruhrgebiet 1930 bis 1960*, vol. 1, Berlin and Bonn, 1983, pp. 31–65.

dramatic than the mere voting figures at first sight reveal.

Two qualifications, however, have to be made. The share of the Centre Party votes no longer reflected the size of the catholic milieu, as had been the case in pre-war times. Church attendance in the Ruhr – or, rather, participation in the Easter communion – did not decrease so much that the figures can fully account for the drop in the Centre Party votes. So one has to conclude that the Centre Party in the Ruhr lost not only the political support of those catholics who had fallen out of the catholic milieu, but to some extent that of church-goers as well. This can partly be ascribed to votes cast for the *Wirtschaftspartei*, which in the 1928 and 1930 Reichstag elections did extremely well in some catholic middle-class districts. But there is also some evidence, supported and illustrated by stories about Italian-style Don Camillo and Peppone relations between catholic priests and communist local activists,[39] that not all catholics who voted for the communists lost contact with the Catholic Church.

The second qualification which has to be made is that the Centre Party, which reached its lowest point in the Reichstag elections of 1928, recovered during the last three elections of the Weimar Republic. Political catholicism closed ranks, accompanied by a remarkable increase in church attendance which lasted until 1935. The rise of National Socialism was apparently perceived by catholics as a threat to the catholic community and reminded them of the *Kulturkampf*. And an indication of the spiritual resources the Centre Party could rely on in the final stage of the Weimar Republic is given by the report that the last meeting of the Witten Centre Party in March 1933 ended with singing the old confessional hymn of catholicism: 'Fest soll mein Taufbund immer stehen.'[40]

Radicalization of the Dominant National Culture: The Rise of the NSDAP in the Ruhr

The partial revival of political catholicism and, except for the last Reichstag election in March 1933, the overall stability of the socialist camp, not surprisingly suggests that one should look elsewhere if one wants to explain Nazi support in this industrial region. True, one has to take into consideration the fact that rather complex voter

39. Bernhard Parisius, *Lebenswege im Revier. Erlebnisse und Erfahrungen zwischen Jahrhundertwende und Kohlenkrise – erzählt von Frauen und Männern aus Borbeck*, Essen, 1984, pp. 137ff.
40. *Wittener Volks-Zeitung*, 9 March 1933.

transitions took place between 1919/28 and 1933. And a closer look at voting behaviour at the ward level at least partly confirms general statistical conclusions. Since the Prussian Landtag elections in 1932 there can be observed some movements from the SPD to the Nazis, notably among metal workers, especially when the 'political coalition' with the SPD was a fairly new one, whereas the miners' milieu, regardless of its political alignment to the SPD, the KPD or the Centre Party, for a long time displayed a remarkable political stability. It took the Nazis until 1933 to get into this milieu. But then some interesting features occur which are perhaps not so surprising if one remembers what has been said about communist constituencies in the 1920s. If one analyses the workers' council elections in the mining industry at the end of March 1933, it appears that the NSDAP (National Socialist Party) was not only especially successful in mining areas which in 1922 had been strongholds of the communist miners' union but also in the milieu of the so-called *Kötterbergleute* which since the 1890s had been dominated by a reformist SPD. The NSDAP was least successful in those mining areas which in the early 1870s had been strongholds of the christian Social movement.[41]

But these interesting developments are mere details compared with the basic fact that it was the old national camp in its broader sense which provided the ground for the Nazi vote. 'In its broader sense' means that non-voters are included. This is appropriate because they had always been a kind of 'national reserve', so to speak the hidden part of the national camp. Habitual non-voters in the Ruhr only went to the polls when Reichstag elections – like those of 1878, 1887 and 1907 – figured as national referenda; the last three Reichstag elections of the Weimar Republic possessed precisely that character and produced nearly the same voting turn-outs.

If one tries to put these findings into a coherent conceptual framework, the most convincing overall explanation is not 'radicalization of the middle classes'[42] or 'radicalization of the uprooted masses',[43] but radicalization of the 'dominant national culture'. What mattered was not social structure as such but culture. The likelihood of voting for the

41. Wolfgang Jäger will give full details in his coming Ph.D. dissertation: 'Ruhrberg-arbeiterschaft und Bergarbeiterbewegung in der Endphase der Weimarer Republik'.
42. Seymour Martin Lipset, 'Fascism – Left, Right and Center', in S. M. Lipset (ed.), *Political Man. The Social Bases of Politics*, Garden City, 1960, pp. 127–79.
43. Reinhard Bendix, 'Social Stratification and Political Power', *American Political Science Review*, 1952, pp. 357–75; Jürgen W. Falter, 'Radikalisierung des Mittelstandes oder Mobilisierung der Unpolitischen? Die Theorien von Seymour Martin Lipset und Reinhard Bendix über die Wählerschaft der NSDAP im Lichte neuerer Forschungs-ergebnisse', in Steinbach, *Probleme politischer Partizipation*, pp. 438–69.

NSDAP was primarily a question of political traditions. This is not to deny that the middle classes were grossly over-represented within the regional Nazi movement.[44] But there is no evidence that manual workers who belonged to the national camp were less inclined to vote for the Nazis than members of the middle classes. The dividing line within the national camp was, it seems, not a social but a religious and a generational one, although this interpretation admittedly is somewhat speculative. In the final stage of the Weimar Republic, the DNVP (German National People's Party) in the Ruhr apparently became a rallying point of protestants with close attachment to the Protestant Church. This had not been the case during the first decade of the Weimar Republic. The new division within the old national camp between DNVP and DVP (German People's Party) was rather a reflection of personal and local circumstances than of the old differences of the 1860s between religious-minded conservatives and more secular-minded liberals. In the end, however, the DNVP seems to have become a somewhat different party.

A cultural hypothesis seems also to be useful if one wants to understand the pattern of resistance to and attraction of Nazism. Looking at voting behaviour in working-class districts between 1930 and 1933 in historical perspective, one might suggest that those KPD voters or SPD voters who from their past or their present had preserved or had acquired close connections with the dominant national culture were also those most likely to vote for the Nazis in 1932 and 1933. So the debate on whether Social Democratic or Communist supporters were most likely to be attracted by the Nazis sounds somewhat abstract. It all depends on what kind of Social Democratic or Communist voters one is speaking about and what their political heritage was.

So it is a cultural explanation – assuming that the rise of Nazism in this industrial area can best be understood as a radicalization of the dominant national culture – which carries a good deal of conviction. The NSDAP took over the place which the National Liberals had occupied in the nineteenth century and was able to increase the old national camp to a size which was reminiscent of the heyday of National Liberalism in the 1870s and 1880s. But by expanding the national camp the Nazis at the same time destroyed it and thereby laid the foundations of a new political society. Right from its beginning, after 1945, it was quite clear in the Ruhr that the political game now

---

44. Wilfried Böhnke, *Die NSDAP im Ruhrgebiet 1920–1933*, Bonn and Bad Godesberg, 1974, p. 225; contrary to Böhnke: Detlef Willi Mühlberger, *The Rise of National Socialism in Westphalia* 1920–1933, London, 1975 (Ph.D. dissertation), p. 363.

Table 4.4. Political camps in the Ruhr, 1919–33

Year of election	Population[1] Total	Catholics %	Labour force[1] Total	Workers %	Eligible voters	Turn-out	Valid votes
1919					1,325,088	86.1	1,136,912
1920					1,638,734	81.8	1,335,395
1924 I					1,889,628	79.5	1,446,602
1924 II	3,325,770	49.7	1,365,285	65.0	1,916,801	78.5	1,476,778
1928					2,088,053	79.0	1,620,602
1930					2,195,319	84.6	1,842,998
1932 I					2,227,050	86.6	1,915,820
1932 II					2,268,937	81.7	1,839,657
1933	3,460,989	49.5	1,371,622	62.9	2,285,837	90.0	2,034,832

1. According to census, 1925 and 1933.
2. Addition of the votes for the German National People's Party, the German People's Party, the German Democratic Party, the Middle Classes Party (Wirtschaftspartei) and the Christian People's Service.
3. Addition of the votes for Social Democrats, Independent Social Democrats and the Communist Party.

Source: Own computations based on the *Statistik des Deutschen Reichs*.

| National camp | | | | Centre Party in % | | Socialist camps[3] in % | |
excl. NSDAP 1. El. vot. Total 2. Val. vot.		incl. NSDAP 1. El. vot. Total 2. Val. vot.		1. El. vot. Total 2. Val. vot.		1. El. vot. Total 2. Val. vot.	
266,314	20.1			323,551	24.4	547,047	41.3
	23.4				28.5		48.1
301,054	18.4			381,085	23.3	590,853	36.1
	22.5				28.5		44.3
337,353	17.9			369,768	19.6	629,236	33.3
	23.3				25.6		43.5
411,607	21.5	430,150	22.4	414,646	21.6	588,063	30.7
	27.9		29.1		28.1		39.8
421,759	20.2	445,212	21.3	388,170	18.6	710,803	34.0
	26.0		27.5		24.0		43.9
377,982	17.2	619,814	28.2	411,964	18.8	751,653	34.2
	20.5		33.6		22.4		40.8
159,264	7.2	617,636	27.7	472,381	21.2	806,302	36.2
	8.3		32.2		24.7		42.1
197,872	8.7	589,263	26.0	449,947	19.8	778,993	34.3
	10.8		32.0		24.5		42.3
205,527	9.0	838,618	36.7	485,849	21.3	709,838	31.1
	10.1		41.2		23.9		34.9

had to be played with new cards. This new constellation in the long history of the Ruhr provided for the first time a real chance for the SPD to become the main political expression of this most industrialized region in Central Europe. And the SPD took its chance.[45]

The Rise of the SPD to Regional Hegemony after the Second World War

The same party which at the last Weimar elections received no more than 12.8% of the Ruhr electorate – in a town like Bottrop no more than 7.8% – scored 29.5% in the first Bundestag elections of 1949 – in Bottrop 26.5%. So the SPD nearly tripled (or more than tripled) its previous Weimar results. With regard to these developments at the polls, one is tempted to say that the Social Democrats were never as successful as in those years when they let the Nazis work for them.

How can one account for the changed voting pattern? The first explanation one thinks of is that the election results in 1949 reflect nothing more than a rearrangement within the socialist camp, the Communists for a number of obvious reasons losing votes and the Social Democrats gaining them.[46] There is some truth in this suggestion. In the long run, the SPD, without doubt, attracted most of the former Communist votes. But in the first years after the war it was different. If one looks at the results of the Landtag elections of 1947 – the first general elections after the war, leaving out the city council elections of 1946 which had some peculiar features – one often finds that the Communists more or less kept their Weimar strength at the ward level whereas at the same time the SPD nearly tripled its Weimar results. Further, if one takes into account the fact that in catholic areas the Christian Democrats were often not much stronger than the old Centre Party[47] and that from the very beginning the FDP (Free Democratic Party)[48] in the Ruhr was only a shadow of the old National

45. Karl Rohe, 'Vom sozialdemokratischen Armenhaus zur Wagenburg der SPD. Politischer Strukturwandel in einer Industrieregion nach dem Zweiten Weltkrieg', *Geschichte und Gesellschaft*, vol. 13, 1987, pp. 508–34.

46. Arno Klönne, 'Die Sozialdemokratie in Nordrhein-Westfalen. Historische Verankerung und heutiges Profil', in Ulrich von Alemann (ed.), *Parteien und Wahlen in Nordrhein-Westfalen*, Cologne, 1985, pp. 69–90, esp. pp. 80, 81.

47. Schmidt, *Zentrum oder CDU*, pp. 154ff.

48. Dieter Hein, *Zwischen liberaler Milieupartei und nationaler Sammlungsbewegung. Gründung, Entwicklung und Struktur der Freien Demokratischen Partei 1945–1949*, Düsseldorf, 1985.

Liberal strength, then there can be no reasonable doubt, although there is no strict proof, that the SPD must have profited considerably from the collapse of the old national camp which had always taken a share of the working-class votes, especially among metal workers.

What had already become apparent in 1947 came fully to the fore at the city council election of 1956 when the outlawed KPD could no longer participate. The SPD was extremely successful and definitely became the political expression of the working class, except for catholic workers who still kept their relationship with the CDU (Christian Democratic Party), the successor to the old Centre Party. From now onwards, it was no longer possible to tell whether a working-class district had been a socialist, communist or national stronghold in pre-war times. There was only one colour left, the mid-red of the Social Democrats.

From the very beginning, the movement towards the SPD was not restricted to the working class. At least among the party activists, one finds quite a lot of people with a middle-class background who in pre-war times would most likely have belonged to the national camp.[49] In addition, there seems to have been a generation effect. In Duisburg, for example, of all elections since the 1960s the SPD achieved its best results among the generation born between 1927 and 1935 – the *Jungvolk* – and the younger Hitler-Youth generation who were between 10 and 18 years old when the war ended.[50] Slightly older were the so-called *neue Lassalleaner*,[51] former members of the Hitler Youth and members of the army with middle-class backgrounds who joined the SPD after the war. As the term *neue Lassalleaner* shows, there was an ideological factor which turned these disappointed young idealists into committed members of the SPD and of a new social and democratic order. And it comes as no surprise that it was the first postwar leader of the SPD, the charismatic Dr Kurt Schumacher – a survivor of a concentration camp – whose combination of democratic socialism,

49. Everhard Holtmann, *Politik und Nichtpolitik. Lokale Erscheinungsformen politischer Kultur im frühen Nachkriegsdeutschland*, Opladen, 1987; Alexander von Plato, 'Erfahrungsstrukturen der Besatzungszeit nicht nur in Nordrhein-Westfalen: Mit alten Köpfen in neue Zeiten', in Gerhard Brunn (ed.), *Neuland: Nordrhein-Westfalen und seine Anfänge nach 1945/46*, Essen, 1986, pp. 9–27; Arno Klönne, *Die deutsche Arbeiterbewegung. Geschichte – Ziele – Wirkungen*, 2nd edn. Dusseldorf and Cologne, 1981, p. 299.
50. Wolfgang Bick, *Konstanz und Wandel des Wahlverhaltens in Duisburg*, Duisburg, 1983 (Amt für Statistik und Stadtforschung (ed.), Daten und Informationen, no. 13).
51. Everhard Holtmann, 'Die neuen Lassalleaner. SPD und HJ-Generation nach 1945', in Martin Broszat et al. (eds), *Von Stalingrad zur Währungsreform. Zur Sozialgeschichte des Umbruchs in Deutschland*, Munich, 1988.

étatism and German patriotism was crucial in integrating these once convinced young National Socialists politically. They were too secular minded to recognize themselves in a christian and catholic interpretation of political and social life as delivered by the regional CDU, which even today has preserved a predominantly catholic character.[52] And they were too socially minded to be attracted by the FDP.

This leads us to another point; namely, the somewhat aloof relations existing between the protestant population in the Ruhr and the regional CDU. True, there were protestants among the regional founders of the CDU, very often former members of the Christian People's Service, very seldom, it seems, former members of the DNVP.[53] But in most parts of the Ruhr the CDU basically remained a successor party to the old Centre Party, adding some protestant elements.

Despite this fact, most protestant members of the middle classes voted for the CDU in the early years of the Federal Republic, as election results in predominantly protestant middle-class areas seem to indicate. But from the very beginning there was a kind of emotional distance between the CDU and regional protestantism, although it took the latter more than a decade to become actively associated with the SPD. This *rapprochement* between SPD and regional protestantism was not caused but supported by the fact that former members of the All-German People's Party, among them the present Prime Minister of North-Rhine-Westphalia, Johannes Rau, joined the SPD in 1957.[54] Most of them – like its founder, Gustav Heinemann, an Essen lawyer and CDU minister in the first Adenauer cabinet and later President of the Federal Republic – had very close affiliations with the Protestant Church. It is evidence of the impact of this *rapprochement* and of the important role of protestant youth organizations as socialization agencies of future SPD élites at that time, that there is a saying today in North-Rhine-Westphalia that the SPD cabinet could foregather as a protestant synod if it felt like it. So there are two Social Democratic intakes of middle-class people which have to be distinguished carefully, although in pre-war days both would most likely have belonged to the national camp: rather secular-minded *neue Lassalleaner* of the Hitler

52. Herbert Kühr, 'Die CDU in Nordrhein-Westfalen. Von der Unionsgründung zur modernen Mitgliederpartei', in Ulrich von Alemann (ed.), *Parteien und Wahlen*, pp. 91–120, esp. p. 116.

53. Clemens Kreuzer, *Union in Bochum. Ein Beitrag zur politischen Geschichte dieser Stadt*, Bochum, 1985, pp. 25ff.

54. Dieter Otten, 'Gustav W. Heinemann und die Transformation der SPD in eine bundesrepublikanische Partei', in Peter Grafe et al. (eds), *Der Lokomotive in voller Fahrt die Räder wechseln. Geschichte und Geschichten aus Nordrhein-Westfalen*, Berlin and Bonn, n.d., pp. 113–19.

Youth generation on the one hand and devoted protestant Christians on the other.

Looking from a historical perspective, one is inclined to state that what happened in the Ruhr after 1945 was a kind of re-unification of the protestant working class and protestant middle class which had split in the 1890s, this time not under a National Liberal but under a Social Democratic banner. There is some truth behind this idea, the more so the more one takes into account the new, overwhelmingly protestant, immigrants from the east and the new miners who all found their political expression in the SPD.[55]

Some qualifications, however, have to be made, mainly because of changes which took place within the catholic camp. There are three changes which have to be looked at closely. Between 1930 and 1935 church attendance among catholics had increased to 53.82% in the Ruhr, but in 1940 it had declined to 44.48% and in 1948 to 40.05%. So although the Nazis were not able to destroy catholic culture, catholic communities were eroded and lost about 13% of their former members.[56] And these were no longer 'natural' voters for the Centre Party, or for its successor, the CDU.

A second change within the catholic camp took place in the early 1960s. Beginning with the Bundestag elections of 1961 and culminating in 1965, the Ruhr SPD showed tremendous growth rates, especially in the predominantly catholic cities of the Ruhr. There were, no doubt, some economic causes, namely the crisis in the coal mining industry,[57] which help to explain this electoral change. However, the whole process can only be understood against the background of cultural and intellectual changes within the Catholic Church.[58] Whatever the detailed reasons may have been, the result was that the SPD for the first time acquired a reasonable amount of catholic voters who did not cut

55. Falk Wiesemann, 'Flüchtlinge in Nordrhein-Westfalen', in Brunn, *Neuland*, pp. 163–73; Alexander von Plato, 'Fremde Heimat. Zur Integration von Flüchtlingen und Einheimischen in die Neue Zeit', in Lutz Niethammer and Alexander von Plato (eds), '*Wir kriegen jetzt andere Zeiten'. Auf der Suche nach der Erfahrung des Volkes in nachfaschistischen Ländern*, Berlin and Bonn, 1985 (*Lebensgeschichte und Sozialkultur im Ruhrgebiet 1930 bis 1960*, vol. 3), pp. 172–219; Mark Roseman, 'Arbeiter in Bewegung. Neubergleute im Ruhrrevier 1945–1958', in Lutz Niethammer et al. (eds), '*Die Menschen machen ihre Geschichte nicht aus freien Stücken, aber sie machen sie selbst*', *Einladung zu einer Geschichte des Volkes in NRW*, Berlin and Bonn, 1984, pp. 192–5.

56. Church attendance is calculated by *Kirchliches Handbuch für das katholische Deutschland*, vol. V–XXV, Freiburg, 1916–62.

57. Karl Lauschke, *Schwarze Fahnen an der Ruhr. Die Politik der IG Bergbau und Energie während der Kohlenkrise 1958–1968*, Marburg, 1984; Werner Abelshauser, *Der Ruhrkohlenbergbau seit 1945. Wiederaufbau, Krise, Anpassung*, Munich, 1984, pp. 87ff.

58. Herbert Kühr, 'Die katholische Arbeiterbewegung im Ruhrgebiet nach 1945', in Karl Rohe and Herbert Kühr (eds), *Politik und Gesellschaft*, pp. 74–92, esp. p. 82.

their ties with the Catholic Church and catholic communities. For the increase in SPD votes was not accompanied by a decline in church attendance. CDU politicians suddenly had to realize that it was now much more difficult to address catholic associations than it had been hitherto. There had admittedly already been individual moves towards the SPD in the 1950s by catholic activists who became frustrated in what they thought of as a *Verbürgerlichung* of the CDU. But it was only in the 1960s that 'alienation' between the CDU and parts of the catholic community in the Ruhr became more widespread.

A third significant change within the catholic electorate was reflected in the 1972 Bundestag elections. The SPD votes in the Ruhr were now more than twice as many as those cast for the CDU. Contrary to the electoral changes in the 1960s, these results must be interpreted against the background of cultural changes, accompanied by a sharp drop in church attendance figures, i.e. a marked reduction of the catholic milieu in the proper meaning of the word. Basically this situation still exists. The former socialist electoral desert of the Kaiserreich and the Weimar Republic has definitely become the regional Social Democratic stronghold in the Federal Republic.

Why Was There a Political Re-Alignment in the Ruhr after 1945?

Was this re-alignment a 'natural' political development which one might have expected? In a sense the answer must be 'yes'. The Nazi era and its concomitants of war, evacuation, destruction of cities, new immigration, etc., accelerated, if not caused, the establishment of social and cultural conditions in the Ruhr which were more favourable to the SPD than those which had existed in the past, the more so the more old political rivals like the Communists and the pre-war Centre Party for internal and external reasons were no longer serious political competitors. And the CDU, despite its early attractiveness as a new party, had some heavy handicaps to carry, partly for historical and partly for social reasons. It was extremely difficult to establish a truly bi-confessional party in a region the cleavage structure of which had for decades been characterized by the catholic–protestant conflict. And it was difficult to keep up catholic political loyalties in a region which had been the centre of social catholicism in Germany when the CDU more and more developed into a conservative bourgeois party. So, the SPD, right from the beginning, was most likely to

Table 4.5. Results of Bundestag elections, 1949–87, in the Federal Republic of Germany (FRG) and the Ruhr

Year of election	Region	Eligible voters FRG / Ruhr	Valid votes FRG / Ruhr	CDU % of eligible voters	CDU % of valid votes	SPD % of eligible voters	SPD % of valid votes	FDP % of eligible voters	FDP % of valid votes
1949	FRG	31,207,600	23,732,398	24.3	31.0	22.9	29.2	9.9	11.9
	Ruhr	2,263,025	1,744,944	23.3	30.2	29.1	37.8	5.5	7.1
1953	FRG	33,120,900	27,551,272	38.9	45.2	24.8	28.8	8.2	9.5
	Ruhr	2,583,196	2,130,006	34.4	41.8	33.1	41.1	5.2	6.4
1957	FRG	33,400,900	29,905,428	44.1	50.2	27.9	31.8	6.8	7.7
	Ruhr	2,817,765	2,363,214	39.4	46.9	36.7	43.8	4.4	5.2
1961	FRG	37,440,700	31,550,901	39.7	45.3	31.8	36.2	11.2	12.8
	Ruhr	2,969,307	2,508,039	33.8	40.0	40.2	47.5	7.5	8.9
1965	FRG	38,510,400	32,620,442	41.3	47.6	34.1	39.3	8.2	9.5
	Ruhr	2,939,581	2,504,577	32.3	37.8	46.0	54.0	4.7	5.5
1969	FRG	38,677,200	32,966,024	40.0	46.1	37.0	42.7	5.0	5.8
	Ruhr	2,823,187	2,401,686	29.6	34.8	48.5	57.0	3.7	4.3
1972	FRG	41,446,300	37,459,750	40.5	45.8	41.4	44.9	7.6	8.4
	Ruhr	2,932,617	2,656,678	27.8	30.7	56.4	62.3	5.6	6.1
1976	FRG	42,058,000	37,822,500	43.7	48.6	38.3	42.6	7.1	7.9
	Ruhr	2,857,695	2,587,848	30.3	33.4	53.7	59.3	5.8	6.4
1980	FRG	43,231,700	37,938,981	39.4	44.5	38.0	42.9	9.4	10.6
	Ruhr	2,822,255	2,473,135	26.7	30.5	51.4	58.7	8.0	9.1
1983	FRG	44,068,700	38,940,687	43.5	48.8	34.0	38.2	6.1	7.0
	Ruhr	2,816,264	2,477,774	30.8	35.0	48.7	55.4	3.6	4.1
1987	FRG	45,290,668	37,861,198	37.0	44.3	31.0	37.0	7.6	9.1
	Ruhr	2,784,762	2,336,392	25.8	30.8	47.0	56.1	4.5	5.3

Source: *Statistik der Bundesrepublik Deutschland.*

Table 4.6. Distances between SPD and CDU in Bundestag elections in the Ruhr cities, 1949–87 (% of valid votes)

Cities	49	53	57	61	65	69	72	76	80	83	87
Duisburg	2.0	−2.8	−7.5	9.6	17.7	23.9	36.7	30.5	32.5	24.5	30.6
Mülheim	6.7	−0.8	−1.4	10.3	15.4	22.8	28.1	21.1	22.8	15.2	17.9
Oberhausen	−0.1	−5.7	−18.5	−2.9	7.9	15.3	28.9	23.6	28.1	20.5	26.8
Bottrop	−7.2	−12.7	−13.2	−10.8	3.7	12.5	26.9	21.2	24.5	16.6	23.3
Essen	5.7	−4.0	−5.2	2.1	11.5	18.5	25.8	19.5	22.6	14.9	19.0
Bochum	6.8	−1.7	−2.2	10.9	20.1	24.5	32.0	26.7	29.1	20.9	26.6
Dortmund	13.2	7.3	6.4	14.7	20.1	26.0	31.4	26.3	28.9	21.0	24.9
Gelsenkirchen	11.6	3.3	0.5	8.7	20.4	24.8	36.9	32.6	33.4	27.2	31.5
Herne	8.7	0.5	−1.1	9.3	20.8	25.0	36.7	33.3	34.2	26.6	31.7
Stadt Recklinghausen	−6.8	−10.0	−12.9	−0.9	8.8	15.7	25.9	19.4	19.6	12.3	18.2
Gladbeck	8.4	0.8	−1.8	5.1	14.5	20.9	34.9	28.6	31.8	24.6	30.1
Castrop	2.7	−4.3	−2.3	6.6	13.1	19.6	32.3	26.8	27.8	19.9	25.7
Lünen	9.5	−2.7	−3.4	6.7	10.6	16.7	29.2	22.2	24.6	14.8	21.7
Witten	19.4	10.5	8.5	20.0	25.0	30.2	37.8	29.5	32.5	24.9	28.0

Source: Own computations based on the *Statistik der Bundesrepublik Deutschland.*

Table 4.7. Differences between SPD strongholds and SPD diasporas in the Ruhr, 1930–87 (% of valid votes)

Reichstag, Bundestag elections	Minimal result SPD	Maximal result SPD	Difference
1930	7.91	32.90	24.99
1932 I	8.50	30.06	21.55
1932 II	9.17	26.34	17.17
1933	8.23	27.29	19.06
1949	28.96	45.41	16.45
1953	35.11	46.71	11.60
1957	36.12	48.47	12.35
1961	39.82	53.24	13.41
1965	48.46	58.02	9.56
1969	52.82	60.55	7.73
1972	58.81	66.14	7.33
1976	55.52	63.78	8.26
1980	54.10	62.75	8.65
1983	51.37	59.51	8.15
1987	50.35	60.38	10.03

Source: Own computations based on the *Statistik der Bundesrepublik Deutschland*.

become the strongest party in the region. An ambitious young politician who, for the sake of argument, would probably have joined the CSU[59] in Bavaria, would quickly evaluate the new situation and decide to become a member of the SPD.

This leads on to the second point. The Nazi era and war had brought about a new political situation which offered new political chances. But chances must be taken and potentials must be realized. And this very much depends on the political mechanisms which are at hand, and the political messages which, consciously or unconsciously, are sent out by political parties either to accommodate to existing mentalities or to change and shape them. The most important political mechanism supporting the political ascendancy of the SPD in the Ruhr was and is the newly created industrial trade unions (*Einheitsgewerkschaften*). Together with the works councils (*Betriebsräte*) and the town halls, the trade unions formed the core of a new social democratic milieu. In a sense it might even be said that the SPD in the Ruhr after 1945 has been nothing other than the continuation of trade unionism by other

59. Alf Mintzel, *Geschichte der CSU. Ein Überblick*, Opladen, 1977.

means.[60] In other words: the Ruhr SPD established its regional hegemony as a highly undogmatic and, to the great embarrassment of
young socialist intellectuals, culturally conservative 'small man's
party' without needing a Godesberg Programme. It very much lived by
articulating the material and emotional concerns of ordinary men and
being an integrated part of their milieu. The immaterial interests must
be emphasized because they are often overlooked. A lot of socialist
intellectuals and regional CDU leaders do not understand the 'real
secret' of the Ruhr SPD, namely that it is rooted not only in the
material interests but in the immaterial interests of 'small men', their
sentiments and resentments and their pride and self-esteem. These
emotional concerns are the very foundation of a 'rain and sunshine'
attachment to the SPD which still exists in the Ruhr. And as long as
these emotional ties exist, the best a CDU councillor who really cares
for his district can hope for is a clap on his shoulder when he enters the
pub in the evening along with the comment: 'You're a nice chap. What
a pity that you're a member of the CDU.'[61]

60. Lutz Niethammer, Foreword, in idem (ed.), *'Hinterher merkt man, daß es richtig war,
daß es schiefgegangen ist'. Nachkriegserfahrungen im Ruhrgebiet*, Berlin and Bonn, 1983 (*Lebensgeschichte und Sozialkultur im Ruhrgebiet 1930 bis 1960*, vol. 2), p. 14; Alexander von Plato,
'Der Verlierer geht nicht leer aus'. Betriebsräte geben zu Protokoll, Berlin and Bonn, 1984.
61.   Wilfried Heimes, 'Die Situation der CDU im Ruhrgebiet', in *Revier-Kultur*, vol. 1,
1986, pp. 47–62, esp. p. 57.

ALF MINTZEL

Political and Socio-economic Developments in the Postwar Era: The Case of Bavaria, 1945–1989

The Case of Bavaria: A Contrast Case to the Ruhr Area

Within the context of our discussion, Bavaria offers, for a number of reasons, a particularly interesting example of regional German party development. From the Kaiserreich throughout the Weimar Republic up until the end of the Third Reich, Bavaria had an essentially agricultural economy, dotted by a few industrial islands (for example, Munich, Augsburg, Nuremberg, Fuerth, Schweinfurt). Following the Second World War, this situation reversed itself as developing high-technology industries made inroads into, and eventually surrounded, agricultural regions.

This rapid, far-reaching industrialization of postwar Bavaria catalysed immense social changes as a modern industrial society emerged from the traditional landscape of farmers, craftsmen, brewers, shopkeepers and priests. As such Bavaria provides a useful contrast to developments within regions such as the Ruhr area, whose highly industrialized economy developed at a much earlier stage.

The changes were also reflected in the Bavarian political landscape as the traditionally fragmented and regionally based party organizations were unified by the hegemony of the Christian Social Union

(CSU). Through the effective utilization of large resources, the CSU, politically the main agent of postwar industrialization, channelled this powerful social current to shape a strong, conservative hegemony. In this respect, therefore, Bavaria presents a sharp contrast to the Ruhr area, where a 'Ruhr-area-social democracy' (Karl Rohe) became, under different circumstances, the dominant political power.

The achievement of political dominance in each of these two instances must be viewed within the complex context of regional developments. In spite of the levelling tendency apparent in national as well as state politics, the regional factor retains its paramount importance. The federal structure of the Federal Republic itself is undoubtedly an important factor in the shaping of regional politics. Karl Rohe's argument, that the Ruhr area has to be understood from a regional rather than a national perspective, is equally valid for Bavaria.[1]

Based upon both empirical and interpretative analyses, I will attempt to explain the particularities of the 'Bavarian case' which have come to light since the War, and I will sketch the stages of economic, socio-economic and political developments.

Bavaria is a product of Napoleonic times and the only historical political entity among the new Länder of the Federal Republic of Germany. Thus we must first examine the historical dimension to the 'Bavarian problem', without which the postwar developments and their historico-political quality cannot properly be understood.

The Historical Background

Three Historical-Political Tradition Zones

From the creation of the Bavarian kingdom in 1806 until its transformation by territorial transfers into an historically new middle-european state some thirteen years later, Bavaria annexed a multitude of old, heterogeneous political cultures, which were administratively divided. Moreover, these were divided into a number of particular socio-cultural and political areas. The new Bavaria embraced three large historico-political zones which have survived to this day: the Franconian zone, the Swabian zone and the zone of Old

---

1. See Karl Rohe, *Vom Revier zum Ruhrgebiet, Wahlen, Parteien, Politische Kultur*, Essen, 1986; idem, 'Wahlanalyse im historischen Kontext. Zu Kontinuität und Wandel von Wahlverhalten', *Historische Zeitschrift* no. 234 (1982), pp. 337–57.

Bavaria.[2] The Franconian zone included the later administrative districts of Upper, Middle and Lower Franconia. The Swabian zone became the present administrative district of Swabia. The Old Bavarian zone comprised the present administrative districts of Upper and Lower Bavaria, as well as the Upper Palatinate. In these new zones, and, in particular, in the Franconian districts and in Swabia, many colourful remnants of the old empire were combined. The Franconian and Swabian zones included numerous former sovereignties, economic organizations and the two main confessions.[3]

With the annexation of the protestant districts Ansbach (in the contemporary administrative district of Middle Franconia) and Bayreuth (now eastern Upper Franconia and the eastern parts of Middle Franconia), and the territories of the old protestant Reich-cities (such as Nuremberg, Rothenburg on the Tauber, Windsheim and Weissenburg), a Franconian-protestant 'corridor' came into being (see Figure 5.1 and 5.2). This stretched from northern Upper Franconia (Hof) across the axis Nuremberg/Fuerth, as far as Rothenburg on the Tauber on the western borderline of Middle Franconia. With a strongly protestant tradition dating back to the Reformation, it split the two-thirds roman-catholic Kingdom of Bavaria, into catholic Main-Franconia, i.e. the dominant catholic Franconian regions along the River Main (today: Lower Franconia and western Upper Franconia with Würzburg and Bamberg) and a primarily catholic southern Bavaria (Old Bavaria and parts of Swabia). In the Upper Palatinate and Upper and Lower Bavaria lies the heart of the former catholic, purely agrarian Bavaria. Exclusively in this area, in Old Bavaria, could one speak of one single Bavarian culture, indeed, of an 'Electoral-Bavarian' (Kurbayrisch) culture. For the country as a whole there had been no integral Bavarian, that is to say, new Bavarian culture. Similarly, there was no integral Franconian consciousness. To the present day there is no integral Franconian political identity, in contrast to the political culture of Old Bavaria.[4]

2. For further information see, for example, Alf Mintzel, 'The Christian Social Union in Bavaria: Analytical Notes on its Development, Role and Political Success', in Max Kaase and Klaus von Beyme (eds), *Elections and Parties. German Political Studies*, vol. 3, London and Beverly Hills, 1978, pp. 192–4.

3. Hanns Hubert Hofmann, *Mittel- und Oberfranken am Ende des Alten Reiches* (1792), Munich, 1954, p. 2; idem, *Franken seit dem Ende des Alten Reiches. Mit 8 Karten und 1 Beilage*, Munich, 1955, VII, p. 3.

4. See Alf Mintzel, 'Besonderheiten der politischen Kultur Bayerns – Facetten und Etappen einer politisch-kulturellen Homogenisierung', in Dirk Berg-Schlosser and Jakob Schissler (eds), *Politische Kultur in Deutschland. Bilanz und Perspektiven der Forschung*, Opladen, 1987, pp. 296/7. Further details, idem, 'Politisch-kulturelle Hegemonie und

Figure 5.1. The principal historical/political tradition zones of Bavaria

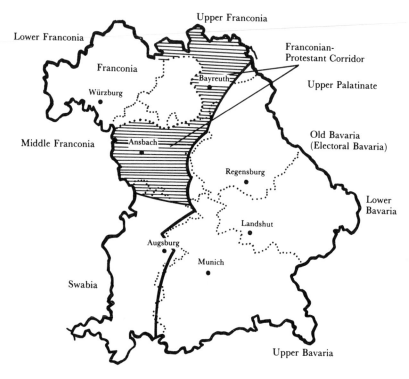

The 7 administration districts (*Regierungsbezirke*) of the Free State of Bavaria today are: Upper Franconia, Middle Franconia, Lower Franconia (the Franconian traditional zone), Upper Palatinate, Lower Bavaria, Upper Bavaria (the Old Bavarian traditional zone), Swabia (the Swabian traditional zone).
Source: Alf Mintzel, *Geschichte der CSU. Ein Überblick*, Opladen, 1977, p. 30.

The Franconian-protestant areas, by means of their particular economic structure and socio-economic circumstances, stood in contrast to both catholic Main-Franconia and the Old Bavarian agrarian area (see Figure 5.2). The district of Nuremburg and north-east Upper Franconia had achieved a notable manufacturing density in the eighteenth century, which was equally as high as that of 'Electoral Saxony' ('Kursachsen'). In protestant Franconia, agrarian small-trade spheres

---

"Gegenkulturen" in Bayern', in Walter Landshuter and Edgar Liegl (eds), *Beunruhigen in der Provinz – Zehn Jahre Scharfrichterhaus*, Passau, 1987, pp. 79–92.

Figure 5.2. The Franconian–protestant corridor and its territories *c.* 1750

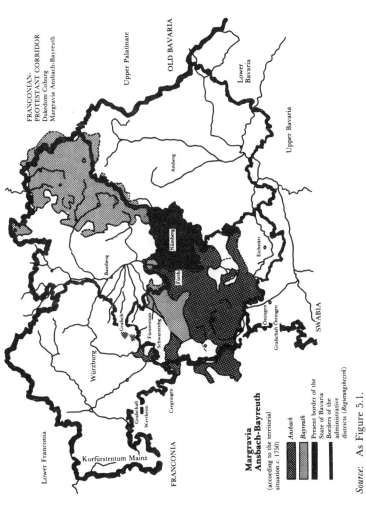

FRANCONIAN–
PROTESTANT CORRIDOR
Dukedom Coburg
Margravia Ansbach-Bayreuth

Upper Palatinate

OLD BAVARIA

Lower
Bavaria

Upper Bavaria

Amberg

Bamberg

Nürnberg

Fürth

Eichstät

Grafsch

Fürstentum
Schwarzenbg

Öttingen

Grafschaft Öttingen

SWABIA

Würzburg

Creglingen

Grafschaft
Wertheim

Kurfürstentum Mainz

Lower Franconia

FRANCONIA

**Margravia
Ansbach-Bayreuth**
(according to the territorial
situation *c.* 1750)

Ansbach

Bayreuth

Present border of the
State of Bavaria

Borders of the
administrative
districts (*Regierungsbezirk*)

Source: As Figure 5.1.

existed, as well as early industrialized environments, with a more clearly-defined class structure. Due to trade politics, the Margravian governments had promoted settlement of their territories with Austrians and French religious fugitives in the eighteenth century, whose opposition to counterreformational catholism had been very strong. Heterogeneity and a large number of regional (sub-)cultures characterized the internal situation of Bavaria. Generally speaking this regional fragmentation was not a Bavarian peculiarity, but was also observable in the other central German states.

Transformation into a Coherent Entity

The new Bavarian state was confronted with the task of integrating into one state the former territories of Franconia and Swabia, as well as the former Old Bavaria, the so-called 'Kurbayern' ('Electoral Bavaria'). The highest principles of Bavarian enlightened state absolutism were domestic unification and centralization, and the strengthening of sovereign authority. Led by a bureaucratic élite, the centralized state became the instrument for the administrative integration of the former territories. The so-called Montgelas-system – named after count Montgelas (1759–1830), leading Bavarian minister under King Max Joseph I – was operated by a highly qualified and competent civil service, which was recruited from all parts of the new state. They were mainly liberal and reform-oriented and to a certain extent anti-clerically disposed. It was they who prepared the ground on the administrative level for the development of an integral Bavarian political unity.[5] In the process of internal Bavarian integration the strong Bavarian state bureaucracy itself became an aspect of the country's political tradition. Territorial and historical-political continuity for more than 180 years furthered this process.

Montgelas's bureaucratic and administrative strategies for political and cultural integration and assimilation (which included secularization, a state-church, the Bavarian army, and the creation of a Bavarian identity out of 'New Bavaria' and 'Old Bavaria') were vigorously resisted by the small, diverse antiquated historical-political cultures. These large traditional zones continued to exist as specific regional

---

5. Gebhardt Jürgen, 'Bayern, Deutschlands eigenwilliger Freistaat – Historisch-gesellschaftliche Aspekte der politischen Kultur in Bayern', in Rainer A. Roth (ed.), *Freistaat Bayern. Die politische Wirklichkeit eines Landes der Bundesrepublik Deutschland*, (Bayerische Landeszentrale für politische Bildungsarbeit), 3. rev. edn, Munich, 1982, pp. 83–104, esp. p. 93.

'symbolic' and 'consciousness' entities (subcultures – as exemplified in architecture and musical traditions).

The demoninational divisions were crucial in forging community identities. After its assimilation into the new Bavarian state the Margravian–Brandenburgian Lutheran Franconia was in a minority position vis-a-vis the catholicism of Old Bavaria and Main-Franconia. The former consequently adopted a defensive position, catalysing one of the key collective experiences which resulted in the development of a Franconian 'stubbornness' *without* the development of a collective consciousness. As a result the catholic Main-Franconian and protestant Margravian areas existed 'independently' of each other.

Impacts on Bavarian Party Constellations and Developments up to 1933

When, towards the middle of the nineteenth century, the Bavarian population gained an independent constitutional voice and began to form political parties, the longevity and vitality of the political cultures of the three traditional zones became apparent in both the Bavarian parties and party-constellations. The Franconian-protestant 'corridor', with its specific history of trade, became a traditional political stronghold of National Liberalism (in particular in western central-Franconia), as well as of Social Democracy. For a long time protestant forces in the corridor prohibited the establishment of a Bavarian catholic party. In catholic Bavaria, as a result of the territorial development mentioned above, at least two main catholic political orientations were created.. One was agrarian-petit-bourgeois, pronouncedly catholic-conservative and Bavarian-patriotic, centred in the Old Bavaria area. The other was a moderately federalistic, more 'Reich'-orientated wing in Swabia and Main-Franconia. In the few urban Bavarian industrial islands (Augsburg, New-Ulm, Nuremberg, Munich, Schweinfurt, Hof-Selb-Muenchberg) Social Democratic and National Liberal strongholds developed. The Bavarian party landscape remained characteristically strongly regionalized.[6]

6. On the development of the new Bavaria with respect to the Bavarian party constellation see for details Dietrich Thränhardt, *Wahlen und politische Strukturen in Bayern 1848–1953. Historisch-soziologische Untersuchungen zum Entstehen und zur Neuerrichtung eines Parteiensystems*, Ed. by Kommission für Geschichte des Parlamentarismus und der politischen Parteien (Beiträge zur Geschichte des Parlamentarismus und der politischen Parteien, vol. 51), Düsseldorf, 1973. Max Spindler, *Handbuch der bayerischen Geschichte*, Vol. IV/1st part, *Das neue Bayern 1800–1970*, Munich: 1974. See, esp., Dieter Albrecht, 'Von

In catholic Bavaria during the Weimar period the strongly catholic and ultra-conservative Bavarian People's Party (Bayerische Volkspartei: BVP) constituted the relative majority party but it always had competitors for the vote in the Bavarian Farming League (Bayerischer Bauernbund) or the Bavarian Farming and Middle-Class League (Bayerischer Bauern- und Mittelstandsbund), both predominantly Old Bavarian catholic interest parties. At Landtag elections the BVP had, as a rule, succeeded in gaining a total of just over 30% of the vote and was thus always dependent on coalition partners, such as the German National People's Party (Deutschnationale Volkspartei: DNVP) and the above-mentioned Bavarian Farming League, in order to form a government. The Franconian-protestant corridor, meanwhile, became the base of the National Socialist German Workers' Party (NSDAP).[7]

Economic and Socio-economic Change after 1945

Belated Full-scale Industrialization and the Development into a High-tech Industrial Economy

Although, as we mentioned earlier, prior to 1945 there had been highly industrialized 'islands' in an otherwise agrarian-craft economy, full industrialization did not occur in Bavaria until after 1945. After 1945, Bavaria developed – in less than two decades – from an agrarian to an industrial state. Thus, this Land exemplifies a regionally specialized instance of a comparatively late transition into a modern industrial economy with a rapidly increasing tertiary sector and high-tech industries.[8]

Between 1957 and 1963 the Bavarian economy entered a new stage

der Reichsgründung bis zum Ende des Ersten Weltkrieges (1871–1918), in Spindler, *Handbuch*, pp. 283–321; Albrecht Schwarz, 'Der vom Bürgertum verführte Freistaat in der Weimarer Republik (1920–1933), in Spindler, *Handbuch*, pp. 454–517; Meinhard Hagmann, *Der Weg ins Verhängnis: Reichstagswahlergebnisse 1919 bis 1933 besonders aus Bayern*, Munich, 1946; Alfred Milatz, *Wähler und Wahlen in der Weimarer Republik* (Schriften aus der Bundeszentrale für politische Bildung, II.66), Bonn, 1968; Peter Claus Hartmann, *Bayerns Weg in die Gegenwart. Vom Stammesherzogtum zum Freistaat heute*, Regensburg, 1989.

7. Jürgen W. Falter, 'Der Aufstieg der NSDAP in Franken bei den Reichstagswahlen 1924–1933. Ein Vergleich mit dem Reich unter besonderer Berücksichtigung landwirtschaftlicher Einflußfaktoren', *German Studies Review*, vol. IX, 1986, pp. 293–318. See also the literature given in note 7.

8. See for details Klaus Schreyer, *Bayern – ein Industriestaat. Die importierte Industrialisierung. Das wirtschaftliche Wachstum nach 1945 als Ordnungs- und Strukturproblem*, Munich and Vienna, 1969. Hans Mayer, 'Probleme und Strukturen der bayrischen Wirtschaft – Bayerns Entwicklung vom Agrar- zum Industriestaat', in Rainer A. Roth (ed.), *Freistaat*

of maturity. The previous preponderance of consumer-goods industries was now followed by a trend towards an advance in the investment-goods industry. The service sector also witnessed above-average growth from 1960 onwards. In these processes of economic change, typical growth industries such as electrical engineering, data-processing, nuclear energy, aviation and space technology, plastics processing and mineral-oil refining played a decisive role. Bavaria experienced, so to speak, a 'belated period of promoterism' (*Gründerzeit*): branch firms were set up and a large number of concerns were also established – increasingly by growth industries – on the periphery of the concentration-areas and in structurally weaker areas.

There were two main phases of this rapid postwar industrialization process. Until the early 1960s Bavaria's economic development was strongly characterized by extensive growth, unparalleled in the Federal Republic. Around 1963 this extensive economic growth changed into an intensive growth. This was also an expression of the increased strength and speed of technical progress (increased capital investment per place of work with a constant level of employment causing an increase in work productivity.) As a corollary of this development, from the beginning of the 1960s the agrarian sector began to shrink even more rapidly. As was to be expected, the number of small farms decreased substantially and the cultivation of farmland became con-centrated in medium-sized holdings.

The specific forms of late full-scale industrialization and the ac-companying process of social restructuring took place under conditions of stability, and were to the advantage of the CSU. Bavaria was spared the great 'social costs' of such processes, despite its rapid late full-scale industrialization and despite radical social change. The great socio-political battles had already been fought. Social tensions and conflicts could, therefore, be absorbed and decisively cushioned in Bavaria. During full-scale industrialization, virtually no industrial proletariat was created, and most certainly not in the former agrarian areas, where the work-force was for the most part accommodated by the 'special case of a late industrialized society with the practised normative behaviour of a property owning bourgeoisie'.[9] This postwar form of industrialization stands in marked contrast to the disruptive impact of industrialization in the nineteenth century.

Bayern. Die politische Wirklichkeit eines Landes der Bundesrepublik (Bayrische Landeszentrale für politische Bildung, A 45), Munich, 1975, pp. 339–48.

9. Klaus Schreyer, 'Bayern – ein Industriestaat', see p. 17 (cf. also p. 20) in connection with pp. 324–5.

The economic and social policies of the CSU were geared towards upholding a dominant middle-class structure. Subsidies and harmonizing strategies served to mitigate the rapid economic process of social transformation and to keep it under conservative control. These policies, owing (or helped at least) by complementary cultural policies, were supported in the late industrialized catholic–conservative areas of Bavaria, in particular, by the catholic church, which contributed decisively to the continuance of traditional patterns of behaviour.

Despite the impact of economic and social change, the political agent of late full-scale industrialization and modernization of Bavaria, the CSU, through its conservative social and cultural policies, created a specific Bavarian variant of industrial society. It is this unusual combination of contradictory elements, that is, the harmonization of pre-industrial and modern industrial forms, which today lends Bavaria its unique character.

Rapid Social Change

The reshuffling of occupations in Bavaria during the period of full industrialization after 1945 displayed the following main trends of typical industrial society (see Figure 5.3 and 5.4, Table 5.1 and 5.2).[10]

(1) The proportion of the working population employed in the sector of agriculture and forestry fell steadily from 37.2% (1946) to 8.1% (1985) whereas the percentage of persons employed in the sector of industry and handicraft rose from 33.6% (1946) to 47.2% (1970) and fell to 42.8% (1985). The industrialization and urbanization of Bavaria spurred a rapid shrinkage process in the agricultural sector. At the same time the 'tertiary sector' (public and private services) gained in importance: whereas in 1946 only 29.2% of the whole working population were employed in this sector, the proportion rose steadily to 49.5% in 1985.

(2) A further main indicator of the complete transformation of the Bavarian agrarian and craft-oriented society into an industrial society was the rapid decrease in the number of self-employed and the increase in (wage-)dependent employment. In the agriculture and forestry sector the farming population became more

10. See for details Alf Mintzel, *Geschichte der CSU. Ein Überblick*, Opladen, 1977, pp. 44–8; idem, *The Christian Social Union in Bavaria*, pp. 196–201.

Figure 5.3. The working population according to economic sector in the Federal Republic of Germany, 1951–85 (%)

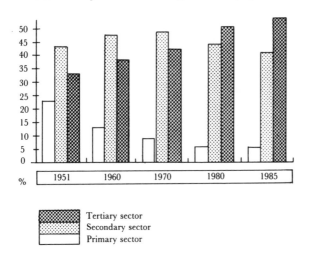

Source: Compiled and computed by the author from official statistics (*Statistische Jahrbücher für die Bundesrepublik Deutschland*, Wiesbaden, 1961, 1971, 1986).

Figure 5.4. The working population according to economic sector in Bavaria, 1961 and 1985 (%)

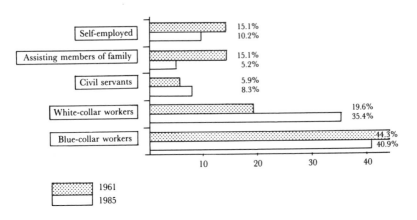

Source: Compiled and computed by the author from official statistics (*Statistische Jahrbücher für Bayern*, Munich, 1972, 1987).

Table 5.1. The working population according to occupational status
1946–85 (in thousands)

Year	Self-employed	Assisting members of family	Civil servants	White-collar workers	Blue-collar workers	Working population
1946						
abs.	799	870	111	628	1,871	4,279
%	18.7	20.3	2.6	14.2	43.7	100
1950						
abs.	782	905	170	588	2,124	4,579
%	17.1	19.8	3.7	12.9	46.5	100
1961						
abs.	714	715	222	932	2,194	4,698
%	15.1	15.1	4.7	19.9	45.0	100
1968						
abs.	637	588	269	1,159	2,115	4,771
%	13.4	12.3	5.7	24.3	44.3	100
1970						
abs.	583	498	356	1,295	2,160	4,894
%	11.9	10.2	7.3	26.5	44.1	100
1982						
abs.	530	313	404	1,714	2,187	5,045
%	10.3	6.1	7.8	33.3	42.5	100
F.A. %	8.7	3.0	8.7	38.3	41.5	
1985						
abs.	533	273	436	1,856	2,145	5,244
%	10.2	5.2	8.3	35.4	40.9	100

Notes: abs. = absolute figure (− total votes)
        F.A. = federal area as a whole.
Source: Compiled by the author from official statistics (*Statistische Jahrbücher für Bayern*, Munich, 1958, 1972, 1981, 1987).

concentrated with the exodus of employed persons. The release of manpower from this sector, however, did not produce an 'agricultural proletariat'.

(3) In this overall process, the group of civil servants and white-collar workers expanded strongly. The proportion of white-collar workers in the total population grew from 16.8% (1946) to 43.7% (1985).

Table 5.2. The working population according to economic sectors 1946–86 (in thousands)

Year	A/F	I/C	Trade finance transport	Public and private services	Working population
1946					
abs.	1,592	1,440	576	672	4,280
%	37.2	33.6	13.5	15.7	100
1950					
abs.	1,398	1,893	640	758	4,571
%	30.6	41.4	14.0	16.6	100
1961					
abs.	1,013	2,088	701	936	4,571
%	21.4	44.1	14.8	19.7	100
F.A. %	13.4	48.1	17.2	21.3	
1968					
abs.	794	2,119	786	1,071	4,771
%	16.6	44.4	16.5	22.5	100
1970					
abs.	646	2,309	772	1,166	4,894
%	13.2	47.2	15.8	23.8	100
F.A. %	7.5	48.9	17.9	25.7	
1982					
abs.	475	2,275	843	1,556	5,148
%	9.2	44.2	16.4	30.2	100
1985					
abs.	425	2,245	869	1,705	5,244
%	8.1	42.8	16.6	32.5	100

Notes: A/F = agriculture and forestry
            I/C = industry and craft
            F.A. = federal area as a whole
Source: Compiled by the author from official statistics (*Statistische Jahrbücher für Bayern*, Munich, 1958, 1972, 1981, 1987).

Facets, Factors and Phases of Political Change

The Persistent Significance of Geographical Distribution Patterns after 1945[11]

Until the 1950s the party landscape, the party constellations and the electoral geography remained strongly influenced by

11. Even after 1945 'the geographical distribution patterns remained more significant

the former socio-political structures and socio-cultural milieus of the three traditional zones. As recently as the 1960s, and as far as social grass-roots and organizational establishments were concerned, there was no really 'integral Bavarian' party, which was equally well 'rooted' in all the traditional zones. The traditional zones and their environments had also survived the Nazi regime. Although the destructive effect of the Nazis on the yet pre-industrial structures and on numerous institutional products of the outdated dignitaries' milieus should not be underestimated, the levelling 'bulldozer' of the NSDAP had merely crippled the driving forces of the traditional zones but had not killed them. After 1945 Bavaria constituted a particularly graphic example of the revitalization and reorganization of the historically outdated milieu-structures. The 'Catholic socio-cultural milieu' in particular was reorganized in an exceedingly effective political manner. When the Americans first relaxed and then ended their restrictions on political life, those old internal Bavarian differences and conflicts came powerfully and vividly once more to light, personified by the popular 'character actors' of the small Bavarian 'World-Stage'. The CSU, which up to 1948/49 had been the principal bourgeois integration party, met with an acute party crisis as a result of the renewed political split in catholic Bavaria. The Bavarian Party (BP), founded in 1946 as a follower party to the Bavarian People's Party (BVP) of the Weimar period, had developed into a dangerous political rival, mostly in Old Bavaria. In the late 1940s and 1950s, the CSU was challenged by the BP (licensed in 1948 on the Bavarian Land level) and ousted from power between 1954 and 1957 by an SPD-led coalition of four other parties (the so-called 'Viererkoalition' of SPD, BP, FDP and the *Refugee Party* BHE.

Many refugees, who during the postwar 'Occupation Democracy' were forced into the licensed parties of 1945/6, wandered off to the refugee parties as a result of the general burden of events, which in turn were related to the aftermath of the war. To a large extent, the Bavarian SPD was and remained the party of the early and already highly industrialized Franconian-protestant districts and the party of the urban industrialized islands of Bavaria. There it also integrated factions of the catholic working class, but without losing its predomi-

---

than the sociological ones', in the language of Infas, i.e. Institute for Applied Social Science, Infas Report on Elections, politogramm 39/40. (*Infas Report Wahlen, Bayern und Hessen, Analysen und Dokumente zu den Landtagswahlen an 27. Oktober*, Bonn and Bad Godesberg, October 1974, p. A 3. Within detailed supporting evidence and also charts in Alf Mintzel, *Die CSU. Anatomie einer konservativen Partei*, Opladen, 1978, pp. 179–93 and pp. 382–426; idem, *Geschichte der CSU*, pp. 415–41; see also in particular Dietrich Thränhardt, *Wahlen und politische Strukturen in Bayern 1948–1953*.

nantly protestant, relatively secular character. The FDP had remained in the anti-clerical tradition, as the party of the Protestant, propertied middle classes of Franconia and the towns. FDP strongholds included the former Margravian Ansbach and Bayreuth, protestant Coburg (which was not integrated into Bavaria until 1920), and the isolated urban areas, which contained a high percentage of senior civil servants and white-collar workers. Behind such superficial statements of electoral analysts stood the 'worlds' of strongly segmented political-cultural circumstances, namely the political cultures of Bavaria.

The Great Internal-Bavarian Political 'Field Re-organization'

In the late 1950s a fundamental change occurred in the formerly strongly segmented, heterogeneous political cultures. The party landscape and electoral landscape in Bavaria became 'black' (conservative) as the CSU set out to become the dominant Bavarian party. For the first time since 1806, a Bavarian party united the forces of political catholicism and succeeded in integrating the divergent regional traditions of Old Bavaria, Franconia and Swabia. The CSU is no longer merely the Bavarian 'party of order and the state' in the sense of being a Bavarian christian conservative voting block; it has become a party of all Bavaria, representative of Bavaria's modernizing industrial state, which the CSU in turn has played a major part in creating.[12]

Both the long-lasting economic prosperity of the Adenauer era, and the CSU's particular political alliance and team-work with the CDU, contributed to the CSU's growing strength in Bavaria. The CSU succeeded in carrying out a political-cultural field re-organization. The old traditional zones and their socio-cultural milieus did not completely disappear from the electoral map, but during the extensive process of socio-structural and political-cultural change they lost their fundamental significance. In the Bavarian parliamentary election of October 1986, and in the German Bundestag elections on 25 January 1987, this process manifested itself very clearly.

In the electoral-sociological analysis of party development, two major phases are discernible. In the 1950s and 1960s the CSU succeeded in winning the 'fraternal struggle' with the Bavarian Party (BP) thereby becoming the indisputable Bavarian majority- and

---

12. Alf Mintzel, 'Gehen Bayerns Uhren wirklich anders?', *Zeitschrift für Parlamentsfragen*, vol. 18, no. 1, March 1987, pp. 77–93. Idem, *Besonderheiten der politischen Kultur Bayerns*. Idem, 'Politisch-kulturelle Hegemonie und "Gegenkulturen" in Bayern'.

Figure 5.5. Regional majorities in the Landtag election, 1950

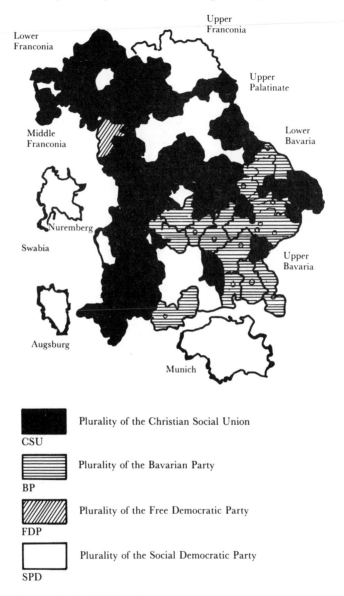

■ **CSU**	Plurality of the Christian Social Union
≡ **BP**	Plurality of the Bavarian Party
▨ **FDP**	Plurality of the Free Democratic Party
□ **SPD**	Plurality of the Social Democratic Party

Source: Cartography by Alf Mintzel.

Figure 5.6. Regional majorities in the Bundestag election, 1953

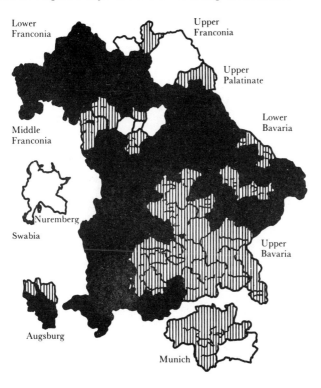

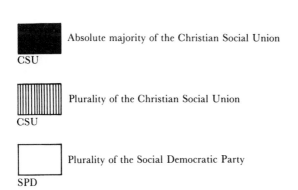

Absolute majority of the Christian Social Union
CSU

Plurality of the Christian Social Union
CSU

Plurality of the Social Democratic Party
SPD

Source: Cartography by Alf Mintzel.

Table 5.3. Results of the Bavarian Landtag elections from 1946 to 1986 (percentage share of votes) according to administrative districts (= election constituencies)

		1946	1950	1954	1958	1962	1966	1970	1974	1978	1982	1986
Upper Bavaria	CSU	48.2	22.1	31.7	40.1	41.3	42.2	52.1	59.6	57.6	55.7	54.3
	SPD	28.7	29.8	30.3	34.6	38.8	39.0	36.9	31.5	30.7	32.2	25.2
	FDP	5.0	6.3	6.3	4.5	5.9	5.8	5.9	6.2	8.1	4.7	4.9
	BP	—	22.0	18.0	11.1	7.4	6.3	2.1	1.2	0.8	1.0	1.0
	Grüne	—	—	—	—	—	—	—	—	—	5.2	9.5
Lower Bavaria	CSU	60.9	29.8	38.4	47.7	53.0	56.5	68.0	72.0	68.5	66.7	60.6
	SPD	25.5	17.9	20.0	20.8	26.6	29.3	24.6	23.1	24.6	25.3	24.4
	FDP	2.1	2.6	2.6	1.9	1.6	1.8	1.4	2.2	3.3	2.6	3.4
	BP	—	27.4	24.5	18.0	10.3	7.5	3.2	1.0	0.4	0.8	0.7
	Grüne	—	—	—	—	—	—	—	—	—	3.6	5.5
Upper Palatinate	CSU	62.7	33.9	47.9	55.8	58.4	58.5	65.3	68.3	63.2	61.9	54.3
	SPD	26.3	25.5	27.5	27.4	31.8	31.6	27.7	24.2	29.4	29.5	31.8
	FDP	1.9	3.8	4.5	3.5	3.2	2.9	2.6	2.9	4.3	2.3	2.4
	BP	—	20.9	9.7	5.6	2.6	1.9	1.5	1.1	0.5	0.7	0.7
	Grüne	—	—	—	—	—	—	—	—	—	4.5	6.3
Upper Franconia	CSU	42.9	19.8	31.5	41.1	44.4	44.6	53.0	58.5	55.5	56.8	55.0
	SPD	36.5	32.1	33.5	36.8	41.4	41.7	39.0	35.6	37.6	36.6	32.8
	FDP	10.9	8.6	9.6	5.6	5.4	4.1	4.1	3.9	4.4	2.3	2.3
	BP	—	17.5	10.9	5.6	2.4	1.4	0.4	0.3	0.3	0.3	0.4
	Grüne	—	—	—	—	—	—	—	—	—	3.0	5.2
Middle Franconia	CSU	38.7	24.0	34.4	39.6	42.6	40.7	46.1	53.7	51.1	51.2	49.6
	SPD	33.9	36.4	33.6	37.7	38.8	38.1	35.3	35.2	38.2	38.5	32.5
	FDP	10.8	13.0	13.2	12.1	11.2	9.0	12.4	8.4	7.6	3.7	4.1
	BP	—	7.8	5.1	2.3	1.1	—	0.5	0.3	0.1	0.1	0.2
	Grüne	—	—	—	—	—	—	—	—	—	5.0	8.3

Lower Franconia											
CSU	64.5	39.6	49.0	55.4	55.2	55.5	61.7	64.8	61.1	60.7	60.1
SPD	23.7	26.5	25.0	26.2	31.4	32.2	31.0	29.2	30.5	31.0	26.7
FDP	3.4	6.7	8.3	5.9	6.1	5.3	4.5	4.3	5.4	3.1	3.5
BP	–	12.3	5.5	3.0	1.6	0.4	0.0	0.1	0.3	0.1	0.3
Grüne	–	–	–	–	–	–	–	–	–	4.0	6.1
Swabia											
CSU	59.6	30.9	43.3	49.5	50.2	52.6	61.8	66.3	63.5	62.8	61.2
SPD	23.0	23.9	22.8	24.7	31.0	31.7	30.1	26.3	27.4	27.3	23.3
FDP	3.6	7.6	5.5	4.7	5.5	4.1	4.4	4.9	5.7	3.4	3.3
BP	–	15.8	14.3	9.1	5.5	3.4	0.8	0.9	0.2	0.3	0.5
Grüne	–	–	–	–	–	–	–	–	–	5.1	7.0
Bavaria											
CSU	52.3	27.4	38.0	45.6	47.5	48.1	56.4	62.1	59.1	58.3	55.8
SPD	28.6	28.0	28.1	30.8	35.3	35.8	33.3	30.2	31.4	31.9	27.5
FDP	5.6	7.1	7.2	5.6	5.9	5.1	5.5	5.2	6.2	3.5	3.8
BP	–	17.9	13.2	8.1	4.8	3.4	1.3	0.8	0.4	0.5	0.6
Grüne	–	–	–	–	–	–	–	–	–	4.6	7.5

Notes: CSU   Christian Social Union
SPD   Social Democratic Party
FDP   Free Democratic Party
BP   Bavarian Party
Grüne   The Greens

Source: Compiled by the author from official election statistics (Bayerisches Landesamt für Statistik und Daten Verarbeitung, Munich).

Alf Mintzel

Table 5.4. Results of the elections for the European Parliament
1979/1984/1989 in Bavaria

Europa	1979		1984		1989	
election	Votes	Percent	Votes	Percent	Votes	Percent
CSU	2,817,120	62.5	2,109,130	57.2	2,324,655	45.4
SPD	1,314,020	29.2	1,017,802	27.6		24.2
Greens	130,797	2.9	250,541	6.8		7.8
FDP	211,531	4.7	145,833	4.0	70,045	4.0
BP	–	–	23,539	0.6		0.8
DVU**	–	–	–	–		1.0
REP	–	–	–	–		14.6

– = did not participate
** DVU = German People's Union

state-party.[13] After 1957 the CSU overwhelmed the BP and emerged as
the dominant political force in Bavaria in both Land and Bundestag
elections.

The CSU found a middle-of-the-road course between traditional
'Bavaria-loyalty' and the necessary, unavoidable opening up and modernization of Bavaria. In fact, a course of federalism was adopted,
which was moderate and well-disposed towards compromise. In the
course of Bavaria's modernization, which the CSU successfully regu-
lated during the Adenauer era, the party transformed itself into a
modern, inter-confessional, broadly-based mass party. It became, as
it were, a political 'big business combine' or 'multi' with a highly
technical and highly communicative political 'production- and market-
ing-system'. The BP on the other hand, which had relied on the
long-established rural population of Bavaria and had represented
ideological and traditionalistic ties, failed as a result of its particularistic defence of outdated structures and its confessional bias
towards catholicism. The second crucial phase followed the formation
of the Social–Liberal coalition in Bonn (1969) and was influenced by
other exogenous factors. The great general CSU breakthrough within
the Franconian-protestant areas and into the urban bourgeoisie, which
had remained partly inaccessible until the end of the 1960s, did not
take place until after 1969 and continued on until the Bavarian par-

13. See for details: Ilse Unger, *Die Bayernpartei. Geschichte und Struktur 1945–1957*
(Studien zur Zeitgeschichte, vol. 16. ed. by Institut für Zeitgeschichte München),
Stuttgart, 1979. Alf Mintzel, 'Die Bayernpartei', in Richard Stöss (ed.), *Parteien-
Handbuch. Die Parteien der Bundesrepublik Deutschland 1945–1980*, vol. 1: AUD bis EEP
(Schriften des Zentralinstituts für sozialwissenschaftliche Forschung der Freien
Universität Berlin, vol. 38), Opladen, 1983, pp. 395–489.

liamentary election in 1986. If the victory in the catholic-Bavarian field brought the CSU very near to the 50% limit, the second phase took it beyond, and indeed far beyond the 60% mark in 1974. The SPD assumed the role of the great loser in this process.

This fundamental process of political-cultural homogenization in Bavaria belongs to the truly dramatic regional-specific developments of political culture in Germany. In an extensive transformational process led by the Bavarian hegemonic party, the CSU, the phenomenon of a single Bavarian political culture was developed for the first time. The political cultures based on the old historic foundations became cultures of the 'third' or 'fourth order'. These 'sub'-cultures are, according to the level of reference, still effective in local behavioural orientation and identity, and in setting local and parochial attitudes.[14] The fundamental process of reaching political-cultural homogeneity in Bavaria was highlighted by the Institute for Applied Social Science (Infas) which, in its analysis of the 1986 Bavarian parliamentary election, observed that: 'Altogether the governmental districts have come nearer together in their political structure.'[15]

This transformation process and the increasingly new political homogeneity has given the CSU a powerful position in the CDU/CSU alliance on the national level. Of course we should not neglect the flamboyant leadership of Franz Josef Strauß until his death (3 October 1988). Certainly it is difficult to imagine the CSU being unified enough to pursue its policies without Strauß. On the other hand, it is impossible to analyse Strauß's pre-eminent position as leader without understanding the structures and traditions in Bavaria that supported him and enhanced his effectiveness, while at the same time setting limits to his freedom of action.

The Development of the CSU and SPD Party Base

The development of the party bases can be taken as an indicator of regional-specific patterns and their social milieus. The decline of the traditional SPD Franconian and urban electoral strongholds through the conquests of the CSU, and the far less dramatic erosion of the CSU strongholds in the Old Bavarian rural areas, indicate a comprehensive standardization of the Bavarian political

14. Mintzel, 'Gehen Bayerns Uhren wirklich anders?', p. 87; idem, 'Politisch-kulturelle Hegemonie und Gegenkulturen in Bayern', pp. 84 and 88.
15. Infas Report on Elections, politogramm no. 39/40, Oct. 1974:A3 (*Infas Report Wahlen no. 39/40, Oct. 1974:A3*).

landscape. The CSU became the dominant party in Bavaria in absolute majority terms (see Figure 5.7 and 5.8). This can also be substantiated by an examination of the organizational picture of both parties. At the grass-roots, both the weakening of former political-cultural forces in the traditional zones and the political-cultural homogeneity of Bavaria are apparent.

With approximately 2,900 local groups (*Ortsverbände*), the CSU is not only well-established in nearly all of the approximately 2,000 political Bavarian communities, but over and above this, it is rooted in many old communities which had existed up until the territorial reform (Gebietsreform 1972). The CSU retained its hereditary party basis and extended itself into former Liberal and Social Democratic milieus. In 1984 the SPD, by contrast, had only 1,742 local groups (*Ortsvereine*) in only 1,317 political communities, that is to say, almost half as many as the CSU. The SPD, furthermore, is not organized in approximately 40% of the political communities. The era of the Social–Liberal coalition in Bonn proved to be a time of catastrophic destabilization for the SPD in its former strongholds. The rapid loss of members rose to thousands (1974–1981 approx. 12,000) and the number of local groups diminished by almost 25%. The claims of the so-called 'dawn-glow' of the Hof SPD Party Rally (1985) became a farce, and the success mark of 35% of the popular vote which the party set itself boomeranged. Only two of 105 direct constituencies were left in 1986 for the SPD. The reduction of the SPD to 27.5% in a Bavarian election, that is thus below the level of 1950 (28%) must be viewed as almost a catastrophe.[16]

The weakness of the Bavarian SPD, which was once the representative of reformism in Social Democracy, can be partly explained in that the SPD allowed its initial progress towards attaining a distinctive Bavarian character and Social Democratic identity to wither away, and that it neglected to develop a specific Social Democratic regional orientation among the political-cultural developments in Bavaria. 'The other Bavaria', which the SPD created as a slogan in the mid-1970s came too late to constitute a comprehensive Bavarian forum and could not be developed in the sense of a specific Bavarian Social Democratic 'anti-culture' in opposition to the 'political hegemony' of the CSU state. The SPD lacked the power to confront the democractic populism of many CSU politicians and was not able to integrate its own organizational units (*SPD-Bezirke*) in an effective way. Owing on the one hand to the centralized, unitary organizational principles which had been

16. Alf Mintzel, 'Gehen Bayerns Uhren wirklich anders?', p. 89.

Figure 5.7. Regional majorities in the Landtag election, 1974

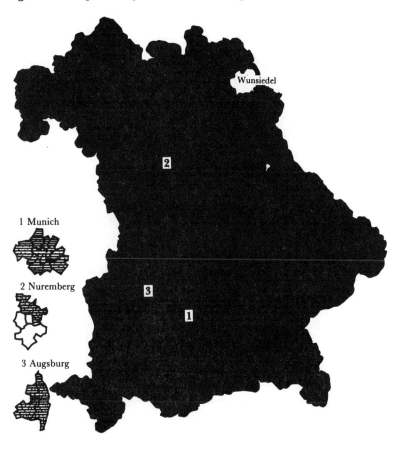

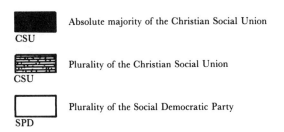

Source: Cartography by Alf Mintzel on the basis of official election statistics.

Figure 5.8. Regional majorities in the Landtag election, 1986

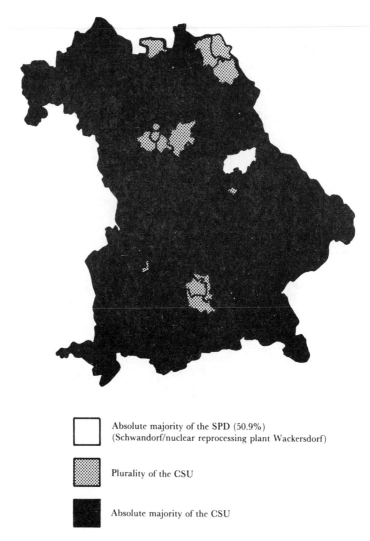

☐ Absolute majority of the SPD (50.9%)
   (Schwandorf/nuclear reprocessing plant Wackersdorf)

▨ Plurality of the CSU

■ Absolute majority of the CSU

Source: Cartography by Alf Mintzel on the basis of official election statistics.

Figure 5.9. Organizational strongholds of the CSU in 1985 according to counties (*Landkreise*) and cities independent of surrounding counties (*kreisfreie Städte*)

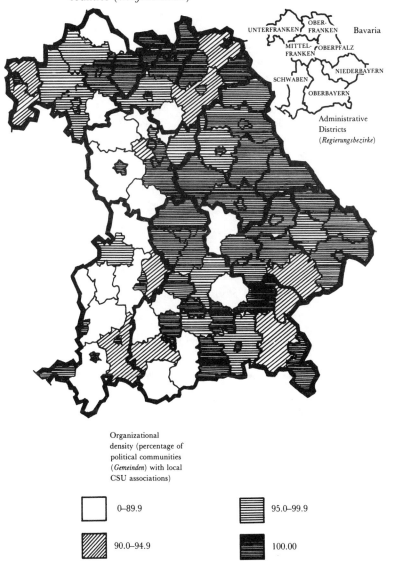

Organizational
density (percentage of
political communities
(*Gemeinden*) with local
CSU associations)

☐ 0–89.9   ▤ 95.0–99.9

▧ 90.0–94.9   ■ 100.00

Source: Cartography by Alf Mintzel on the basis of statistics on party organization provided by the political parties.

Figure 5.10. Organizational strongholds of the SPD in 1985 according to counties (*Landkreise*) and cities independent of surrounding counties (*kreisfreie Städte*)

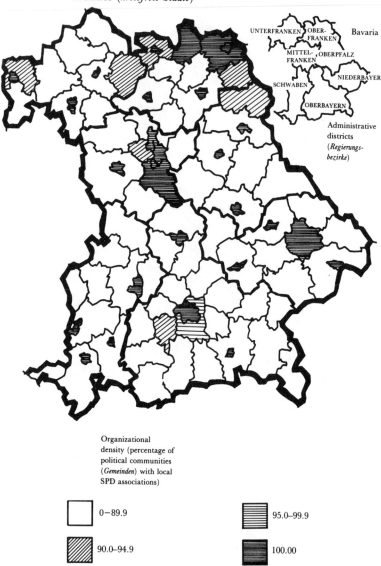

Organizational
density (percentage of
political communities
(*Gemeinden*) with local
SPD associations)

☐ 0–89.9		▤ 95.0–99.9
▨ 90.0–94.9		▬ 100.00

Source: Cartography by Alf Mintzel on the basis of statistics on party organization provided by the political parties.

cemented in a 100 year history of organizational conservatism, and, on the other hand, to a constitutional-political basic principle, the Bavarian SPD was able neither to become an autonomous regional-state party, nor to attain a significant increase in its regional-state organization, let alone enforce a special parliamentary status in Bonn.

In Bavaria the three SPD districts dating from the nineteenth century were retained (Franconia, Southern Bavaria, Lower Bavaria/ the Upper Palatinate). After 1945 they could neither be developed into a comprehensive Franconian, nor a southern Bavarian nor a 'comprehensive Bavarian SPD identity with a Bavarian Social Democratic "Anti-Culture"'. Rather the old inner-Bavarian political cleavages were widely conserved, fostering regional encapsulation. After 1945, powers within the Bavarian Social Democratic Party committed themselves to strengthening the regional associations inwardly and outwardly in the hope of achieving more effective representation. This endeavour met with little success. The failure of the SPD party reform in 1971 and 1985 put an end to these efforts for the time being. In contrast, the CSU had long before recognized the eminent political importance of possessing an efficient organizational apparatus, and had declared party reform to be a permanent task.

The Bases of the Small Parties

The Free Democractic Party (FDP)

The FDP, which had hoped to unify the weak political liberal tendencies within Bavaria, had great difficulty in retaining its identity within the context of the socio-political changes engineered by the CSU. After the departure of Thomas Dehler, the leading spokesman of the anti-clerical tradition in Bavarian liberalism, the FDP increasingly sought to accommodate to the conservative hegemony. As a result, the party lost its secular anti-clerical function to the same extent that the CSU lost its catholic clerical character and developed instead into the modern inter-confessional state party of Bavaria. The FDP was unable to realize its so-called 'second-enlightenment' in the face of the overwhelming strength of conservative/christian interests. The creation of the Social–Liberal coalition in Bonn (1969), and the temporary predominance of the social–liberal wing of the FDP on the national level, put the national-liberal-oriented FDP in Bavaria in a precarious position. Many of the National Liberals went over to the

CSU causing a political *Besitzerwechsel*, i.e. a change of political 'land-lords', in many traditional FDP areas. The CSU became the new political 'landlord' in national-liberal-oriented areas.[17]

Since 1982 the FDP is no longer represented in the Bavarian Land-tag. In the 1986 Landtag election it received only 3.8% of the vote. In the 1987 Bundestag election it received only 6.2% of the second vote, compared with CSU total of 55.8%.

The advent of the ultra-right Republikaner in the late eighties and their ability to attract the nationalist vote also threatens the national-liberal-oriented FDP in Bavaria. The 1990 Landtag election will prob-ably leave the FDP as a negligible political factor in Bavaria. The peculiar political and cultural circumstances in Bavaria prohibit the FDP from serving as either a corrective factor in a coalition or a means to achieving a majority, much less as a means to achieving a change of party coalition. Below the state level, however, it should be noted that the FDP maintains a regional and local presence, above all in urban areas such as Munich, Augsburg/Friedberg and Nuremberg/Fuerth/Erlangen.[18]

The Greens ('Die Grünen')

It would be incorrect to identify the ecology movement in Bavaria completely with 'The Greens' (Die Grünen). The election of The Greens is also an act of diffuse or concrete protest against the trinity of State, 'State–Party' and 'The Church'. It is directed against the powerful unity of this 'unholy Trinity', which reinforces the 'cul-tural hegemony' and values of the industrial system in Bavaria.

If, however, any effective opposition to the conservative power-cartel could succeed in creating a viable 'counter-culture' to the CSU's 'political hegemony', then, even if strongly influenced by youth, this opposition appears to be the Greens. This party and its numerous related groups, which in 1984 had already become the third political power in Bavaria at the Landtag election, reached, contrary to their own lower expectations, 7.5% in the 1986 election, giving them the status of a parliamentary delegation (*Fraktion*) in the Bavarian parlia-ment. This anti-movement is politically active almost everywhere, but

17. See Karl Rohe, *Historischer Wandel von Wahlverhalten*, p. 350.
18. This information is based on results of a current research project on 'Party organization in the social context of Bavaria' conducted by Alf Mintzel, University of Passau (see Fig. 5.11).

Figure 5.11. Organizational base of the FDP in Upper Franconia, 1985 according to political communities (*Gemeinden*)

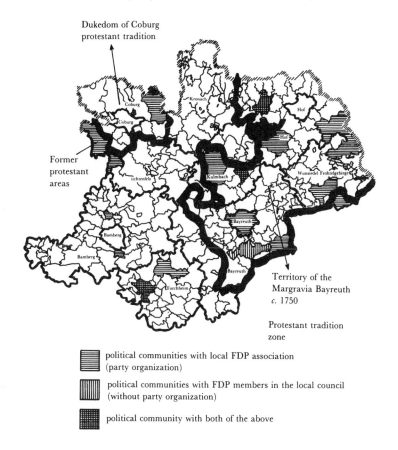

political communities with local FDP association (party organization)

political communities with FDP members in the local council (without party organization)

political community with both of the above

Source: Cartography by Alf Mintzel on the basis of statistics on party organization provided by the political parties.

particularly in areas where the consequences of rapid industrialization, demographic concentration and power supply technology (energy policies) appear most clearly. These areas include the urban conglomerations of Munich, Nuremberg/Fuerth, Aschaffenburg, Augsburg and New Ulm, centrally located areas with particular 'service' functions, and crucial areas with special environment concerns such as motorway-construction, atomic power production and waste disposal, and the destruction of the countryside.[19] Everywhere in such areas the Greens receive support to a modest extent from the population, particularly from young voters.

The rise and the activities of the Greens in Bavaria show that the Free-State, despite all its particularities, does display many general Federal Republican characteristics and developments. Bavaria is not immune to the extensive economic development and cultural processes (weakening of patriarchy, women's emancipation, the increasing move away from the church) which characterize the Federal Republic as a whole. After 1945 Bavaria witnessed a further thrust toward secularization (such as the general enforcement of the values of the industrial system, increase in the divorce rate, increase in abortions, decrease in the number of children, etc.). On the other hand, the situation of the Greens in the context of the Bavarian party constellation does show some significant Bavarian features: the party, or at least the majority faction known as 'Realos', are not only confronted with a strongly formed, integrative and ideologically conservative environment, but also with a weak and withering Social Democracy. The dilemma is that in winning ground in those places where the SPD has its bases and fields of recruitment, the Greens have damaged the already weak opposition and cannot combat the overwhelming power of the conservative party any more effectively than the Social Democrats.

'The Republicans' ('Die Republikaner')

The structural hegemony of the CSU, which since the 1970 Landtag election has been expressed in the CSU's absolute majority and in the concomitant powerlessness of Bavaria's opposition parties, was threatened for the first time in the 1989 elections for the European Parliament. The Republicans (REP) won 14.6% of the vote and thereby pushed the CSU below the magic 50% threshold. Even if the addition of the electoral results for the SPD (24.2%), Greens (7.8%), FDP (4.0%), REP (14.6%) and Bavarian Party (BP 0.8%) is merely a mathematical game, the power relationship of 51.4% (SPD+Greens+FDP+REP+BP) to 45.4% (CSU) leaves the impression that the CSU's hegemony in Bavaria has been broken, or at least has reached its limits. As to the Republican factor, there are various forces at work here that require further analysis. A serious analysis does not yet exist. Only one thing can be argued with some

---

19. This information is based on the results of a current research project. See note 18.

certainty: it would be a gross oversimplification to interpret the Republicans' success as purely a Neo-Nazi 'comeback' led by unrepentant extremists. Within the Bavarian population there has always existed an inclination to the view the 'ideal' party as somewhat further to the right. A portion of this vote, which had earlier been bound to the CSU through the populism of Franz Josef Strauß, has been bound to the Republicans through the ultrarightist popularism of Republican party leader Franz Schönhuber. It cannot yet be said whether or not we are dealing with a temporary factor on the right-hand political margin. There always have been right-wing groups which have not been fully absorbed. In any case, Bavaria was conspicuous among the Länder of the Federal Republic in the 1989 elections for the European Parliament in that here the Republican portion of the vote reached double digits. In North Rhine Westphalia, where the SPD has remained dominant, the Republicans could only manage 4.1%. Thus the respective regional peculiarities of the Federal Republic have surfaced once again.

The Conservative Shaping of Linguistic and Figurative Bavarian State Symbols

Full industrialization, demographic concentration, mechanization and the far-reaching impact of the mass-media were strong erosive powers which levelled historic political entities and their social milieus. Bavaria's landscape, the rural-catholic social order, was subject to a broad process of destruction and re-organization. But precisely this development into a modern and industrially expansive state, which in the final analysis is propagated and observed as a Bavarian achievement, helped to consolidate the integral Bavarian pattern of identity. The transformation and creation of historical structures was not dependent on the forms of the process of industrialization as such. It was instead dependent on the political and institutional strategies of local, regional and national elites, and on how traditional middle-class society reacted to extensive socio-economic structural transformation as it adapted itself to the macro-transformation. The CSU-elites in fact succeeded in integrating the various traditional zones and social milieus. In its own terms, the CSU bulldozed them and welded them together by means of social-structuring-power into a new state-Bavarian society.

The development of the CSU into a political agent for modernization and its own adaptation into a modern party with power to shape the social-structuring itself,[20] demonstrates that 'political culture' and 'political hegemony' cannot only be seen as something which grows and becomes out-dated in historical periods, but that it is to be considered as something which is created as a product of a goal-orientated state and party politics, which seeks to secure and extend sovereignty. The dramatic struggle between the CSU and BP in the conservative, catholic milieu of Old Bavaria resulted in a change of political 'landlords'. The CSU became, in an historic perspective, the successor of the Bavarian People's Party (BVP) and the BP, but then continued to integrate the former regions into a state-wide organization under its own hegemony.

The CSU succeeded in fact in tying its party identity with that of Bavaria, and this not only in the eyes of the Bavarian public. Nowadays, this identity is not only a propagandistic 'work of CSU art', not a persuasive pipe-dream for the population by the state-party, but a reality, to which the party propaganda and state-Bavarian image-making machinery can relate. The party that created 'beautiful Bavaria', and backed this with an existing Bavarian state tradition, holds fast to the regime's linguistic and figurative symbols. The Bavarian national symbol of the 'Lion' and the blue 'Diamond' are employed as party-symbols, and it is not even necessary to add the CSU's name.

In fact nearly everyone knows which party is meant. 'We in Bavaria CSU "82"', 'Politics for Bavaria, for the Federal Republic, for Europe' are catchy, symbolically pithy phrases. In Bavaria and elsewhere, a positive chain of associations runs as follows: beautiful Bavaria – CSU – Strauß – modern industry. 'Beautiful Bavaria' and 'the countryside', are catch-all headings for various, sometimes contradictory political philosophies. The 'Bavarian countryside' has symbolic power for conservative as well as for progressive or alternative orientated people. On one hand it stands for traditional security, and on the other, for a concrete utopia, for romantic withdrawal and ecology. The 'hunting-ground preservationists', the recently termed 'conservationists', the foresters and agrarians as well as the majority of conservative ecologists vote for the state-party – their party.

20. See Aline Kuntz, 'The CSU and the Vicissitudes of Modernity: An End of Bavarian Exceptionalism', *German Politics and Society*, June 1988, no. 14, *Political Parties in the FRG*, pp. 13–18. Idem, *Conservatives in Crisis: The Bavarian Christian Social Union and the Ideology of Antimodernism* (Thesis presented to the Faculty of the Graduate School of Cornell University August 1987). See also Alf Mintzel, 'Conservatism and Christian Democracy in the Federal Republic of Germany', in Zig Layton-Henry (ed.), *Conservative Politics in Western Europe*, London and Basingstoke, 1982, pp. 131–59, esp. 'The Development of Conservatism in Modern Germany: The Role of the CSU', pp. 143–56.

The CSU has increasingly created its own social environment, mainly by means of goal-directed organizational politics. In other words, the party itself constructs its own foundation and creates a new, frequently segmented and far-reaching informal type of interest articulation. The party controls and regulates new social conditions by means of associations and informal networks, it creates and renews in this way its political culture in advance. This constitutes a new form of party, growing into 'its own' society. The CSU, initially the sum of outdated structures and energies, became on the state level the creator of a regional, state-Bavarian 'political culture' and continues to contribute incessantly to its texture and transformation. In Bavaria the clocks don't tick differently, but other historico-social and political conditions and industrial social forms of developments have had, after 1945, a particular 'Bavarian effect'.

My analyses of the economic, socio-economic and political developments in Bavaria support the validity of Karl Rohe's argument for an analysis of 'voting behaviour from an historical context'.

Three levels continually manifest themselves: social structure, consciousness/attitude and (organizational and institutional) transmission. Each level has its own dynamic of historical change which does not necessarily harmonize with the others. The relationship among these levels and to politics has to be considered as an important variable that in time can produce decisive changes.[21]

In retrospect, it is evident that the CSU was able to create the internal consensus instrumental to its political success through the highly effective integration of regional Bavarian socio-historical traditions with a progressive strategy – which identified the party as an agent of productivity and prosperity. The CSU's ability to integrate the old (traditional) with the new (social-engineering) was accomplished through a constant Bavarian focus, in which the goals of the party reinforced and became those of the state. It can furthermore be argued that Bavarian unity as it exists today, is a product of this CSU strategy. This is not to say that regional differences have been eliminated, but rather that the party has been able to create a unifying state of image over and above these interests.

To conclude, a concrete example of the party's success in creating a sense of a 'Bavarian interest' is worth noting. In Bonn the CSU Landesgruppe is represented as an element distinct from the CDU.

---

21. See Karl Rohe, *Wahlanalyse im historischen Kontext*, p. 354.

This development is unique in the history of the parliamentary system of the Federal Republic of Germany and as such further underlines the leitmotiv of this chapter, namely the consolidation of the regional factor as a key to an understanding of postwar Bavarian politics.

KARL SCHMITT

Religious Cleavages in the West German Party System: Persistence and Change, 1949–1987

At times, historians, political scientists and sociologists have difficulty in assessing the 'religious factor' in politics. This applies to research on modern German history as well. One major example is that many are unable to come to grips with the Centre Party, the most important confessional political organization before 1933. The Centre Party 'does not really fit most of the generalizations which have become commonplace about the Wilhelmine political system'.[1] Within the party system of the Weimar Republic it is felt to be a 'foreign body'.[2] Therefore, it is not surprising that the most stable party in both the Kaiserreich and the Weimar Republic is the 'least studied' and 'least understood'[3] of the major political formations in Germany: 'A disembodied political phenomenon.'[4]

Similar observations concern research on postwar developments. The political role of the churches, although prominent, is largely *terra incognita* in German political science. Psephologists have difficulty in

1. Richard J. Evans, Introduction, in idem (ed.), *Society and Politics in Wilhelmine Germany*, London and New York, 1978, p. 30.
2. Erhard Blankenburg, *Kirchliche Bindung und Wahlverhalten*, Olten and Freiburg, 1967, p. 148.
3. James J. Sheehan, 'Klasse und Partei im Kaiserreich: Einige Gedanken zur Sozialgeschichte der deutschen Politik', in Otto Pflanze and Elisabeth Müller-Luckner (eds), *Innenpolitische Probleme des Bismarck-Reiches*, Munich and Vienna, 1983, p. 9.
4. David Blackbourn, 'The Problem of Democratization: German Catholics and the Role of the Centre Party', in Evans, *Society and Politics*, p. 161.

179

accepting that confessional factors continue to influence voting behaviour.[5]

This helplessness in the face of the 'religious factor' may be explained by certain traditions in historiography and social research, which focused attention on the horizontal social structures brought about by radical economic change, and regarded all other, vertical, differentiations within society as secondary. It was but a small step from here to the theoretical distinction between 'real' and 'apparent' conflicts.

In the extreme, this approach makes it possible to view confessional, regional, ethnic or linguistic conflicts as 'diversionary' fronts which distract from the 'real' conflict, for instance the class struggle. In this view, a confessional party lacks legitimacy, is an 'error of history'.[6] A worker who votes for a confessional party instead of a class party manifests a 'false consciousness' and is but a victim of the manipulations of the ruling classes. Even when it is accepted that confessional conflicts are real and legitimate, they are often treated as a transitional stage in the development towards a society in which dividing lines are defined in terms of struggles over the distribution of material goods.

The survival, indeed the renaissance of diverse ethnic, regional, linguistic and confessional particularisms in the industrialized states, and the failure of numerous attempts in the Third World to build homogeneous national states in accordance with European ideals, have relativized the generally accepted theories on the nature of social conflict. Social levelling, better communication and increased prosperity have not only not hastened the disappearance of non-economic qualitative identities but have in many instances even strengthened them. At any rate, there is little support for the view that economically based conflicts must automatically and increasingly dominate all others.[7]

5. See for instance the sarcastic remark of Franz Urban Pappi, 'Konstanz und Wandel der Hauptspannungslinien in der Bundesrepublik', in Joachim Matthes (ed.), *Sozialer Wandel in Westeuropa*, Frankfurt and New York, 1979, p. 472: 'Wenn sich der Faktor Religion bei einer Bundestagswahl wieder als wichtig herausgestellt hat, tröstet sich [*sic*] mancher damit, daß dies demnächst ja anders werden müsse.'

6. David Blackbourn, 'Die Zentrumspartei und die deutschen Katholiken während des Kulturkampfes und danach', in Pflanze and Müller-Luckner, *Innenpolitische Probleme*, p. 74: 'Zeitweise hat man direkt den Eindruck, als glaubten die Historiker, das Zentrum dürfe es "eigentlich" gar nicht gegeben haben.'

7. See Theodor Hanf, 'Un son de cloche! Essai sur confession et style politique en Allemagne', *Revue d'Allemagne*, vol. 16, 1984, pp. 266–80, and Arend Lijphart, 'Religious versus Linguistic versus Class Voting: The "Crucial Experiment" of Comparing Belgium, Canada, South Africa and Switzerland', *American Political Science Review*, vol. 73, 1979, pp. 442–58.

Such considerations suggest that it is reasonable to resist theoretical prejudice in the nature of social conflicts and to abandon any deterministic view of history. Instead, it is advisable to base analysis of societies and political systems on a far wider concept of interest so as to include both material as well as spiritual matters.[8] Which interests clash, which conflicts lead to the formation of groups and which do not, which become political, which divisions predominate and how established divisions precondition the rise of potential new divisions – answers to all these questions are, in this view, purely a matter of empirical enquiry.[9] Therefore, in the following analysis, confessional conflicts are treated as genuine, real and legitimate, like any other. What needs closer attention is, on the one hand, the historical constellations in which confessional conflicts break out, those in which they weaken or in which they disappear; and, on the other, the factors which determine the mobilizing potential of these conflicts and their permanent institutionalization.

1945: Renaissance of Confessional Politics?

The West German party system as it was established after 1945 and in the lasting form it had found by the mid-1950s did not start with a *tabula rasa*. In many respects it is a continuation of the prewar constellation.[10] Three elements of the traditional constellation deserve closer attention in our context.

Firstly, the party system which emerged during the Kaiserreich and which existed until the rise of the NSDAP (National Socialist Party) at the end of the Weimar Republic reflected the confessional divisions which had existed in Germany since the Reformation. Of the four main political formations, three (Conservatives, Liberals and Social Democrats) drew their support almost exclusively from the protestant population. One (the Centre Party) represented the catholic population.

Secondly, there was a confessional asymmetry in the traditional

8. See Karl Rohe, 'Vom alten Revier zum heutigen Ruhrgebiet. Kontinuität und Wandel einer regionalen politischen Gesellschaft', in idem (ed.), *Vom Revier zum Ruhrgebiet. Wahlen – Parteien – Politische Kultur*, Essen, 1986, pp. 15–19.
9. See the seminal work of Seymour M. Lipset and Stein Rokkan (eds), *Party Systems and Voter Alignments*, New York and London, 1967.
10. For a systematic comparison of pre-war and postwar elections see Jürgen W. Falter, 'Kontinuität und Neubeginn', *Politische Vierteljahresschrift*, vol. 22, 1981, pp. 236–63.

constellation. The confessional split within the party system did not mean that all parties regarded themselves as representatives of a particular confession. This was true only of the catholic Centre Party. In contrast to the situation in other confessionally divided countries, such as Switzerland and the Netherlands, none of the political groupings supported by the protestant population regarded itself first and foremost as a protestant party, let alone as *the* party of protestantism. The asymmetrical politicization of the confessional conflict thus meant that the confessional divide was a pre-eminently political factor for catholics alone, who isolated themselves from the only negatively defined protestants. Thus for the protestants, party affiliation was not a matter of religious affiliation but one of social status or ideological orientation. For them the decisive cleavages existed not between the confessions but within the protestant section of the population.

Although to this extent the cleavages did at least partially overlap, there was little competition between the parties. This is the third important feature of the traditional German party system. Each party was rooted in its own more-or-less closed subsociety, each of which had all the essential characteristics of a subculture (common *Weltanschauung* – common way of life, group identity) and was structurally differentiated to an extent which ensured its cohesion and survival as an independent unit. Consequently, the existence of the parties was bound up with their respective subsocieties or subcultures. In short: it was not individuals who elected parties but subcultures.[11]

This background enables us to formulate more precisely the question of stability and change in the confessional element in the postwar party system. Were the basic conditions, which had earlier been responsible for the emergence of confessional conflicts and confessional subcultures, still present after 1945? Were there still subcultures, particularly the catholic one, and, if not, did they re-emerge after 1945? Was the party system again based on subcultures? And, finally, presuming that there had been structural changes in the party system, how did the voters react to them?

Let us start by contrasting the pre–1933 situation with that of the Federal Republic when it was founded. What were the major conditions conducive to confessional conflicts in both situations?

First of all, we have to remember the way confessional conflicts were

---

11. This aspect was first systematically discussed by M. Rainer Lepsius, 'Parteiensystem und Sozialstruktur. Zum Problem der Demokratisierung der deutschen Gesellschaft', in Wilhelm Abel et al. (eds), *Wirtschaft, Geschichte und Wirtschaftsgeschichte, Festschrift zum 65. Geburtstag von Friedrich Lütge*, Stuttgart, 1966, pp. 371–93.

originally politicized.[12] Although the confessional split had existed in Germany since the Reformation, its politicization in the nineteenth century surprised most contemporaries. The *amicabilis compositio*, an elaborate system for peacefully regulating confessional conflicts, had functioned successfully over two centuries. It took the Congress of Vienna to destroy the main pillars of this system – i.e. numerical balance between the confessions and confessional segregation by territory *cujus regio ejus religio*. Now large, compact catholic territories passed to the protestant German states, above all to Prussia. The protestant ascendancy culminated in 1871 with the proclamation of the German Empire, from which catholic Austria was excluded.

From this time onwards, German catholics not only lived in states ruled, with few exceptions, by protestant dynasties; they felt themselves very much to be second-class citizens in the 'Holy Protestant Empire' (as Adolf Stoecker termed it), in which they formed a one-third minority. Subjected to state interference in their religious worship, socially backward compared with the dominant protestant business classes and the protestant state bourgeoisie, culturally marginalized, suspected to be unpatriotic because of their religious allegiance to a supranational leader in Rome – German catholics found themselves very much on the defensive and regarded the confessional cleavage as the common denominator of the conflicts in which they had become involved. In the perception of the catholic masses, the Catholic Church hierarchy's struggle against the state for its rights, the struggle to preserve a catholic cultural identity and the struggle of the minority for equal rights all combined to a confessional confrontation, to a struggle between catholics and protestants.

The struggle did not end in a catholic victory. But the conditions of the cease-fire were favourable. Owing to its firm leadership and a reorganized, streamlined church administration, the catholic population emerged from the *Kulturkampf* with its unity almost completely intact. The conflicts with liberalism and the state had moulded it into a tight subculture with its own clearly defined consciousness, in which the Centre Party stood out as a tower of strength, seeming to many to be the 'temporal expression of the rock upon which the Church was founded'.[13]

12. For an overview, see the excellent reader by Anton Rauscher (ed.), *Der soziale und politische Katholizismus. Entwicklungslinien in Deutschland 1803–1963*, Munich, 1981, and Karl Gabriel and Franz-Xaver Kaufmann (eds), *Zur Soziologie des Katholizismus*, Mainz, 1980.
13. Rudolf Morsey, 'Katholizismus und Unionsparteien in der Ära Adenauer', in Albrecht Langner (ed.), *Katholizismus im politischen System der Bundesrepublik 1949–1963*, Paderborn, 1978, p. 34.

In these circumstances it is not surprising that German protestantism did not develop a similar subculture with its own political representation.[14] As protestants were in the majority anyway, and the
protestant princes were simultaneously heads of the established church
in their respective states, there was no need for a defensive strategy.
Essential preconditions for such a strategy were lacking as well. Each of
the established protestant churches in the various states was its own
authority and churches themselves were often incorporated in the state
apparatus. Hence, they were unsuitable as mobilizing and integrating
factors. In addition, they lacked a theology which could have imparted
legitimacy to a protestant political organization.

Comparing this scenario with the years after 1945, we notice that
essential elements, which had previously contributed to the politicization of the confessional cleavages, are missing. The factor of greatest
consequence in the Federal Republic was the change in the confessional ratio. As a result of the partition of Germany after the Second
World War, the confessional equilibrium in West Germany resembled
that in the Holy Roman Empire established by the Treaty of Westphalia three centuries earlier. Thus, the German catholics were now
liberated from their minority status. There was no longer any objective
foundation for a defensive attitude. Thus the catholics 'discovered'[15]
the second German republic and could 'for the first time in a German
federal state feel politically at home'.[16] Conversely, the protestants
found themselves rather on the defensive. The prominent protestant
church leader Martin Niemöller expressed this emotional state when
he referred to the Federal Republic as 'in the final analysis . . . [a]
Catholic state conceived in Rome and born in Washington'.[17]

Furthermore, with the disappearance of Prussia from the political
map, the reason for the German catholics' traditionally anti-centralist,
anti-Prussian feelings had disappeared too. Their traditional demand
for parity in public life, in particular in the civil service – already
largely fulfilled in the Weimar Republic – no longer seemed to en-
counter problems in the new circumstances.

Only three elements of the old conflict potential remained: the level

14. See Wolf-Dieter Hauschild, 'Volkskirche und Demokratie', in Dieter Oberndörfer
and Karl Schmitt (eds), *Kirche und Demokratie*, Paderborn, 1983, pp. 33–49.
15. Gerhard Schmidtchen, *Protestanten und Katholiken. Soziologische Analyse konfessioneller
Kultur*, Berne and Munich, 1973, p. 245.
16. Karl Forster, 'Deutscher Katholizismus in der Ära Adenauer', in Dieter Blumenwitz et al. (eds), *Konrad Adenauer und seine Zeit*, vol. 2, Stuttgart, 1976, p. 497.
17. Interview with *New York Herald Tribune*, 14 December 1949; reprinted in *Kirchliches
Jahrbuch*, vol. 76, 1949, pp. 240ff.

of state support to ensure the continued existence of the catholic subculture (e.g. confessional schools and church tax), the recognition of certain ethical demands as binding on the state (e.g. abortion and marriage laws) and, finally, a state guarantee that the church would retain its character as an autonomous organization.

However, what set the course in the immediate postwar years was not so much the fact that the potential sources of conflict were fewer and less important, but rather the vitality of the catholic subculture. It had survived the 'National Socialist bulldozer'[18] relatively intact. Moreover, its remaining structures were now refortified. Confessional schools, closed by the National Socialists, were reopened and associations prohibited during the Hitler regime were refounded. Also the subculture maintained its clearly defined identity by such means as the prohibition on confessionally mixed marriages. In short, despite the changed circumstances the traditional strategy of the confessional subculture was retained.[19]

There was one major exception to that strategy: the catholic party did not re-emerge. Instead, the interconfessional CDU/CSU (Christian Democratic Party) was formed together with sections of protestantism – primarily Lutheran – which had been politicized by their experiences under National Socialism. But as the strategy of a united front also applied to party politics, this decision did not require a fundamental restructuring of political activity. The loyalties of organized catholicism were transferred from the defunct Centre Party to the CDU/CSU. In pastoral letters at election time, the bishops supported this party just as openly as they had previously supported the Centre Party. Just as important for the CDU/CSU as the official church commendation was the close personal and organizational involvement with the catholic associations. This enabled it, as it had the Centre Party previously, to keep its own organizational infrastructure to a minimum, reactivating it shortly before elections.

This renaissance of pre-war patterns of political behaviour was not limited to the catholic population, but was found throughout the 'new' party system. In the other subcultures, too, enough of the old substance

18. Alf Mintzel, *Die Volkspartei. Typus und Wirklichkeit*, Opladen, 1983, p. 245. For a discussion of continuity and change in the catholic subculture, see Herbert Kühr, 'Katholische und evangelische Milieus. Vermittlungsinstanzen und Wirkungsmuster', in Dieter Oberndörfer, Hans Rattinger and Karl Schmitt (eds), *Wirtschaftlicher Wandel, religiöser Wandel und Wertwandel. Folgen für das politische Verhalten in der Bundesrepublik Deutschland*, Berlin, 1985, pp. 245–61.

19. Klaus Gotto, 'Zum Selbstverständnis der katholischen Kirche im Jahre 1945', in Dieter Albrecht et al. (eds), *Politik und Konfession. Festschrift für K. Repgen zum 60. Geburtstag*, Berlin, 1983, pp. 465–81.

had survived to enable personal, organizational and programmatic continuity. Both social democracy and liberalism reconstituted themselves as political parties representing a *Weltanschauung*, reviving some of the anti-clerical elements of their pre-war traditions. On the whole, the German party system survived the National Socialist regime remarkably well. All the major postwar parties retained traditions inherited from prewar formations. Although the foundation of the CDU/CSU bridged the old confessional split within the German party system between a closed catholic segment and a sociologically and ideologically differentiated protestant segment – thereby overcoming the asymmetry in confessional politicization – the way parties were linked to society had not changed fundamentally: they remained centred on their respective subcultures.

Emancipation of Parties – Disintegration of Subcultures

In the 1950s this constellation may have seemed stable enough to contemporaries. Today, with hindsight, it is clear that the constellation of parties at the birth of the Federal Republic already contained the germs of a fundamental change which became manifest at the end of the 1950s and is still in progress. This change may best be described as a process of parties becoming independent of and breaking away from their respective subcultures. It was a process which proceeded from both sides, the parties and the subcultures.

The parties broke with the old system in that the CDU/CSU as a political formation united representatives from more than one subculture. This, as it turned out, was the beginning of the end of a party system based on subcultures, and in the long run knocked the bottom out of the catholic strategy of a united front. Adenauer's style of government speeded up this development. Although he enjoyed the support of the catholic subculture, he did not let it determine his policies. For him, the CDU was not a 'Christian missionary society'[20] but an instrument to secure a majority for his policies. This paved the way from the Weimar system of proportional government towards an essentially Anglo-Saxon system of alternating party governments.[21]

---

20. Quoted from Anneliese Poppinga, *Konrad Adenauer. Geschichtsverständnis, Weltanschauung und politische Praxis*, Stuttgart, 1975, p. 80.
21. See Rudolf Wildenmann, 'Die soziale Basis der Herrschaft Konrad Adenauers', in Blumenwitz et al., *Konrad Adenauer*, pp. 275–84.

The success of the CDU/CSU's strategy forced a process of imitation upon the SPD (Social Democratic Party). The SPD had little prospect of escaping from its '30% tower' unless it went beyond the boundaries of its own subculture. It took this step with the Godesberg Programme in 1959. By formally abandoning its claim to be the party of a specific *Weltanschauung*, the SPD aimed at middle-class and catholic voters.

Corresponding with the changes in the parties there were significant changes within the subcultures themselves. Although they all experienced changes to a greater or lesser extent, the focus of the following section will be on the processes within the catholic segment.[22]

The first of these concerned its relations with its political representative, the CDU/CSU. In the course of the past decades, a trend towards pluralization has gained ground within both the hierarchy and lay organizations. As the church's influence on policies of the CDU/CSU – whose 'Christian' character became increasingly controversial as ideologies in general lost ground – was limited, the church perceived a close identification with these policies as a threat to its credibility. Spurred on by the momentum within the church as a whole (in particular by the Second Vatican Council), this perception has led since the mid-1960s to a weakening of the coalition between organized catholicism and the CDU/CSU, and a more relaxed relationship between the church and the SPD.

As a result of proposed legislation of the centre left coalition and the elements of the FDP programme critical of the churches (*Kirchenthesen*), there has been a *rapprochement* between the church and the CDU/CSU, starting in the mid-1970s. Yet this has not completely reversed the process of pluralization. Today's relatively close relationship between the church and the CDU/CSU has a quality that differs from the one in the 1950s. It no longer implies unquestioned support but relies on agreement about individual questions of policy. This agreement varies considerably from one issue to another. Thus it is now inconceivable that the CDU/CSU could claim, as it once did, a monopoly in representing the positions of the church. In addition, within the catholic lay associations 'pluralism has reached a stage where it is no longer possible to regard Church organizations as the natural reserve army of the CDU'.[23]

While the political profile of the subculture has been losing its sharp

22. For an overview, see Klaus Gotto, 'Wandlungen des politischen Katholizismus seit 1945', in Oberndörfer et al., *Wirtschaftlicher Wandel*, pp. 221–44.
23. Herbert Kühr, 'Lokalpartei und Kirche', in H. Kühr et al. (eds), *'Lokalpartei und vorpolitischer Raum*, Melle, 1982, p. 97.

contours, a second process has been taking place: shrinkage and dilution. The boundaries between the two large confessions have blurred and the confessional cleavages have lessened. One unmistakable sign of this is the growing number of interconfessional marriages. Decisive developments in this respect have been the disappearance of regions almost exclusively inhabited by members of a single confession and the abolition of confessional schools. Other factors have helped to weaken the awareness of a special catholic identity: catholics were no longer a minority, the increasingly influential mass media were confessionally neutral, the gaps in education and status between catholics and protestants were closing and, finally, catholics collaborated with protestants in both the CDU/CSU and the unified national trade union system German Federation of Labour (Deutscher Gewerkschaftsbund – DGB). Moreover, active church involvement fell dramatically (regular church attendance dropped by half) and everyday life became increasingly deritualized. The closed catholic subculture of the 1950s no longer exists.

The postwar situation of German protestantism[24] differed from the prewar situation in two respects. On the one hand, for the first time in its history, protestantism had a national institution representing all the regional churches, the Protestant Church in Germany (Evangelische Kirche in Deutschland – EKD), and could thus act as a united body. On the other hand, the *Kirchenkampf* during the National Socialist era had taught protestants the fundamental lesson that protestant christians and the Protestant Church could not evade political responsibility; indeed, that the political dimension is an elementary aspect of christian existence. However, despite the politicization of protestantism and, with the formation of the CDU/CSU, the first-ever option for them of a specifically christian party, the church leadership has never officially supported a particular party but preferred to maintain neutrality. At the same time, prominent protestants, including theologians, church officials and members of the synod, have been active on different sides of the party spectrum: from Hermann Ehlers, Eugen Gerstenmaier and Gustav Heinemann to Richard von Weizsäcker and Erhard Eppler.

On the whole, postwar protestantism, particularly institutionalized protestantism, is characterized by a strong polarization. This

24. See Wolfgang Huber, *Kirche und Öffentlichkeit*, Stuttgart, 1973, and Trutz Rendtorff, 'Protestantismus zwischen Kirche und Christentum', in Werner Conze and M. Rainer Lepsius (eds), *Sozialgeschichte der Bundesrepublik Deutschland*, Stuttgart, 1983, pp. 410–40.

Figure 6.1. Confessional composition of marriages (Baden-Württemberg)

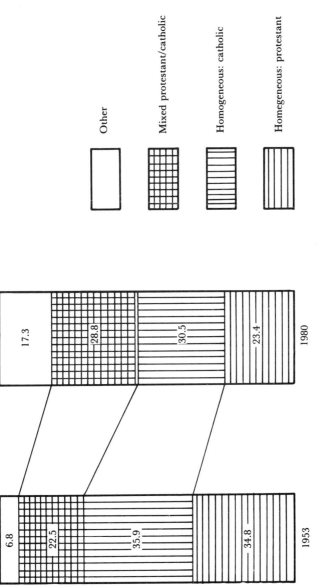

Other

Mixed protestant/catholic

Homogeneous: catholic

Homegeneous: protestant

17.3

28.8

30.5

23.4

1980

6.8

22.5

35.9

34.8

1953

Source: Unpublished statistics of the Statistische Landesamt Baden-Württemberg.

Figure 6.2. Church attendance on Sundays (% of catholics)

¹ 1938: Territory of the Reich.
1949–65: Federal Republic without Berlin.
1969–: Federal Republic including Berlin (West).

Source: *Kirchliches Handbuch*, vols XXII–XXVII; unpublished statistics of the Sekretariat der Deutschen Bischofskonferenz.

polarization is much stronger than that of the pluralist catholicism of the 1980s, let alone the closed catholicism of the 1950s. One cause of these cleavages – apart from the traditional differences between Lutheran and Reformed Churches – is the revival within German protestantism of a strong current which strives directly to translate christian ethical principles into political decisions. As the confrontation between Heinemann and Adenauer in the early 1950s demonstrated,[25] this approach has remained foreign to the CDU/CSU, which has a very different understanding of what 'christian politics' means. The group of protestant politicians who think along Heinemann's lines eventually joined the SPD. This was a major factor opening up the SPD to broad circles of institutionalized protestantism, though neutralist disapproval of Adenauer's commitment to the West as well as protestant confessional feeling against the dominantly catholic CDU/CSU also played a part.

25. Compare Andreas Hillgruber, 'Heinemanns evangelisch-christlich begründete Opposition gegen Adenauers Politik 1950–1952', in Albrecht et al., *Politik und Konfession*, pp. 503–17.

The Voters: Stability in an Unstable World or Postponed Change?

Looking back over the developments since the 1950s, one can observe two interacting processes. On the one hand, there is the erosion of subcultures which had previously survived decades of sometimes dramatic political change and, on the other hand, the development of the major parties into parties independent of their traditional subcultures (*Volksparteien*). This change may suggest the conclusion that there was a corresponding decline in the importance of the 'religious factor' in voting behaviour, perhaps to a point where it becomes negligible.

But does this conclusion square with reality? Have the shrinkage of the catholic subculture, the changed attitudes of the church hierarchy towards the parties, the pluralistic trends in the lay associations and the blurring of the ideological profiles of the parties really levelled differences in voting behaviour between the confessions? Has the CDU/CSU lost its 'catholic' character? Has the Godesberg Programme enabled church-going protestants and catholics to vote for the SPD? In short, have the German political parties lost their confessional contours since 1945?

Representative surveys of voting behaviour in the Federal Republic since 1953 provide answers to these questions.[26] The most important results of a comparative evaluation of these studies for the three and a half decades between 1953 and 1987 can be summarized in six points.[27]

(1) In 1953 the voting behaviour of German catholics was startlingly similar to that in the Weimar Republic. The CDU/CSU shares of the catholic vote on both the national and the state levels were surprisingly close to those of the Centre Party. The catholics' prewar united front had been preserved. The CDU/CSU had indeed inherited the political loyalties of the catholic voters. Continuity among the protestant population had also been preserved in so far as not religion but other criteria remained dominant in determining its voting behaviour. Although the CDU/CSU was able to win a majority of those voters outside the Social

---

26. See the longitudinal studies by Franz Urban Pappi, 'Parteiensystem und Sozialstruktur in der Bundesrepublik', *Politische Vierteljahresschrift*, vol. 14, 1973, pp. 191–213; idem, 'Sozialstruktur, gesellschaftliche Wertorientierungen und Wahlabsicht', *Politische Vierteljahresschrift*, vol. 18, 1977, pp. 195–229; Kendall L. Baker, *Germany Transformed. Political Culture and the New Politics*, Cambridge and London, 1981, and Manfred Berger et al., 'Die Konsolidierung der Wende. Eine Analyse der Bundestagswahl 1987', *Zeitschrift für Parlamentsfragen*, vol. 18, 1987, pp. 253–84.

27. For a detailed analysis see Karl Schmitt, *Konfession und Wahlverhalten in der Bundesrepublik Deutschland*, Berlin, 1989.

Table 6.1. Catholic vote in 1924 and 1953 (%)

	German Reich/ Federal Republic		Baden and Württemberg		Bavaria	
1924[1]						
Centre Party/BVP	55.3		66.2		44.0	
DDP	3.1		5.6		2.7	
DVP	4.0		9.6		1.5	
DNVP	8.4		3.5		9.4	
Bavarian Peasant League	3.5		–		13.5	
SPD	12.1		8.9		16.6	
KPD/USPD	6.7		3.3		5.7	
1953[2]						
CDU/CSU	52.3	(54.8)	61.7	(65.6)	45.2	(47.6)
Centre Party	3.8	(4.3)	1.8	(2.2)	0.3	(–)
FDP	5.4	(5.8)	7.2	(7.7)	3.6	(3.9)
SPD	23.4	(23.5)	16.9	(19.1)	24.7	(23.5)
KPD	0.6	(0.6)	0.5	(0.5)	0.5	(0.3)
BHE	4.8	(0.3)	4.5	(0.3)	5.1	(0.3)
Bavarian Party	5.8	(6.8)	–	–	17.9	(21.9)
DP	2.2	(2.2)	1.4	(2.2)	1.3	(1.3)
Total	1217	(994)	222	(163)	392	(311)

BVP	– Bavarian People's Party
DDP	– German Democratic Party
DVP	– German People's Party
DNVP	– German National People's Party
SPD	– Social Democratic Party
KPD	– German Communist Party
USPD	– Independent Socialist Party of Germany
CDU	– Christian Democratic Union
CSU	– Christian Social Union
FDP	– Free Democratic Party
BHE	– Refugee Party
DP	– German Party

[1] Percentages of catholic valid votes.
Source: Johannes Schauff, *Das Wahlverhalten der deutschen Katholiken im Kaiserreich und in der Weimarer Republik*, 1928, ed. with a new introduction by Rudolf Morsey, Mainz, 1975, pp. 115ff.
[2] Party preference percentages of catholic respondents in Unesco survey 1953. Figures in brackets: without refugees. N = total number of cases
Source: Unesco Study 1953 (study No. 145 of the Zentralarchiv für empirische Sozialforschung, University of Cologne).

Democratic subculture, it had the support of only one-third of the protestant electorate as a whole. Thus, although the confessional asymmetry characteristic of the German party system had weakened, it had not disappeared.

(2) Taking the postwar period as a whole, the differences in the voting behaviour of catholics and protestants have neither disappeared nor have they undergone dramatic change. Support for the CDU/CSU remained remarkably stable between 1953 and 1987: 30% to 40% of protestants voted CDU/CSU; the figure for catholics fluctuated around 60%. The SPD's share of total votes rose continually from 1953 to 1972. But, with the increase coming from both confessions, the decisive point is that for the major parties the magnitude which separates the share of vote in both confessions has remained virtually constant over more than thirty years. Hence, confessional affiliation has not only not lost its significance for voting behaviour in the Federal Republic, but – in view of the weakening influence of other socio-structural characteristics such as social class[28] – has become the most important single determinant of voting behaviour.

(3) The increase in support for the SPD up to the early 1970s in both the catholic and protestant electorate, came in neither case from workers but from salaried employees and civil servants. Thanks to its attractiveness to large sections of these strata, in 1972 the SPD received more votes than the CDU/CSU for the first (and up to now only) time in the history of the Federal Republic. Decisive for this electoral development was the uninterrupted growth of the relative importance of the salaried employees and civil servants – the 'new middle class'. Its share of the working population almost doubled between 1950 (21%) and 1970 (38%); by the end of the 1970s it outnumbered workers.

This means that, contrary to expectations, catholic workers were not responsible for the growth in SPD support. This is remarkable, particularly in view of the fact that it could not be taken for granted that the catholic working class would stay with the CDU/CSU. If anything, the constellation within the CDU/CSU militated against this. Whereas in the old Centre Party all strata were relatively evenly represented, in the CDU/CSU the linkage with middle-class protestantism meant a relative loss of weight within the party for the catholic working class, i.e. a shift to the right. However, this new position as a structural

28. See Hans-Joachim Veen and Peter Gluchowski. 'Tendenzen der Nivellierung und Polarisierung in den Wählerschaften von CDU/CSU und SPD von 1959–1983. Eine Fortschreibung', *Zeitschrift für Parlamentsfragen*, vol. 14, 1983, pp. 545–55.

Figure 6.3. Votes for the CDU by confession

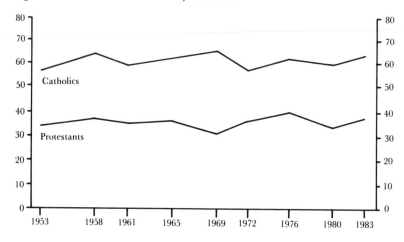

Source: Based on mass surveys archived in the Zentralarchiv für empirische Sozialforschung, University of Cologne, study nos. 145, 455, 57, 314, 525, 840, 1135,
1000, 1275, 1536.

Figure 6.4. Votes for the SPD by confession

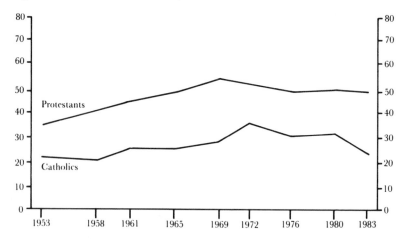

Source: As Figure 6.3.

Figure 6.5. Votes for the SPD: protestants by occupation

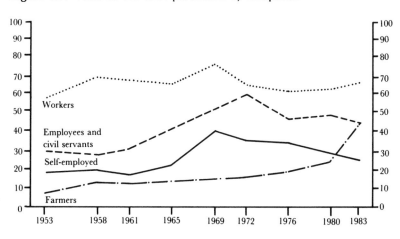

Source: As Figure 6.3.

Figure 6.6. Votes for the SPD: catholics by occupation

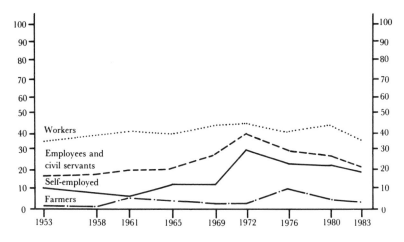

Source: As Figure 6.3.

minority did not alienate catholic workers massively from the CDU/CSU: it retained the loyalties of the overwhelming majority of religious catholic workers.

In other words, the hopes the SPD had placed in its Godesberg Programme were not fulfilled. Abandoning its programmatic *Weltanschauung* at Godesberg was not enough to bridge the distance between the SPD and catholic workers close to their church.

(4) The correlation between religious involvement and changes in party preference differed for the two confessions. Among the protestants there was a relatively even, constant drift to the SPD between 1953 and 1965, irrespective of the degree of religious commitment. By contrast, among the catholics the shift towards the SPD occurred in phases; that among devout catholics took place relatively late (i.e. between 1969 and 1972) and was relatively limited. This means that the core of what was left of the catholic subculture remained relatively stable, with only, as it were, the ice melting at the edges.

In addition, the growth in catholic support for the SPD reflected a general quantitative shift towards the category 'non-religious', i.e. a decrease in religious involvement in general. All in all, however, the increase in the SPD share of the total vote as a consequence of the postwar decline in religious commitment among catholics was much less dramatic (approximately 5%) than the decline itself – hence the widely shared opinion that the SPD rose to become the strongest party in 1972 mainly because of the decline of religious commitment must be treated with reservation.

(5) After what has been said above, it should not come as a surprise that not only the respective parties' share of votes in each of the confessions but also the relative weight of the confessional groups among the voters of each party has remained remarkably constant in the course of the past decades. For the two large parties there have been only slight shifts in the confessional profile. The CDU/CSU has remained a predominantly catholic party, the SPD even more so a protestant one. However, this relative stability should not close our eyes to the fact that there have been considerable shifts within the CDU/CSU electorate in the past decades. In 1953 the CDU/CSU was justified in calling itself a 'christian party', in so far as three-quarters of its voters practised their religion with at least some regularity. Regularly practising catholics constituted the largest single block of almost half the party's vote; together with regularly practising protestants they formed an absolute majority of CDU/CSU voters. Today, practising catholics constitute only one-quarter, and together with practising

Figure 6.7. Votes for the SPD: protestants by church attendance

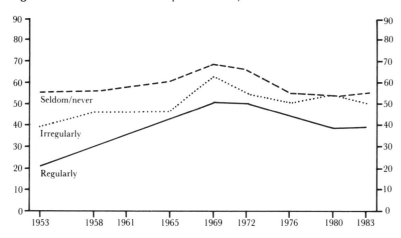

Source: As Figure 6.3.

Figure 6.8. Votes for the SPD: catholics by church attendance

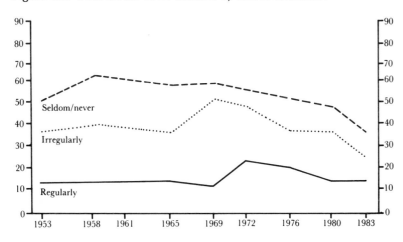

Source: As Figure 6.3.

protestants only one-third, of CDU/CSU voters. Thus, even among CDU/CSU supporters practising christians are in a minority, a fact which has not been without consequences for the party programme and strategy.

In contrast to the two major parties, there have been marked changes in the confessional base of the FDP. Traditionally, it was a protestant party, but it is no longer such. Until the late 1960s only one-quarter of its support was catholic. From the time when it entered into a coalition with the SPD in 1969 the gap narrowed continuously, a process which even the FDP theses on the churches in the early 1970s could not stop. In the 1983 elections, after it had broken with the SPD to form a coalition with the CDU/CSU, the FDP had a catholic majority among its supporters for the first time.

Confessional structures among Green voters deviate markedly from those of the 'traditional' parties. Although there is speculation about the religious roots of the peace movement, the Green Party has the least religious profile of all parties. Only 10% of its voters are regularly practising christians, and 20% of its voters do not belong to any church at all (the average in the population is 9%).

(6) There is a paradox in the postwar development as a whole. On the one hand, the catholic subculture has shrunk enormously and its political contours have blurred. On the other hand, the majority of catholic voters have remained loyal to the CDU/CSU, as a result of which there has been little levelling of confessional differences in voting behaviour.

This paradox can be explained if one assumes a long-term process of change. In the first phase, which has still not run its full course, the ground is prepared for changes in voting behaviour, though the changes themselves are not yet apparent. Under this assumption, there is a time gap between the loosening of religious ties and the consequences of this in terms of partisan affiliation. There is a large probability that catholics who at some point in their lives stop practising their religion remain catholics in a sociological sense. The sociological effect of secularization manifests itself only in the next generation.

Support for this assumption is found in interesting behavioural differences within the group of non-practising catholics. A far greater proportion of those who declare that religion played an important role in their upbringing tend to support the CDU/CSU than of those who declare that religion did not play an important role in their family.

In terms of electoral sociology, the stability of the CDU/CSU share of the catholic vote is assumed to be based on the fact that among

Table 6.2. Recruitment patterns of parties 1953–87 (%)

	1953	1961	1965	1969	1972	1976	1980	1983	1987
CDU/CSU									
Protestants	36	37	40	32	41	41	38	38	37
Catholics	62	61	59	67	56	57	59	59	59
Other	2	2	2	1	3	3	3	4	4
Difference between catholics and protestants	26	24	19	35	15	16	21	21	22
SPD									
Protestants	57	60	64	62	58	61	59	62	56
Catholics	37	34	31	32	35	34	33	29	37
Others	6	6	5	6	6	5	8	9	7
Difference between catholics and protestants	20	26	33	30	23	27	26	33	19
FDP									
Protestants	67	65	67	73	65	64	59	45	56
Catholics	29	28	29	27	24	28	34	48	36
Other	4	7	4	–	11	8	7	6	8
Difference between catholics and protestants	38	37	38	46	41	36	25	−3	20

Source: As Figure 6.3.

secularized catholics party affiliation through membership of the catholic subculture has been transformed into 'genuine' affiliation, i.e. affiliation based on personal preference. The party affiliation itself remains intact. But its character has changed in the course of the individual's development. The catholic subculture functions, so to speak, as midwife to a 'genuine' affiliation, i.e. the individual's own CDU/CSU ties. The influence of the subculture lives on in such 'heirlooms', even when its power to shape political identities has weakened with the passing of time.

This transformation of CDU/CSU ties via church affiliation into 'genuine' CDU/CSU ties cannot be taken for granted. A prerequisite is the postwar party constellation of the Federal Republic, which, in contrast to the Netherlands, for instance,[29] made it possible for a person to leave the subculture but to continue voting for the party representing that same subculture. The decision of the leaders of catholicism not to re-form the Centre Party in 1945 but to found an interconfessional party instead was crucial for this development. Paradoxically, the choice of this new approach made it possible to preserve the confessional differences in the voting behaviour of German voters to the present day. As a result of precisely this decision in 1945, the CDU/CSU has been able to cushion the potential loss of support which has resulted from the accelerating process of secularization within the catholic population since the 1960s. The dual character of the CDU/CSU as a party of the catholic subculture, on the one hand, and as a party aiming at all sections of voters to the right of the SPD, on the other, maintains the loyalty of those catholics who have remained in their subculture, and at the same time makes it possible for a large proportion of other catholics to loosen their religious ties without abandoning their traditional party affiliation.

This dual character of the CDU/CSU was cemented right from the beginning by Adenauer's determination to use his party as a vehicle for national policy and not for the interests of a subculture. This was the reason behind his refusal (and that of his successors) to raise the *bona particularia* of organized catholicism to become central political objectives of the christian party and pursue them at all costs. Accordingly, the relative 'unanimity of the catholic vote', apparent even today, is not to be understood as an expression of a '*Kulturkampf* without opponents',[30] but as precisely the opposite, namely as the consequence of the CDU/CSU's refusal to regard the *Kulturkampf* as the essence of its policies. In short, the continuation of confessionalism in voting behaviour is due to the deconfessionalization of the parties.

In this view, the postwar development must be seen as a period of transition. It is doubtful whether its stability will continue in the long term. The process of transforming the CDU/CSU affiliation derived from the catholic subculture into a 'genuine' affiliation is not a *perpetuum mobile*, for two reasons. Firstly, it presumes that membership of a subculture existed in the first place. But this premise is more and more doubtful. The likelihood of future generations being socialized into their church is decreasing rapidly over time. In 1982 only one-quarter

---

29. See Rudy B. Andeweg, *Dutch Voters Adrift. On Explanations of Electoral Change 1963–1977*, Leiden, 1982.
30. Blankenburg, *Kirchliche Bindung*, p. 169.

of catholics between the ages of 18 and 30 (as compared with 56% of those aged 60 or more) said they had been brought up in a religious atmosphere. Secondly, there is a time limit on the assumed phase shift: voting behaviour can reflect an early religious socialization only as long as a socialized generation is still alive.

Will the CDU/CSU be able to retain its inheritance from the catholic subculture by its own efforts? Crucial in this respect are the conditions which determine the passing on of party affiliations from one generation to the next. A deeply rooted subculture like the catholic one influences many aspects of life and can, provided it is still intact, pass on a party affiliation almost automatically, i.e. largely independently of the specific policies of the party affiliated with it. In contrast, the ability of a party to ensure that a 'genuine' affiliation is passed on from one generation to the next is limited. It can try to consolidate its own terrain by creating its own subculture with a specific milieu-like character. But the prospects of such an effort are limited by the fact that politics does not play a central role in the lives of the majority of the population. Hence, if the party affiliation of socially 'floating' voters is to be retained and passed on, the parties will have to rely on an incalculable resource – the persuasive power of their political performance.

FRANZ URBAN PAPPI

New Social Movements and the Traditional Party System of the Federal Republic of Germany

New social movements[1] seem to be more of a challenge to the established party system in West Germany than in other Western nations. After a long period of a stable three-party system, the Greens began to have an effect in the late 1970s and were able to enter the federal parliament in 1983 for the first time. During the same year the peace movement was very successful in mobilizing support against the deployment of medium-range missiles in West Germany, even if finally it could not change the deployment policy of the federal government. From time to time we took notice of large demonstrations of the anti-nuclear movement, strongly supported by the Green Party, and step by step the politicians who had backed the build-up of nuclear power plants up to then began to retreat from their former strong position.

If we want to explain the strong position of the new social movements in Germany, as compared with other nations, we might be tempted to look back to sociological explanations of the National Socialist movement. Writing in 1942, Talcott Parsons paid special attention to the formality of German social life outside the family. 'The element of formalism in the patterning of the basic institutional system of Germany, . . . seems to indicate a stronger general tendency to romanticism than exists in the Anglo-Saxon countries, in that insti-

1. For the definition of 'social movement' as the term is used in this article, see p. 206.

tutionalized status tends to absorb less of the individual's emotional attachments.'[2] This romanticism was fruitful soil for the 'fundamentalist' revolt of the Nazis 'against the whole tendency of rationalization in the Western world'.[3] Even if some goals of the new social movements have a fundamentalist flavour, a direct comparison of these movements with the Nazi movement would not be very fruitful. At the political level these two types of movements do not have much in common. But when we consider the social conditions inducing people to support movements instead of parties or interest groups, we may nevertheless find social-structural similarities between Germany in 1930 and in 1980 which are responsible for an alienation of middle-class youth and perhaps of women from established social institutions. Parsons focused on these two groups, which had to suffer severe strains because older conservative values, 'especially in defining the role of youth, of sex relationships and of women, could not serve as an adequate basis of institutional integration'.[4]

After this historical reminiscence, it is time to narrow our analysis to the immediate options for political action and look for explanations at a more concrete level of analysis. I shall start my analysis with a discussion of the possible relationships between new social movements and the Green Party. In the next section I review the traditional strongholds of the established parties to find out in which social-structural niche the Green Party will be able to establish itself on a permanent basis. We shall then be able to speculate about the future of the German party system in the last section.

I shall use survey data gathered as part of a 1987 election study[5] on adherents of new social movements and voting behaviour as empirical evidence for some of my arguments.

The Movement Sector

A Short History

Political protest movements in West Germany have a history which can be traced back to the early 1950s. In those years the

2. Talcott Parsons, 'Democracy and Social Structure in Pre-Nazi Germany', in idem (ed.), *Essays in Sociological Theory*, Glencoe, Ill., 1954 (1942), p. 121.
3. Ibid., p. 123.
4. Ibid., p. 122.
5. Zentral Archiv für empirische Sozialforschung der Universität zu Köln, *Wahlstudie 1987*, Part 2, *Panel-Studie* (ZA-Nr. 1537).

SPD tried to mobilize citizens against German rearmament and the deployment of nuclear weapons on German territory. When the SPD (Social Democratic Party) came to terms with the Western integration of the Federal Republic, the Easter marches of the 1960s were organized by independent groups outside the established party system. Among these the Socialist German Student Association (Sozialistischer Deutscher Studentenbund: SDS) as the former student organization of the Social Democrats, played a prominent role. It was debarred from the SPD after the passing of the Godesberg Programme and developed into a radical core group of the student movement of the late 1960s. The ideology of the SDS was not communist or socialist in the orthodox sense, but influenced by the critical theory of the Frankfurt School. These students advocated a revolution in all aspects of life, not just in the economic and political system, but they favoured decentralization and were opposed to the bureaucratic structures of communist states. Even after the executive committee of the SDS announced, on 21 March 1970, that it was dissolving its organization, its influence both on the newly formed communist splinter groups and the citizens' initiative movement must be considered substantial. The citizens' initiative movement gained momentum in the 1970s with a growing concern for a more decentralized planning process in the area of urban renewal and for environmental issues in general. When the federal government decided in 1973 to expand its nuclear energy programme, many citizens' initiatives were founded by people living in the neighbourhood of prospective sites of the nuclear power plants and these groups were supported by movement activists from all over Germany. The names of villages like Wyhl, Brokdorf and Gorleben became known as sites of large demonstrations. Members of the diverse groups fighting the construction of nuclear power plants and also other large construction projects such as new airports joined forces, for example with adherents of the ecological movement to found the party of the Greens. After electoral successes in some states, the federal party was founded in January 1980 but gained only 1.5% in the second ballot in the 1980 federal election. In 1983 the percentage was up to 5.6, and in January 1987 7.9% of voters voted in favour of the candidate lists of this party.

The self-chosen role of the Greens is to serve as the party of the movement sector and to advocate the movement goals in the federal and state parliaments. This party is thus the intervening force between the new social movements and the traditional party system. Before we discuss the type of relationship between the Greens and the movement sector, we have first to define social movements and answer the question of which phenomena we want to subsume under this concept.

Social Movements Defined

Social scientists use three dimensions to define social movements: goals, organizational characteristics and forms of collective action. The common characteristics of social movements are that they involve a population subgroup which is not formally organized but has nevertheless some in-group feeling because the insiders are committed to the same goals or ideology in favour of a more or less radical social change; this commitment and common feeling is strengthened by joint collective actions such as demonstrations. Some authors argue that new social movements can first of all be characterized by their loose organizational forms; they function socially as a network of networks.[6] Melucci proposes the term 'movement networks', that is 'networks of "informal" relationships connecting core individuals and groups to a broader area of participants'.[7] Other authors emphasize the type of goals advocated by new social movements, some following, for instance, Inglehart's concept of post-materialist concerns[8] in which they see a common denominator of the diverse movements.[9] The fight against modern large-scale bureaucracies often has a defensive character whereas emancipation movements are more offensive, fighting for the rights of certain groups which they legitimize in terms of universalistic human values. Among the new social movements only the feminist groups are rooted in the tradition of modern emancipation.[10]

The term 'movement' is not only a social science concept but is used as an identifying label by the groups themselves. In Germany, social scientists and leaders within the movement sector seem to agree that it makes sense to categorize the people demonstrating against nuclear power plants, the diverse peace groups, young people advocating an alternative life-style, radical ecologists and feminists as new social

6. Friedhelm Neidhardt, 'Einige Ideen zu einer allgemeinen Theorie sozialer Bewegungen', in Stefan Hradil (ed.), *Sozialstruktur im Umbruch*, Opladen, 1985, pp. 193–204.
7. Alberto Melucci, 'An End to Social Movements? Introductory paper to the session on "new social movements and change in organizational forms"', *Social Science Information*, vol. 23, 1984, p. 828.
8. Ronald Inglehart, *The Silent Revolution: Changing Values and Political Styles Among Western Publics*, Princeton, NJ, 1977.
9. See Max Kaase, 'Soziale Bewegungen zwischen Innovation und Antimodernismus', University of Mannheim, unpublished manuscript, 1986.
10. Jürgen Habermas, *Theorie des kommunikativen Handelns*, vol. 2, Frankfurt 1981, p. 578.

movements. As authors such as Raschke[11] have argued, this categor- ization also seems justified from the analytic perspective of the social sciences. Since the major goals of these diverse groups are different I shall distinguish the anti-nuclear from the peace movement and these two from the womens' movement and so on. These single movements can be combined in a movement sector, the acting parts of which are the single movements; a complete sector organization is not assumed.

Movements and Parties: Types of Relationships

In modern democracies the function of interest articulation is normally performed by interest groups. I consider movements as functional alternatives to interest groups when the access to normal lobbying activities is blocked for certain interests or groups. These interests are then articulated by movements which challenge the estab- lished system and have to rely on their own forces when mobilizing their potential followers through efforts of collective action. The policy areas of ecological issues, which were first articulated by ecological movements, are today the domains of public interest groups in the US, whereas German interest groups seem to be less pluralistically struc- tured and have higher thresholds of access for new groups. Movements are, therefore, a more viable alternative.

The Green Party did not originally consider itself to be a 'normal' party within a parliamentary system. Many of its supporters preferred direct democracy, which they tried to practise at least within their party. The best-known example in this respect is the rotation scheme for Green members of parliament, who were supposed to return their mandate after two years and clear the way for other spokesmen of the Green grass-roots. In terms of the function of interest aggregation, the Green Party has the option either to perform this function in the usual way – in this case as the parliamentary representative of the move- ment sector – or to combine it with the function of interest articulation and act itself as a mobilizing agent for the central concerns of the new movements. The fundamentalist and the realist wings of the party are the respective advocates of these two options for the further develop- ment of the party.

When we cross-classify the party and movement options, that is the dimensions of interest aggregation and interest articulation, the result- ing cells of this fourfold table describe four possible scenarios for the

11. Joachim Raschke, *Soziale Bewegungen*, Frankfurt 1985.

relationship between the new social movements and the Green Party (see Figure 7.1). At the same time, the type of relationship determines the future development of the movement sector. We should explicitly mention that we assume that the new social movements and the Green Party are separate actors, even if they co-operate closely from time to time.

This close co-operation has to be the consequence of the choice of option 1,1 shown in Figure 7.1 by movements and party. Both actors try to mobilize the movement sympathizers within the general population, and as they are different agents of the same movement sector they will have success if they co-operate. Severe conflicts would raise the question of whether these agents actually do belong to the same movement. But if they are able to co-operate closely they may mobilize large segments of the general population and achieve some of their goals.

Periods of high mobilization are always an exception and in contrast to normal periods of day-to-day politics. During periods of demobilization it may be either the party or the movements which follow first the track of institutionalized forms of policy making. If the movements are the first to change their character and turn into interest groups, the party can perform the role of the avant-garde of the movement (option 1,2). This has been the role of Leninist parties within the labour movement when trade unions had already decided in favour of piecemeal progress instead of revolutionary change. For the new social movements in Germany, I think it is less likely that the movements will turn into public interest groups than that the Green Party will give up its role as an active mobilizing agent.

This alternative (2,1) seems to be the most likely outcome of the conflict between the realists and fundamentalists within the Green Party, whereas the movements are still playing the role of mobilizing collective actors. Under this combination of options, one could interpret the role of the party as an umbrella organization of the movement sector, aggregating the diverse interests of the single movements and trying to enlarge the appeal of this sector within the general electorate.

The last logical possibility (option 2,2) is a normal division of labour between interest-articulating and interest-aggregating organizations which both use the institutionalized channels of the input structure of the political system. Thus 'normal politics' would be the final outcome. I do not predict that for the near future.

How will the relationship between party and movements develop in the near future? The outcome depends in part on political decisions of

Figure 7.1. Possible relationships between the new social movements and the Green Party

Party 'Die Grünen'	Movements	
	mobilizing collective actors (1)	interest groups politics (2)
mobilizing agent (1)	close co-operation, periods of high mobilization	party as avant-garde
parliamentary representative of movement sector (2)	party as umbrella organization	division of labour, normal politics

the party, in part on the dynamic of the further developments of the movements and finally on the reaction of the sympathizers of the movement sector who are not themselves active participants either of the movements or of the Green Party. The Green Party itself seems to be still ambiguous about which direction it should go in. The core groups of at least some of the new movements, for instance the anti–nuclear movements, try to maintain a certain level of mobilization to prove their force as independent movements, but they are, of course, dependent on the official government policy which is backing nuclear energy for the foreseeable future. In this situation one can ask what are the constraints for the further development of the Greens with respect to the larger group of sympathizers. It is this question which I shall try to answer.

The Degree of Overlap between Adherents of Different Movements

One condition is important both at the elite level and at the level of voters. The Greens are the only party trying to represent the movement sector exclusively, but there exist different movements, at least with regard to the different contents of their goals. One question is to what extent the adherents of the different movements are overlapping. If they are overlapping to a large extent, then mobilization of the movement sector is easier than in the other case. When the single movements are not overlapping, mobilization of one movement does not imply a mobilization of the other movements at the same time. Then a party strategy of being an umbrella organization for all new social movements irrespective of their current mobilization level would make more sense. When the adherents are overlapping the party will reach more adherents with a consistent mobilization strategy.

The amount of overlapping among the sympathizers of the different movements can be tested empirically. I measured subjective membership in three movements, that is in the anti-nuclear, the peace and the women's movements, by asking the same type of question, which was used to measure subjective class or party identification: 'Do you think of yourself as an adherent of the women's movement?' The respondents answering 'Yes' were asked whether they go to demonstrations or meetings of this movement. We call respondents who also answered 'Yes' to this question active adherents, and the ones who said 'Yes' to the first question only passive adherents. The peace movement had its largest group of sympathizers in February 1987, 19% passive and 5% active adherents. The anti-nuclear movement follows as the second largest movement, with 15% passive and 4% active adherents. The women's movement is the smallest one: 9% of the female and 4% of the male respondents identified with this movement; the figures for active participation are still lower, 2% for women and 1% for men.

With these data it makes sense to test the following model. The three questions identifying adherents and non-adherents can be interpreted as different indicators of the latent variable 'subjective membership in a unitary movement'. The indicators differ in their difficulty; a man answering 'Yes' to the question about whether he thinks of himself as a member of the women's movement has to have a higher degree of movement identification than one identifying only with the peace movement. But apart from the different difficulty of the questions, they are supposed to measure the same underlying dimension of movement membership. Technically speaking, we can test these assumptions by applying a Rasch scaling model,[12] and since we already know that the difficulty of identifying with the women's movement is greater for men than for women we have to stratify the respondents according to gender. The test of this model has a negative result. The assumption of a unitary social movement is not justified for passive adherents.

This situation changes when we test the same model for the classification 'active adherents versus other respondents'. Now we get a positive result; that is, the activists of the different movements fit into one latent dimension of movement activity; even the composition of men and women is the same with respect to the different degrees of

12. Otin Dudley Duncan, 'Rasch Measurement in Survey Research: Further Examples and Discussion', in Charles F. Turner and Elizabeth Martin (eds), *Surveying Subjective Phenomena*, vol. 2, New York, 1984.

movement activity. Only the percentages that agree with the different items for the peace and the feminist movements differ according to gender.[13]

We can draw two conclusions from these results. Firstly, a strategy for the Greens to act as a mobilizing agent is not hopeless from the beginning because they can target at the overlapping activist groups at the core of the different new movements. Secondly, stressing the most radical demands of a movement as its mobilizing agents may be detrimental to campaign efforts to win a large number of voters from the mere sympathizers to the different movements; they may be deterred from supporting a party pushing too vehemently in one direction, especially when non-institutionalized means are used. Thus the umbrella strategy seems to have advantages as a purely electoral strategy, but in this case we have to consider the competition between the parties. The Greens are not the only attractive alternative for voters who sympathize with one or the other of the new social movements.

Voters Between the Movement Sector and the Party System

The first information we need in this section is very simple. How many passive and active identifiers with the new movements chose the Green Party in the last federal election and how attractive are the established parties to these voters? The second question is as follows. How exclusively do the Greens depend at the polls on the movement sector? These two questions are answerable by using the same cross-tabulation previously looked at, the percentages being computed column- and row-wise.

Even though there are data available for three movements, I shall present only analyses concerning the anti-nuclear movement. Of the three movements, the mobilization was highest for this one. The emergency caused by the Chernobyl disaster had not yet been forgotten and the activists of the anti-nuclear movement had a high visibility in the mass media. Among voters, the correlation between movement identification and preferences for movement goals was highest for this movement, too. I interpret this as a consequence of the high level of mobilization.

13. See Franz Urban Pappi, 'Neu soziale Bewegungen und Wahlverhalten in der Bundesrepublik', Institut für Soziologie der Universität Kiel, unpublished manuscript, 1984.

The political distinctiveness of the active adherents of the anti-nuclear movement is quite visible (see Table 7.1, column percentages). Almost two-thirds of this group voted for the Greens in the last federal election; one-third voted for the Social Democrats. The political distinctiveness of the passive identifiers is less clear but even this group favours one party overwhelmingly; this is not the Greens but the SPD. This situation is similar in the peace movement, so that we can draw the conclusion that the Greens are first of all the party of movement activists, even though the activists do not dominate within the Green electorate, owing to the small size of this group. Only 36% of the Green voters are activists of the anti-nuclear movement; another 37% are passive identifiers. But if we add these two percentages we see that the overall movement distinctiveness of the Greens (row percentages) is quite high.

This marks the main difference between the party and the SPD. Even though the Social Democrats are quite attractive to passive identifiers, the movement distinctiveness of this party is low. Three-quarters of its voters are not adherents of the anti-nuclear movement. In periods of high movement mobilization this may cause problems for the SPD, because a policy which is attractive to movement identifiers may alienate the majority of its voters. In periods of medium-to-low mobilization, the SPD seems to be in a better position to compete for voters from the movement sector than the Greens. The dilemma for the Greens is the choice between the option to maximize their attractiveness for the small group of movement activists and the option to broaden its supporters, which may help the SPD more than the Greens. Evaluated from this perspective, the arguments of the fundamentalists in favour of the strategy to act as a mobilizing agent are strengthened. But this is a viable option only for periods of high movement mobilization, which is dependent on many exogenous factors and not only on the self-stimulation of movement activists.

There have always been cycles of political protest phenomena and we could argue that the current cycle of ecological protest which began in the late 1970s is already in a downswing. Thus the Greens as a party of a transient protest vote will not be able to establish themselves as a permanent component of the German party system.[14] Other authors reach contrary conclusions. They interpret the Greens as a party of the

14. See Wilhelm P. Bürklin, 'Governing Left Parties Frustrating the Radical Non-Established Left: The Rise and Inevitable Decline of the Greens', *European Sociological Review*, vol. 3 (September), 1987, pp. 109–26, for these arguments.

Table 7.1. Identification with the anti-nuclear movement and party choice (second ballot of the Bundestag election in 1987)

Party	Non-identifiers		Passive identifiers		Active identifiers		Σ	
	%	%	%	%	%	%	%	%
CDU/CSU	97	48	3	9	—	—	100	40
SPD	74	35	23	60	3	30	100	38
FDP	84	6	16	6	—	—	100	6
Greens	28	2	37	17	36	62	100	7
Other	67	1	11	1	22	4	100	1
Non-voters	85	8	14	7	2	4	100	8
Σ	81	100	15	100	4	100	100	N = 1285

Cramer's V = 0.397.

Source: 1987 German election study, third panel wave (Zentralarchiv für empirische Sozialforschung, University of Cologne) study no. 1537.

new politics of a post-industrial age[15] or as the representatives of new social classes – for instance a 'knowledge' class.[16] Associated with these contrary positions is a diverging interpretation of cross-sectional age differences in voting behaviour. All available empirical data are revealing one unambiguous result: the Greens have their social-structural stronghold among the better educated young voters. Bürklin[17] interpreted this finding as a life-cycle phenomenon. Owing to a tight labour market for people with university degrees, the social integration of this group into normal adult positions both in the economic and other spheres of life is delayed, giving rise to dissatisfaction and protest behaviour. Thus these non-established groups do not feel represented by the traditional parties and are voting for the Greens at present. But 'it is concluded that the electoral support of the Greens will decline drastically as soon as the unemployment situation eases and the Social Democratic Party has redefined its role as spokesman of the less-integrated political left'.[18]

The long-term perspective for the Greens changes dramatically when we assume, firstly, that the age effect has to be interpreted as a generational effect and if we add, secondly, that the generations growing up under conditions of post-industrialism acquire value orientations which are contradictory to the ideologies of the traditional parties. These parties should be able to adjust their programmes to the new conditions but they cannot surpass the Greens as the party of post-modernism.

It is very difficult to test these contradictory hypotheses empirically. An analysis design in which cohort and ageing effects can be separated has to rely on data from historical periods when the Green Party had not been founded. One can, of course, test whether the traditional social cleavages of the German party system are withering away among the younger generations. It is possible to find some empirical evidence supporting this hypothesis,[19] but only among the youngest generations for which a separation of cohort and age effect is almost impossible. The models which best fit these data have to include a generational

15. See Russell J. Dalton, 'The West German Party System Between Two Ages', in R. J. Dalton, Scott C. Flanagan and Paul Allen Beck (eds), *Electoral Change in Advanced Industrial Democracies*, Princeton, NJ, 1984.

16. See, e.g. Johan Galtung, 'The Green Movement: A Social-Historical Exploration', *International Sociology*, vol. 1, no. 1, pp. 75–90.

17. See Bürklin, 'Governing Left Parties'.

18. Ibid., p. 110.

19. Franz Urban Pappi and Peter Mnich, 'Social Structure and Part Choice in the Federal Republic of Germany since the 1960s', Institute für Soziologie der Universität Kiel, unpublished manuscript, 1987.

effect as an important determinant of voting behaviour, but for the youngest age groups we detected some period-specific fluctuations of votes, which become settled in a specific direction when the cohort reaches about 30 years of age. The period since the entry of the Greens into the party system is, therefore, too short to make solid predictions about the stable party preferences of the youngest of today's generations.

In this situation I refrain from long-range predictions about the chances of the Green Party and concentrate instead on its middle-range perspectives, paying attention first of all to the role of the new social movements in this respect.

Social-Structural Determinants of Movement Identification and Voting Behaviour

The stable points of gender and occupation will be compared. Age is omitted because the descriptive findings are known and the theoretical interpretation would be ambiguous for cross-section data. I shall first investigate which social groups support the new social movements most, again using the anti-nuclear movement as an example. In so far as identification with a movement can be interpreted as a sign of dissatisfaction with traditional politics, this first analysis will uncover the social-structural locations of the dissatisfied. I shall try to find out whether dissatisfaction is linked to the class situation of the respective groups which could provide a more permanent basis for different forms of political alienation from the established system. In a second step I shall describe the voting behaviour of these social structural groups. The agreement between movement identification and party choices for gender and occupational groups will tell us whether the Greens do profit from this dissatisfaction and what their chances are of gaining a more stable social structural basis within the electorate.

The occupational structure of post-industrial societies is changing gradually, mainly owing to processes of cohort replacement. In designing an occupational classification it is important to be careful to treat occupations typical of modern societies as a separate category. For my purposes a good starting point is the social class schema developed by John Goldthorpe[20] and applied to voting behaviour by

20. John H. Goldthorpe, *Social Mobility and Class Structure in Modern Britain*, Oxford, 1980.

Heath.[21] Among white-collar occupations, Heath, Jowell and Curtice distinguish between the salariat and routine non-manuals. I adopt his latter category – of clerks, sales personnel and secretaries – but divide the former by separating out top managers and top civil servants. The remaining part of the first category consists of professionals and semi-professionals. The fourth group encompasses the small self-employed, together with the owners of small and middle-size farms; we call this group the petty bourgeoisie. Manual workers are treated as one large category, the working class.

In earlier voting studies researchers have used the occupation of the household head as an indicator of the class position of respondents. But since the concept of the head of household became ambiguous with the increase in the number of married women in the labour force, I decided to rely on the present or last occupation of the respondent. Empirically, the decision to use the occupation of the respondent instead of the occupation of the household head is justified by the stronger relationship of the former with voting behaviour. Of respondents, 6.5% never had an occupation of their own; 85% of this group were elderly women.

A specially meaningful category of respondents' occupation is the group of students and apprentices who are still in the preparatory phases of their careers. Since the overwhelming majority in this group are students, I apply this term to designate the category. This category provided a reminder that the age composition of the occupational groups may have an effect. It was, therefore, necessary to test whether age would change the main results of the following analyses. This was not the case and the tables showing the results are therefore omitted.

Which segments of the occupational structure sympathize most with the anti-nuclear movement and are, therefore, most alienated from the present policies concerning nuclear energy (see Figure 7.2)? These are, above all, the students and, secondly, the professionals – that is, the students of yesterday. The petty bourgeoisie and the executives are least favourable towards the anti-nuclear movement. It is difficult to say whether these results are related to the class situation of these groups. Some authors argue that employees not engaged in manufacturing but in people- or client-oriented occupations are more critical of the economic growth policy of the industrial age. An alternative interpretation would be that growing occupational groups are more influenced by the generational value change going on mainly among the better educated, that is among people who spent a long period of their lives within the educational system.

21. Anthony Heath, Roger Jowell and John Curtice, *How Britain Votes*, Oxford, 1985.

Figure 7.2. Occupation and gender predicting anti-nuclear movement identification

% identifiers

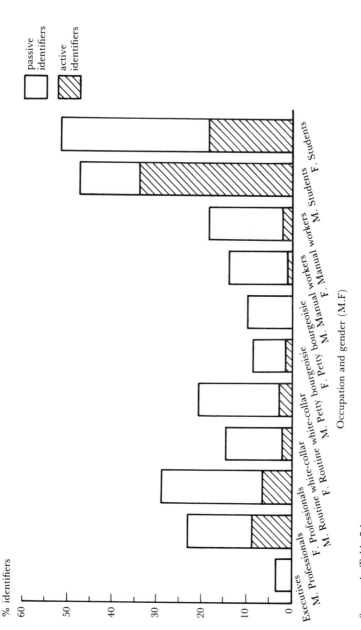

Executives
M. Professionals
 F. Professionals
  M. Routine white-collar
   F. Routine white-collar
    M. Petty bourgeoisie
     F. Petty bourgeoisie
      M. Manual workers
       F. Manual workers
        M. Students
         F. Students

Occupation and gender (M.F)

passive identifiers

active identifiers

Source: As Table 7.1.

What is interesting is that in every occupational group women identify more with the anti-nuclear movement than men (overall identification). This may be a hint that the less-settled members of a social class are in general more alienated from established politics, and that the fastest growing occupations, mainly the professional and routine white-collar occupations, encompass a larger share of less-settled positions whose incumbents identify more with challenger groups. We cannot test this hypothesis so the link between class position and movement identification remains missing. But as long as a party has certain social-structural strongholds, whatever the reasons, that party can rely on the forces of normal politics which will turn the supporting group into a party clientele.

Up to now I have commented only on the percentages of overall identification. The shares of active identifiers do not show the same pattern across occupation and gender as the adherents in general. The main difference is that among the students and the professionals the male activists outnumber the female ones. Altogether, general movement identification is more a female prerogative, at least when occupation is controlled, and movement activity more a male affair.

When we now compare the Green vote within the different social-structural groups (see Figure 7.3) with the identification profiles, we are first impressed by the similarities. The Green vote is highest in those groups with the highest percentage of anti-nuclear movement adherents. Among students and professionals men and women are choosing the Greens to the same extent. Among men activity level is a good predictor of party preference, whereas women prefer the Greens overproportionally compared with their activity level. This is especially true for routine white-collar women.

Among men the small self-employed seem to be an exception to the general close connection between activity level and the Green vote. It may well be that some small shop owners and farmers chose the Greens in 1987 as a protest party because they were dissatisfied with the agricultural policy and not because they were against nuclear energy.

When we combine the Green vote and SPD vote into a general left vote, we observe two different gender patterns. Among the traditional occupational groups of the working class and the petty bourgeoisie, men vote more left than women. Among white-collar occupations this pattern is reversed. Here the party preference pattern is the same as the movement identification profile for gender differences. I draw the strong conclusion from this finding that among white-collar groups the SPD is attractive for the same reasons as the Greens, as a party more of

Figure 7.3. Occupation and gender predicting party choice

% SPD and Greens

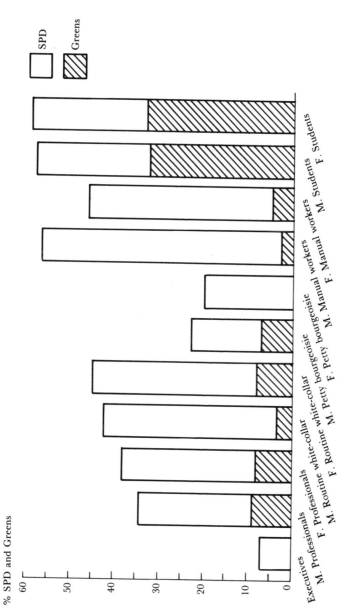

SPD

Greens

Executives   M. Professionals   F. Routine white-collar   M. Petty bourgeoisie   F. Manual workers   M. Students
    F. Professionals   M. Routine white-collar   F. Petty bourgeoisie   M. Manual workers   F. Students

Occupation and gender (M.F)

Source: As Table 7.1.

the new than the old left. This statement is perhaps too strong for routine white-collar employees whose SPD share is higher than that of the professionals, thus reflecting conditions of traditional class cleavages too. But my main argument is that, if the Greens and the SPD compete for votes, then it will be first of all among white-collar employees. And if we take into account as a second precondition that the SPD is most successful not among active movement adherents but among passive sympathizers – who are more likely to be female than male – then the conclusion must be that the future of the Greens as a party in parliament will be decided by middle-class women who may, in the long run, find the SPD more attractive and sensitive to their concerns than the Greens.

Conclusion

I have already reached the speculative part of my paper, but I would like to present a little more evidence to support my conclusions. I have focused on the anti-nuclear movement because of its high mobilization level. Compared with its 3.9% activists, only 1.6% of all respondents said that they participated in demonstrations and visited meetings of the women's movement. Comparatively few people preferred the movement goal of a preferential treatment of female applicants for positions in which women have been under-represented until now. One may wonder whether feminists will ever reach high levels of mobilization for their movement, on account of the absence of a large enough core activist group, especially among women. But one should distinguish movements which reach quick and intense mobilization with hard tactics, perhaps using violent means, from other movements which grow more silently via soft, consciousness-raising techniques. The women's movement belongs to this second type. Under the conditions of soft mobilization techniques, the prospects of the SPD in attracting young white-collar women will be better than those of the Greens. The alliance between the SPD and the female white-collar employees seems to have a solid base in the still existing occupational disadvantages of women in professional and routine white-collar occupations, where women earn less than men and have poorer chances of upward mobility. The empirical evidence I have already mentioned is that even activists of the women's movement have a higher probability of being SPD voters than Green voters.

I started this paper with a reminiscence about Parsons's argument regarding the severe strains to which the young and women were exposed under the German value system. I am not sure whether strains of interpenetration between the formal social status system and the emotional needs of personalities can explain the tendency of young and female Germans to sympathize with the new movements. I prefer a social-structural explanation. German society is, in parts, well organized, causing problems for those who are trying to get access to those parts. 'Credentialism' or stress on formal qualification is an important factor in careers and even interest groups have to be licensed in order to get formal access to the federal government. High thresholds of access to the established system create problems for outsiders. These are, of course, the young and women, who are giving up their traditional roles.

The general conclusion must, therefore, be that because of the stability and sometimes rigidity of the established channels of interest articulation and aggregation, the movement sector is functioning as a safety valve at the periphery of the established system. The new social movements and the Greens are not a major challenge to the established party system, enforcing a new dimension in addition to the left–right continuum of this system and thereby threatening also the CDU/CSU and the FDP. The Greens are a party of the left competing for votes mainly with the Social Democrats. They are not able to gain major support from the voters at the centre and right positions of the underlying ideological dimension. The SPD has to bear the burden of discussing politics with the Greens, partly endorsing and partly ignoring policy options advocated by new social movements. As the major opposition party at present, its opportunities to remain attractive to the less active identifiers with the new social movements seem to be quite good and there may be a chance in the near future that the SPD and the Greens together will gain a majority of votes in a federal election. These prospects will be enhanced the more the social and economic policy of the present government of CDU/CSU and FDP antagonizes the unions and their traditional working-class members. Thus these groups which normally do not support the new social movements will be forced into a coalition of the new and old left because of their common, yet differently motivated, opposition to the liberal-conservative government.

Until now the Greens could afford a policy of 'self-limiting radicalism',[22] that is, they acted both as a mobilizing agent of the

---

22. See Elim Papadakis, 'Social Movements, Self-Limiting Radicalism and the Green Party in West Germany', *Sociology*, vol. 22 (August), 1988, pp. 433–54.

movement sector in times of high mobilization and as a parliamentary representative of this same sector in normal times. Should they ever enter a coalition government with the SPD, this alternating strategy may no longer be possible and the Greens may develop into an umbrella organization of the movement sector, having a broader spectrum of potential voters than today but one which also leans towards the SPD. Then it will be up to the SPD whether it can integrate old and new left elements within one large party or not. Only in the latter case will the Greens remain an enduring option within the German four-party system.

Bibliography

I General

Albertin, Lothar, and Werner Link (eds), *Politische Parteien auf dem Wege zur parlamentarischen Demokratie in Deutschland. Entwicklungslinien bis zur Gegenwart*, Düsseldorf, 1981

Albrecht, Dieter et al. (eds), *Politik und Konfession. Festschrift für K. Repgen zum 60. Geburtstag*, Berlin, 1983

Becker, Winfried (ed.), *Die Minderheit als Mitte. Die Deutsche Zentrumspartei in der Innenpolitik des Reiches 1871–1933*, Munich, 1986

Best, Heinrich (ed.), *Politik und Milieu. Wahl- und Elitenforschung im historischen und interkulturellen Vergleich*, St Katharinen, 1989

Büsch, Otto, Monika Wölk and Wolfgang Wölk (eds), *Wählerbewegung in der deutschen Geschichte. Analysen und Berichte zu den Reichstagswahlen 1871–1933*, Berlin, 1978

Büsch, Otto (ed.), *Wählerbewegung in der Europäischen Geschichte. Ergebnisse einer Konferenz*, Berlin, 1980

Büsch, Otto, and Peter Steinbach (eds), *Vergleichende europäische Wahlgeschichte. Eine Anthologie*, Berlin, 1983

Dix, Arthur, *Die deutschen Reichstagswahlen 1871–1930 und die Wandlungen der Volksgliederung*, Tübingen, 1930

Fenske, Hans, *Wahlrecht und Parteiensystem. Ein Beitrag zur deutschen Parteiengeschichte*, Frankfurt, 1972

——, *Der liberale Südwesten. Freiheitliche und demokratische Traditionen in Baden und Württemberg 1790–1933*, Stuttgart, 1981

Franz, Günther, *Die politischen Wahlen in Niedersachen, 1867 bis 1949*, 2nd edition, Bremen, 1957

Fricke, Dieter (ed.), *Die bürgerlichen Parteien in Deutschland. Handbuch der Geschichte der bürgerlichen Parteien und anderer bürgerlicher Interessenorganisationen vom Vormärz bis zum Jahre 1945*, 2 vols, Leipzig, 1968/70

Fricke, Dieter et al. (eds), *Lexikon zur Parteiengeschichte. Die bürgerlichen und kleinbürgerlichen Parteien und Verbände in Deutschland (1789–1945)*, 4 vols, Leipzig, 1983/84

Fricke, Dieter, 'Die politische Organisation der bürgerlichen Gesellschaft in Deutschland von 1789 bis zur Gegenwart in der BRD. Aufgaben und Probleme ihrer historischen Erforschung', *Jenaer Beiträge zur Parteiengeschichte*, 1987, pp. 14–50

Günther, Wolfgang (ed.), *Sozialer und politischer Wandel in Oldenburg*, Oldenburg, 1981

—— (ed.), *Parteien und Wahlen in Oldenburg. Beiträge zur Landesgeschichte im 19. und 20. Jahrhundert*, Oldenburg, 1983

Hofmann-Göttig, Joachim, *Emanzipation mit dem Stimmzettel. 70 Jahre Frauenwahlrecht in Deutschland*, Bonn, 1986

Huber, Ernst Rudolf, *Deutsche Verfassungsgeschichte seit 1789*, 7 vols, Stuttgart, 1957–84

Immerfall, Stefan, *Territorium und Wahlverhalten. Zur Erklärungskraft geoökonomischer und geopolitischer Entwicklungsprozesse*, Ph. D., Passau, 1989

Kaack, Heino, *Geschichte und Struktur des deutschen Parteiensystems*, Cologne, 1971

Kaiser, Jochen-Christoph, *Arbeiterbewegung und organisierte Religionskritik. Proletarische Freidenkerverbände in Kaiserreich und Weimarer Republik*, Stuttgart, 1981

Kühr, Herbert, 'Katholische und evangelische Milieus: Vermittlungsinstanzen und Wirkungsmuster', in Dieter Oberndörfer, Hans Rattinger and Karl Schmitt (eds), *Wirtschaftlicher Wandel, religiöser Wandel und Wertwandel*, Berlin, 1985

Langewiesche, Dieter, *Liberalismus in Deutschland*, Frankfurt, 1988

Lavies, Ralf-Rainer, *Nichtwählen als Kategorie des Wahlverhaltens. Empirische Untersuchung zur Wahlenthaltung in historischer, politischer und statistischer Sicht*, Düsseldorf, 1973

Lehnert, Detlef, *Sozialdemokratie zwischen Protestbewegung und Regierungspartei 1848–1983*, Frankfurt, 1983

Lepsius, M. Rainer, 'Parteiensystem und Sozialstruktur: Zum Problem der Demokratisierung der deutschen Gesellschaft (1966)', in Gerhard A. Ritter, *Die deutschen Parteien vor 1918*, Cologne, 1973, pp. 56–80

——, 'Wahlverhalten, Parteien und politische Spannungen', *Politische Vierteljahresschrift*, vol. 14, 1973, pp. 293–313

Lönne, Karl-Egon, *Politischer Katholizismus im 19. und 20. Jahrhundert*, Frankfurt, 1986

Naßmacher, Hiltrud, 'Auf- und Abstieg von Parteien. Ansätze zur vergleichenden Betrachtung von Etablierung und Niedergang von Parteien im Wettbewerb', *Zeitschrift für Politik*, vol. 36, 1989, pp. 169–90

Naßmacher, Karl-Heinz, 'Zerfall einer liberalen Subkultur. Kontinuität und Wandel des Parteiensystems in der Region Oldenburg', in Herbert Kühr (ed.), *Vom Milieu zur Volkspartei. Funktionen und Wandlungen der Parteien im kommunalen und regionalen Bereich*, Königstein, 1979, pp. 30–134

Neugebauer-Wölk, Monika, *Wählergenerationen in Preußen zwischen Kaiserreich und*

Republik, Berlin, 1987

Nöcker, Horst, *Der preußische Reichstagswähler in Kaiserreich und Republik 1912 und 1924. Analyse, Interpretation, Dokumentation. Ein historisch-statistischer Beitrag zum Kontinuitätsproblem eines epochenübergreifenden Wählerverhaltens*, Berlin, 1987

Nuhn, Heinrich, *Wahlen und Parteien im ehemaligen Landkreis Hersfeld 1867–1970. Eine historisch-analytische Längsschnittstudie*, Ph. D., Marburg, 1988

Oberndörfer, Dieter and Karl Schmitt (eds), *Parteien und regionale politische Traditionen in der Bundesrepublik Deutschland*, Berlin, 1989

Pappi, Franz Urban, *Wahlverhalten und politische Kultur*, Meisenheim, 1970

——, 'Die konfessionell-religiöse Konfliktlinie in der deutschen Wählerschaft. Entstehung, Stabilität und Wandel', in Dieter Oberndörfer, Hans Rattinger and Karl Schmitt (eds), *Wirtschaftlicher Wandel und Wertwandel. Folgen für das politische Verhalten in der Bundesrepublik*, Berlin, 1985, pp. 263–90

Ritter, Gerhard A., *Staat, Arbeiterschaft und Arbeiterbewegung in Deutschland*, Berlin, 1980

Rohe, Karl, 'Konfession, Klasse und lokale Gesellschaft als Bestimmungsfaktoren des Wahlverhaltens – Überlegungen und Problematisierungen am Beispiel des historischen Ruhrgebiets', in Lothar Albertin and Werner Link (eds), *Politische Parteien auf dem Weg zur parlamentarischen Demokratie in Deutschland*, Düsseldorf, 1981, pp. 109–26

——, 'Wahlanalyse im historischen Kontext. Zu Kontinuität und Wandel von Wahlverhalten', *Historische Zeitschrift*, vol. 234, 1982, pp. 337–57

——, 'Die Vorgeschichte: Das Parteiensystem in den preußischen Westprovinzen und in Lippe-Detmold 1871–1933', in Ulrich v. Alemann (ed.), *Parteien und Wahlen in Nordrhein-Westfalen*, Cologne, 1985, pp. 22–47

——, *Vom Revier zum Ruhrgebiet. Wahlen – Parteien – Politische Kultur*, Essen, 1986

—— in collab. with Wolfgang Jäger and Uwe Dorow, 'Politische Gesellschaft und Politische Kultur im Ruhrgebiet 1848–1987', in Dietmar Petzina et al. (eds), *Das Ruhrgebiet im Industriezeitalter*, vol. 2, Düsseldorf, 1990

——, 'Regionale politische Kultur: ein sinnvolles Konzept?', in Dieter Oberndörfer and Karl Schmitt (eds), *Parteien und regionale politische Traditionen in der Bundesrepublik Deutschland*, Berlin, 1990

Schmidtchen, Gerhard, *Protestanten und Katholiken. Soziologische Analyse konfessioneller Kultur*, Berne, 1973

Schmitt, Karl (ed.), *Wahlen, Parteieliten, politische Einstellungen. Neuere Forschungsergebnisse*, Frankfurt, 1989

Sheehan, James, *German Liberalism in the Nineteenth Century*, Chicago, 1978

Steinbach, Peter, 'Stand und Methode der historischen Wahlforschung. Bemerkungen zur interdisziplinären Kooperation von moderner Sozialgeschichte und den politisch-historischen Sozialwissenschaften am Beispiel der Reichstagswahlen im deutschen Kaiserreich', in H. Kaelble et al., *Probleme der Modernisierung in Deutschland. Sozialhistorische Studien zum 19. und 20. Jahrhundert*, Opladen, 1978, pp. 171–234

——, 'Historische Wahlforschung', *Archiv für Sozialgeschichte*, vol. 21, 1981, pp. 499–526

——, 'Modernisierungstheorie und historische Beteiligung. Zur Analyse politischer Partizipation im langfristigen Wandel', in H. Kaelble et al. (eds), *Arbeit, Mobilität, Partizipation, Protest. Gesellschaftlicher Wandel in Deutschland im 19. und 20. Jahrhundert*, Opladen, 1986, pp. 36–65

Thränhardt, Dietrich, *Wahlen und politische Strukturen in Bayern 1848–1953. Historisch-soziologische Untersuchungen zum Entstehen und zur Neuerrichtung eines Parteiensystems*, Düsseldorf, 1973

Urwin, Derek, 'Germany: Continuity and Change in Electoral Politics', in Richard Rose (ed.), *Electoral Behavior: A Comparative Handbook*, New York, 1974, pp. 109–70

Vogel, Bernhard, and Peter Haungs, *Wahlkampf und Wählertradition. Eine Studie zur Bundestagswahl von 1961*, Cologne, 1965

Vogel, Bernhard, Dieter Nohlen and Rainer-Olaf Schultze, *Wahlen in Deutschland. Theorie – Geschichte – Dokumente 1848–1970*, Berlin, 1971

Weitzel, Kurt, 'Konfessionelle Parteien in Rheinhessen 1862–1933', *Archiv für Hessische Geschichte und Altertumskunde*, vol. 41, 1983, pp. 151–96

Zang, Gert (ed.), *Arbeiterleben in einer Randregion. Die allmähliche Entstehung der Arbeiterbewegung in einer rasch wachsenden Industriestadt. Singen am Hohentwiel 1895–1933*, Constance, 1987

II Kaiserreich and Historical Origins

Aschoff, Hans-Georg, *Welfische Bewegung und politischer Katholizismus 1866–1918. Die Deutschhannoversche Partei und das Zentrum in der Provinz Hannover während des Kaiserreiches*, Düsseldorf, 1988

Becker, Winfried, 'Kulturkampf als Vorwand: Die Kolonialwahlen von 1907 und das Problem der Parlamentarisierung des Reiches', *Historisches Jahrbuch*, vol. 106, 1986, pp. 59–84

Bendikat, Elfi, *Wahlkämpfe in Europa 1884 bis 1889. Parteiensysteme und Politikstile in Deutschland, Frankreich und Großbritannien*, Wiesbaden, 1988

——, 'Politikstile, Konfliktlinien und Lagerstruktur im deutschen, britischen und französischen Parteiensystem des späten 19. Jahrhunderts', *Politische Vierteljahresschrift*, vol. 30, Opladen, 1989, pp. 482–502

Best, Heinrich, 'Politische Modernisierung und parlamentarische Führungsgruppen in Deutschland 1867–1918', *Historische Sozialforschung*, vol. 13, 1988, p. 5–75

——, *Die Männer von Bildung und Besitz. Struktur und Handeln parlamentarischer Führungsgruppen in Deutschland und Frankreich 1848/49*, Düsseldorf, 1989

Blackbourn, David, *Class, Religion and Local Politics in Wilhelmine Germany. The Centre Party in Württemberg before 1914*, Wiesbaden, 1980

——, 'Die Zentrumspartei und die deutschen Katholiken während des Kulturkampfes und danach', in Otto Pflanze (ed.), *Innenpolitische Probleme des Bismarck-Reiches*, Munich, 1983, pp. 73–94

——, 'Peasants and Politics in Germany 1871–1914', *European History Quarterly*, vol. 14, 1984, pp. 47–75

Boll, Friedhelm, *Massenbewegungen in Niedersachsen 1906–1920. Eine sozialgeschicht-liche Untersuchung zu den unterschiedlichen Entwicklungstypen Braunschweig und Hannover*, Bonn, 1981

Brandt, Hartwig, *Parlamentarismus in Württemberg 1819–1870. Anatomie eines deut-schen Landtags*, Düsseldorf, 1987

Breuilly, John, 'Liberalismus oder Sozialdemokratie? Ein Vergleich der briti-schen und deutschen politischen Arbeiterbewegung zwischen 1850 und 1875', in Jürgen Kocka (ed.), *Europäische Arbeiterbewegungen im 19. Jahrhundert. Deutschland, Österreich, England und Frankreich im Vergleich*, Göttingen, 1983, pp. 129–66

Büsch, Otto, 'Parteien und Wahlen in Deutschland bis zum Ersten Weltkrieg: Gedanken und Thesen zu einem Leitthema für Forschung und Unterricht über die Geschichte der "Industriegesellschaft" im 19. und frühen 20. Jahrhundert', *Abhandlungen aus der Pädagogischen Hochschule Berlin*, vol. 1, 1974, pp. 178–264

Chickering, Roger, *We Men Who Feel Most German: A Cultural Study of the Pan-German League 1886–1914*, Boston, 1984

Claggett, William et al., 'Political Leadership and the Development of Political Cleavages: Imperial Germany, 1871–1912', *American Journal of Political Science*, vol. 26, 1982, pp. 643–64

Conrad, Horst et al. (eds), *Preußische Parlamentarier. Ein Photoalbum 1859–1867*, Düsseldorf, 1986

Conze, Werner, 'Politische Willensbildung im deutschen Kaiserreich als For-schungsaufgabe historischer Wahlsoziologie', in Helmut Berding et al. (eds), *Vom Staat des Ancien Régime zum modernen Parteienstaat. Festschrift für Theodor Schieder*, Munich, 1978, pp. 331–47

Ditt, Karl, *Industrialisierung, Arbeiterschaft und Arbeiterbewegung in Bielefeld 1850–1914*, Dortmund, 1982

Dorneich, Julius, *Franz Josef Buß und die katholische Bewegung in Baden*, Freiburg, 1979

Dowe, Dieter, 'Zur Frühgeschichte der Arbeiterbewegung im Bergischen Land bis 1875', in K. Düwell and W. Köllmann (eds), *Rheinland – Westfalen im Industriezeitalter*, vol. 2, Wuppertal, 1984, pp. 148–69

Ehrle, Peter Michael, *Volksvertretungen im Vormärz. Studien zur Zusammensetzung. Wahl und Funktion der deutschen Landtage im Spannungsfeld zwischen monarchischem Prinzip und ständischer Repräsentation*, 2 vols, Frankfurt, 1979

Evans, Richard J. (ed.), *Society and Politics in Wilhelmine Germany*, London, 1978

Fairbairn, Brett, *The German Elections of 1898 and 1903*, Ph. D., Oxford, 1987

Geller, Helmut, 'Sozialstrukturelle Voraussetzungen für die Durchsetzung der Sozialform "Katholizismus" in Deutschland in der ersten Hälfte des 19. Jahrhunderts', in Karl Gabriel and Franz-Xaver Kaufmann (eds), *Zur Soziologie des Katholizismus*, Mainz, 1980, pp. 66–88

Grünthal, Günther, *Parlamentarismus in Preußen 1848/49–1857/58. Preußischer Kons-titutionalismus – Parlament und Regierung in der Reaktionsära*, Düsseldorf, 1982

Guttsmann, W. L., *The German Social Democratic Party, 1875–1933: From Ghetto to*

Government, London, 1981

Hamerow, Theodore S., 'The Elections to the Frankfurt Parliament', *The Journal of Modern History*, vol. 33, 1961, pp. 15–32

——, *The Social Foundations of German Unification*, 2 vols, Princeton, 1969/72

Haunfelder, Bernd, and Klaus E. Pollmann (eds), *Reichstag des Norddeutschen Bundes 1867–1870. Historische Photographien und biographisches Handbuch*, Düsseldorf, 1989

Herzig, Arno, 'Organisationsprobleme der Sozialdemokratie im Ruhrgebiet im 19. Jahrhundert', in Ludger Heid and Julius H. Schoeps, *Arbeit und Alltag im Revier*, Duisburg, 1985, pp. 6–21

——, D. Langewiesche and A. Sywottek (eds), *Arbeiter in Hamburg*, Hamburg, 1983

Hiery, Hermann, *Reichstagswahlen im Reichsland. Ein Beitrag zur Landesgeschichte von Elsaß-Lothringen und zur Wahlgeschichte des Deutschen Reiches 1871–1918*, Düsseldorf, 1986

Hirschfelder, Heinrich, *Die bayerische Sozialdemokratie 1864–1914*, 2 vols, Erlangen, 1979

Hunt, James Clark, *The People's Party in Württemberg and Southern Germany 1890–1914*, Stuttgart, 1975

Immerfall, Stefan, and Peter Steinbach (eds), 'Politisierung und Nationalisierung deutscher Regionen im Kaiserreich', in Dirk Berg-Schlosser and Jakob Schissler (eds), *Politische Kultur in Deutschland. Bilanz und Perspektiven der Forschung*, Opladen, 1987, pp. 68–79

Klein, Thomas, 'Reichstagswahlen und -abgeordnete der Provinz Sachsen und Anhalts 1867–1918: Ein Überlick', in W. Schlesinger (ed.), *Festschrift für Friedrich von Zahn, vol. 1: Zur Geschichte und Volkskunde Mitteldeutschlands*, Cologne, 1968, pp. 65–141

Langewiesche, D., *Liberalismus und Demokratie in Württemberg zwischen Revolution und Reichsgründung*, Düsseldorf, 1974

——, 'Die Anfänge der deutschen Parteien. Partei, Fraktion und Verein in der Deutschen Revolution von 1848/1849', *Geschichte und Gesellschaft*, vol. 4, 1978, pp. 324–61

—— (ed.), *Die deutsche Revolution von 1848/49*, Darmstadt, 1983

Lipp, Carola, and Wolfgang Kaschuba, 'Wasser und Brot. Politische Kultur im Alltag der Vormärz- und Revolutionsjahre', *Geschichte und Gesellschaft*, vol. 10, 1984, pp. 320–51

Loth, Wilfred, *Katholiken im Kaiserreich. Der politische Katholizismus in der Krise des wilhelminischen Deutschlands*, Düsseldorf, 1984

Mann, Bernhard, *Biographisches Handbuch für das Preußische Abgeordnetenhaus 1867–1918*, Düsseldorf, 1988

McLeod, Hugh, 'Protestantism and the Working Class in Imperial Germany', *European Studies Review*, vol. 12, 1982, pp. 323–44

Na'aman, S., *Der deutsche Nationalverein*, Düsseldorf, 1987

Niehuss, Merith, 'Parteien, Wahlen und Arbeiterbewegung in München 1890–1910', in Friedrich Prinz and Marita Kraus (eds), *München um 1900*,

Munich, 1988

Nipperdey, Thomas, *Die Organisation der deutschen Parteien vor 1918*, Düsseldorf, 1961

——, *Religion im Kaiserreich. Deutschland 1870–1918*, Munich, 1988

Nolan, Mary, *Social Democracy and Society: Working Class Radicalism in Düsseldorf 1890–1920*, New York, 1981

Obenaus, Herbert, *Anfänge des Parlamentarismus in Preußen bis 1848*, Düsseldorf, 1984

Offermann, T., *Arbeiterbewegung und liberales Bürgertum in Deutschland, 1850–1863*, Bonn, 1979

——, 'Die regionale Ausbreitung der frühen deutschen Arbeiterbewegung 1848/49–1860/64', *Geschichte und Gesellschaft*, vol. 13, 1987, pp. 419–47

Padtberg, B.-C., *Rheinischer Liberalismus in Köln während der politischen Reaktion in Preußen nach 1848/49*, Cologne, 1985

Pflanze, Otto (ed.), *Innenpolitische Probleme des Bismarck-Reiches*, Munich, 1983

Pollmann, Klaus Erich, *Parlamentarismus im Norddeutschen Bund 1867–1870*, Düsseldorf, 1985

——, 'Arbeiterwahlen im Norddeutschen Bund 1867–1870', *Geschichte und Gesellschaft*, vol. 15, 1989, pp. 164–95

Pulzer, Peter, *The Rise of Political Anti-Semitism in Germany and Austria*, New York, 1964

Rauscher, Anton (ed.), *Der soziale und politische Katholizismus. Entwicklungslinien in Deutschland 1803–1863*, Munich, 1981

Ritter, Gerhard A., *Die Arbeiterbewegung im wilhelminischen Deutschland*, 2nd edition, Berlin, 1963

—— (ed.), *Die deutschen Parteien vor 1918*, Cologne, 1973

——, *Wahlgeschichtliches Arbeitsbuch. Materialien zur Statistik des Kaiserreiches 1871–1918*, Munich, 1980

——, *Die deutschen Parteien 1830–1914. Parteien und Gesellschaft im konstitutionellen Regierungssystem*, Göttingen, 1985

——, 'Die Sozialdemokratie im deutschen Kaiserreich in sozialgeschichtlicher Perspektive', *Historische Zeitschrift*, vol. 249, 1989, pp. 295–362

—— (ed.), *Der Aufstieg der sozialistischen Arbeiterorganisationen zur Massenbewegung im deutschen Kaiserreich*, Munich, 1990

Rohe, Karl, 'Konfession, Klasse und lokale Gesellschaft als Bestimmungsfaktoren des Wahlverhaltens. Überlegungen und Problematisierungen am Beispiel des historischen Ruhrgebiets', in Lothar Albertin and Werner Link (eds), *Politische Parteien auf dem Weg zur parlamentarischen Demokratie in Deutschland. Entwicklungslinien bis zur Gegenwart*, Düsseldorf, 1981, pp. 106–26

——, 'Die verspätete Region. Thesen und Hypothesen zur Wahlentwicklung im Ruhrgebiet vor 1914', in Peter Steinbach (ed.), *Probleme politischer Partizipation im Modernisierungsprozeß*, Stuttgart, 1982, pp. 231–52

——, 'Die Ruhrgebietssozialdemokratie im Wilhelminischen Kaiserreich und ihr politischer und kultureller Kontext', in Gerhard A. Ritter (ed.), *Der Durchbruch der Sozialdemokratie zur Massenbewegung*, Munich, 1990

Rossmeisl, Dieter, *Arbeiterschaft und Sozialdemokratie in Nürnberg 1890–1914*, Nuremberg, 1977

Saldern, Adelheid von, *Auf dem Wege zum Arbeiter-Reformismus. Parteialltag in sozialdemokratischer Provinz Göttingen 1870–1920*, Frankfurt, 1984

Schieder, W. (ed.), *Liberalismus in der Gesellschaft des deutschen Vormärz*, Göttingen, 1983

Schloßmacher, Norbert, *Düsseldorf in der Bismarckzeit. Politik und Wahlen, Parteien und Verbände*, Düsseldorf, 1985

Schröder, Wilhelm Heinz, *Sozialdemokratische Reichstagsabgeordnete und Reichstagskandidaten 1898–1918. Biographisch-Statistisches Handbuch*, vol. 2, Düsseldorf, 1986

Schulte, Wolfgang, *Struktur und Entwicklung des Parteisystems im Königreich Württemberg. Versuche zu einer quantitativen Analyse der Wahlergebnisse*, Ph. D., Mannheim, 1970

Schwentker, Wolfgang, *Konservative Vereine und Revolution in Preußen 1848/49. Die Konstituierung des Konservatismus als Partei*, Düsseldorf, 1988

Sepaintner, Fred Ludwig, *Die Reichstagswahlen im Großherzogtum Baden. Ein Beitrag zur Wahlgeschichte im Kaiserreich*, Frankfurt, 1983

Sheehan, James J., 'Klasse und Partei im Kaiserreich: Einige Gedanken zur Sozialgeschichte der deutschen Politik', in Otto Pflanze (ed.), *Innenpolitische Probleme des Bismarck-Reiches*, Munich, 1983, pp. 1–24

Siemann, W., *Die deutsche Revolution von 1848/49*, Frankfurt, 1985

Specht, Fritz, and Paul Schwabe, *Die Reichstagswahlen von 1867–1903. Eine Statistik der Reichstagswahlen nebst den Programmen der Parteien und einem Verzeichnis der gewählten Abgeordneten*, 2nd edition, Berlin, 1904

Sperber, Jonathan, *Popular Catholicism in 19th Century Germany*, Princeton, 1984

Steinbach, Peter, *Wahlen im deutschen Kaiserreich. Studien zur Mobilisierung und Politisierung der Wählerschaft im 19. Jahrhundert. Zugleich ein Beitrag zur regionalspezifischen Rezeption der Politik unter Berücksichtigung modernisierungsspezifischer Fragestellungen*, Habil., Berlin, 1978

Suval, Stanley, *Electoral Politics in Wilhelmine Germany*, Chapel Hill, 1985

White, Dan S., *The Splintered Party. National Liberalism in Hessen and the Reich, 1867–1918*, Cambridge, Mass., 1976

Wölk, Monika, *Der preußische Volksschulabsolvent als Reichstagswähler 1871–1912. Ein Beitrag zur Historischen Wahlforschung in Deutschland*, Berlin, 1980

Zwahr, Hartmut, *Zur Konstituierung des Proletariats als Klasse. Strukturuntersuchungen über das Leipziger Proletariat während der industriellen Revolution*, Berlin, 1978

——, 'Die deutsche Arbeiterbewegung im Länder- und Territorienvergleich 1875', *Geschichte und Gesellschaft*, vol. 13, 1987, pp. 448–507

III   Weimar Republic

Allen, William S., *The Nazi Seizure of Power: The Experience of a Single German Town, 1930–1945*, revised edition, New York, 1984

Broszat, Martin et al. (eds), *Bayern in der NS-Zeit*, vol. 1: *Soziale Lage und politisches Verhalten der Bevölkerung im Spiegel vertraulicher Berichte*, Munich, 1977

—— (eds), *Bayern in der NS-Zeit*, vol. 2: *Herrschaft und Gesellschaft im Konflikt, Teil A*, Munich, 1979

—— (eds), *Bayern in der NS-Zeit*, vol. 3: *Herrschaft und Gesellschaft im Konflikt, Teil B*, Munich, 1981

—— (eds), *Bayern in der NS-Zeit*, vol. 4: *Herrschaft und Gesellschaft im Konflikt, Teil C*, Munich, 1981

—— (eds), *Bayern in der NS-Zeit*, vol. 5: *Die Parteien KPD, SPD, BVP in Verfolgung und Widerstand*, Munich, 1983

—— (eds), *Bayern in der NS-Zeit*, vol. 6: *Die Herausforderung des Einzelnen. Geschichten über Widerstand und Verfolgung*, Munich, 1983

Broszat, Martin, 'Zur Struktur der NS-Massenbewegung', *Vierteljahresheft für Zeitgeschichte*, vol. 31, 1983, pp. 52–76

Buchloh, Ingrid, *Die nationalsozialistische Machtergreifung in Duisburg. Eine Fallstudie*, Duisburg, 1980

Burnham, Walter Dean, 'Political Immunization and Political Confessionalism: The United States and Weimar Germany', *The Journal of Interdisciplinary History*, vol. 4, 1973, pp. 1–30

Childers, Thomas, 'The Social Bases of the National Socialist Vote', *Journal of Contemporary History*, vol. 11, 1976, pp. 17–42

——, 'Inflation, Stabilization and Political Realignment in Germany 1919–1928', in Gerald D. Feldman et al. (eds), *Die deutsche Inflation. Eine Zwischenbilanz*, Berlin, 1982, pp. 409–31

——, *The Nazi Voter. The Social Foundations of Fascism in Germany, 1919–1933*, Chapel Hill, 1983

—— (ed.), *The Formation of the Nazi Constituency 1919–1933*, London, 1986

Evans, Richard J., and Dick Geary (eds), *The German Unemployed. Experiences and Consequences of Mass Unemployment from the Weimar Republic to the Third Reich*, London, 1987

Falter, Jürgen W., and Dirk Hänisch, 'Die Anfälligkeit von Arbeitern gegenüber der NSDAP bei den Reichstagswahlen 1928–1933', *Archiv für Sozialgeschichte*, vol. 26, 1986, pp. 179–216

Falter, Jürgen W., et al., 'Arbeitslosigkeit und Nationalismus. Eine empirische Analyse des Beitrages der Massenerwerbslosigkeit zu den Wahlerfolgen der NSDAP 1932 und 1933', *Kölner Zeitschrift für Soziologie und Sozialpsychologie*, vol. 35, 1983, pp. 525–54

Falter, Jürgen, W., Thomas Lindenberger and Siegfried Schumann, *Wahlen und Abstimmungen in der Weimarer Republik. Materialien zum Wahlverhalten 1919–1933*, Munich, 1986

Falter, Jürgen W., and Reinhard Zintl, 'The Economic Crisis of the 1930's and the Nazi Vote', *Journal of Interdisciplinary History*, vol. 19, 1988, pp. 55–87

Falter, Jürgen W., 'Die Wählerpotentiale politischer Teilkulturen 1920–1933', in Detlev Lehnert and Klaus Megerle (eds), *Politische Identität und nationale Gedenktage. Zur politischen Kultur in der Weimarer Republik*, Opladen, 1989, pp. 281–305

Fischer, Conan, *Stormtroopers: A Social, Economic, and Ideological Analysis 1929–35*, Winchester, Mass., 1983

——, 'Turning the Tide? The KPD and Right Radicalism in German Industrial Relations, 1925–8', *Journal of Contemporary History*, vol. 24, 1989, pp. 575–97

Grill, Johnpeter H., *The Nazi Movement in Baden, 1920–1945*, Chapel Hill, 1983

Hagtvet, Bernt, 'The Theory of Mass Society and the Collapse of the Weimar Republic: A Re-Examination', in Stein U. Larsen et al. (eds), *Who were the Fascists? Social Roots of European Fascism*, Oslo, 1980

Hamilton, Richard F., *Who Voted for Hitler?*, Princeton, 1982

——, 'Hitler's Electoral Support: Recent Findings and Theoretical Implications', *Canadian Journal of Sociology*, vol. 11, 1986, pp. 1–34

Hänisch, Dirk, *Sozialstrukturelle Bestimmungsgründe des Wahlverhaltens in der Weimarer Republik. Eine Aggregatdatenanalyse der Ergebnisse der Reichstagswahlen 1924 bis 1933*, Duisburg, 1983

Heberle, Rudolf, *Landbevölkerung und Nationalsozialismus*, Stuttgart, 1963

Hennig, Eike, 'Regionale Unterschiede bei der Entstehung des deutschen Faschismus. Ein Plädoyer für "mikroanalytische Studien" zur Enforschung der NSDAP', *Politische Vierteljahresschrift*, vol. 21, 1980, pp. 152–73

—— (ed.), *Hessen unterm Hakenkreuz. Studien zur Durchsetzung der NSDAP in Hessen*, Frankfurt, 1983

——, 'Die Wahlentwicklung im Landkreis Kassel (1928–1933). Ein Hinweis zur Diskussion der politischen Kultur im "roten Landkreis"', *Zeitschrift des Vereins für hessische Geschichte und Landeskunde*, vol. 92, 1987

Hoffmann, Herbert, *Im Gleichschritt in die Diktatur? Die nationalsozialistische 'Machtergreifung' in Heidelberg und Mannheim 1930 bis 1935*, Frankfurt, 1985

Horstmann, Johannes, 'Katholiken und Reichstagswahlen 1920–1933. Ausgewählte Aspekte mit statistischem Material', *Jahrbuch für Christliche Sozialwissenschaften*, vol. 26, 1985, pp. 63–95

——, 'Katholiken, Reichspräsidentenwahlen und Volksentscheide. Ausgewählte Aspekte zum Wahlverhalten der Katholiken in der Weimarer Republik mit statistischem Material', *Jahrbuch für christliche Sozialwissenschaften*, vol. 27, 1986, pp. 61–93

Jones, Larry Eugene, 'Die Rückwirkungen der Inflation auf die Entwicklung des deutschen Parteiensystems in der Weimarer Republik', in Otto Büsch and Gerald D. Feldman (eds), *Historische Prozesse der deutschen Inflation 1914 bis 1924. Ein Tagungsbericht*, Berlin, 1978, pp. 288–95

——, 'Inflation, Revaluation and the Crisis of Middle-Class Politics. A Study of the Dissolution of the German Party System 1923–1928', *Central European History*, vol. 12, 1979, pp. 143–69

——, 'The Dissolution of the Bourgeois Party System in the Weimar Republic', in Richard Bessel and E. J. Feuchtwanger (eds), *Social Change and Political Development in Weimar Germany*, London, 1981

Kater, Michael, 'Methodologische Überlegungen über Möglichkeiten und Grenzen einer Analyse der sozialen Zusammensetzung der NSDAP von

1925 bis 1945', in Reinhard Mann (ed.), *Die Nationalsozialisten. Analysen faschistischer Bewegungen*, Stuttgart, 1980, pp. 155–85

——, *The Nazi Party. A Social Profile of Members and Leaders 1919–1945*, Cambridge, Mass., 1983

——, 'Generationskonflikt als Entwicklungsfaktor in der NS-Bewegung vor 1933', *Geschichte und Gesellschaft*, vol. 11, 1985, pp. 217–43

Kaufmann, Doris, *Katholisches Milieu in Münster 1928–1933. Politische Aktionsformen und geschlechtsspezifische Verhaltensräume*, Düsseldorf, 1984

Kershaw, Ian, 'Ideology, Propaganda, and the Rise of the Nazi Party', in Peter D. Stachura (ed.), *The Nazi Machtergreifung*, London, 1983, pp. 162–81

Koshar, Rudy, 'Two "Nazisms": The Social Context of Nazi Mobilization in Marburg and Tübingen', *Social History*, vol. 7, 1982, pp. 27–42

——, *Social Life, Local Politics and Nazism: Marburg 1880–1935*, Chapel Hill, 1986

——, 'From Stammtisch to Party: Nazi Joiners and the Contradictions of Grass Roots Fascism in Weimar Germany', *Journal of Modern History*, vol. 59, 1987

Kühr, Herbert, *Parteien und Wahlen im Stadt- und Landkreis Essen in der Zeit der Weimarer Republik. Unter besonderer Berücksichtigung des Verhältnisses von Sozialstruktur und politischen Wahlen*, Düsseldorf, 1973

Lepsius, M. Rainer, *Extremer Nationalismus. Strukturbedingungen vor der nationalsozialistischen Machtergreifung*, Stuttgart, 1966

Lohmöller, Jan-Bernd et al., 'Unemployment and the Rise of National Socialism. Contradicting Results from Different Regional Aggregations', in Peter Nijkamp (ed.), *Measuring the Unmeasurable*, Dordrecht, 1985, pp. 357–70

Lucas, Erhard, *Zwei Formen von Radikalismus in der deutschen Arbeiterbewegung*, Frankfurt, 1976

Maehl, William H., *The German Socialist Party. Champion of the First Republic 1918–1933*, Philadelphia, 1986

Mann, Reinhard (ed.), *Die Nationalsozialisten. Analysen faschistischer Bewegungen*, Stuttgart, 1980

Manstein, Peter, *Die Mitglieder und Wähler der NSDAP 1919–1933. Untersuchungen zu ihrer schichtmäßigen Zusammensetzung*, Frankfurt, 1988

Martiny, Martin, 'Sozialdemokratie und junge Generation am Ende der Weimarer Republik', in Wolfgang Luthardt (ed.), *Sozial demokratische Arbeiterbewegung und Weimarer Republik. Materialien zur gesellschaftlichen Entwicklung 1927–1933*, vol. 1, Frankfurt, 1978, pp. 56–64

Meckstroth, Theodore W., *Conditions of Partisan Realignments. A Study of Electoral Change*, Ph. D., Minnesota, 1972

Milatz, Alfred, *Wähler und Wahlen in der Weimarer Republik*, Bonn, 1965

Mühlberger, Detlef Willi, *The Rise of National Socialism in Westphalia 1920–1933*, Ph. D., London, 1975

Neumann, Sigmund, *Die Parteien der Weimarer Republik. Mit einer Einführung von Karl Dietrich Bracher*, 4th edition, Stuttgart, 1977

Noakes, Jeremy, *The Nazi Party in Lower Saxony*, London, 1971

Passchier, Nico, 'The Electoral Geography of the Nazi Landslide. The Need

for Community Studies', in Stein U. Larsen et al. (eds), *Who were the Fascists?*
Social Roots of European Fascism, Oslo, 1980, pp. 283–300

Paul, Johann, *Vom Volksrat zum Volkssturm: Bergisch-Gladbach und Bamberg*,
Bergisch-Gladbach, 1988

Rauh-Kühne, Cornelia, *Ettlingen 1918–1939, Wirtschaft, Gesellschaft und Politische
Kultur in einer südwestdeutschen Kleinstadt. Fragmentierte Gesellschaft und Nationalsozialismus*, Ph. D., Tübingen, 1989

Ritter, Gerhard A., 'Kontinuität und Umformung des deutschen Parteiensystems 1918 bis 1920', in Gerhard A. Ritter, *Arbeiterbewegung, Parteien und
Parlamentarismus. Aufsätze zur deutschen Sozial- und Verfassungsgeschichte des 19.
und 20. Jahrhunderts*, Göttingen, 1976, pp. 116–57

Rosenhaft, Eve, *Beating the Fascists? The German Communists and Political Violence
1929–1933*, Cambridge, 1983

Rünger, Gabriele, *Wer wählte die NSDAP? Eine lokale Fallstudie im Kreis Euskirchen
an Hand der Ergebnisse der politischen Wahlen 1920–1933*, Ph. D., Bonn, 1984

Ruppert, Karsten, 'Der Politische Katholizismus im Rheinland und in West-
falen zur Zeit der Weimarer Republik', in K. Düwell and Wolfgang
Köllmann (eds), *Vom Ende der Weimarer Republik bis zum Land Nordrhein-
Westfalen*, Wuppertal, 1984, pp. 76–97

Schanbacher, Eberhard, *Parlamentarische Wahlen und Wahlsystem in der Weimarer
Republik. Wahlgesetzgebung und Wahlreform im Reich und in den Ländern*,
Düsseldorf, 1982

Schlegel-Batton, Thomas, 'Politische Kultur der Mittelschichten im Übergang
zum Nationalsozialismus', in Dirk Berg-Schlosser and Jakob Schissler (eds),
*Politische Kultur in Deutschland: Bilanz und Perspektiven der Forschung (Politische
Vierteljahresschrift*, special issue: vol. 18), Opladen, 1987, pp. 112–22

Schnabel, Thomas (ed.), *Die Machtergreifung in Südwestdeutschland. Das Ende der
Weimarer Republik in Baden und Württemberg 1928–1933*, Stuttgart, 1982

——, 'Wer wählte Hitler?', *Geschichte und Gesellschaft*, vol. 8, 1982, pp. 116–33

Shiveley, W. Philipps, 'Party Identification, Party Choice and Voting Stability:
The Weimar Case', *American Political Science Review*, vol. 66, 1972, pp.
1203–25

Stachura, Peter D., 'Der kritische Wendepunkt? Die NSDAP und die Reichstagswahlen vom 20. Mai 1928', *Vierteljahreshefte für Zeitgeschichte*, vol. 26,
1978, pp. 66–99

—— (ed.), *Unemployment and the Great Depression in Weimar Germany*, London,
1986

Stokes, Lawrence D. (ed.), *Kleinstadt und Nationalsozialismus. Ausgewählte Dokumente zur Geschichte von Eutin 1918–1945*, Neumünster, 1984

Striesow, Jan, *Die Deutschnationale Volkspartei und die Völkisch-Radikalen 1918–1922*,
2 vols, Frankfurt, 1981

Winkler, Heinrich August, *Der Schein der Normalität. Arbeiter und Arbeiterbewegung
in der Weimarer Republik 1924 bis 1930*, Berlin, 1985

——, *Von der Revolution zur Stabilisierung, Arbeiter und Arbeiterbewegung in der
Weimarer Republik 1918 bis 1924*, 2nd edition, Berlin, 1985

——, *Der Weg in die Katastrophe. Arbeiter und Arbeiterbewegung in der Weimarer Republik 1930 bis 1933*, Berlin, 1987

Zofka, Zdenek, *Die Ausbreitung des Nationalsozialismus auf dem Land*, Munich, 1979

IV Federal Republic

Baer, Christian-Claus, and Erwin Faul (eds), *Das deutsche Wahlwunder*, Frankfurt, 1953

Baker, Kendall L., *Germany Transformed. Political Culture and the New Politics*, Cambridge, Mass., 1981

Becker, Winfried, *CDU und CSU 1945–1950. Vorläufer, Gründung und regionale Entwicklung bis zum Entstehen der CDU-Bundespartei*, Mainz, 1987

Berger, Manfred et al., 'Bundestagswahl 1976: Politik und Sozialstruktur oder: Wider die falsche Einheit der Wahlforschung', *Zeitschrift für Parlamentsfragen*, vol. 8, 1977, pp. 197–231

——, 'Die Konsolidierung der Wende. Eine Analyse der Bundestagswahl 1987', *Zeitschrift für Parlamentsfragen*, vol. 18, 1987, pp. 253–84

Bethscheider, Monika, *Wahlkampfführung und politische Weltbilder: eine systematische Analyse des Wahlkampfes der Bundesparteien in den Bundestagswahlkämpfen 1976 und 1980*, Frankfurt, 1987

Blankenburg, Erhard, *Kirchliche Bindung und Wahlverhalten. Die sozialen Faktoren bei der Wahlentscheidung in Nordrhein-Westfalen 1961 bis 1966*, Olten, 1967

——, 'Die politische Spaltung der westdeutschen Arbeiterschaft', *Archives Européennes de Sociologie*, vol. 10, 1969, pp. 3–24

Brand, K.-W. et al., *Aufbruch in eine andere Gesellschaft. Neue soziale Bewegungen in der Bundesrepublik*, Frankfurt, 1983

Brand, W., and H. Honolka, *Ökologische Betroffenheit, Lebenswelt und Wahlentscheidung*, Opladen, 1987

Brinkmann, Heinz-Ulrich, 'Wahlverhalten der "neuen Mittelschicht" in der Bundesrepublik', *Aus Politik und Zeitgeschichte. Beilage zur Wochenzeitung Das Parlament*, vol. B 30–1, 1988, pp. 19–32

Buchhaas, Dorothee, *Die Volkspartei. Programmatische Entwicklung der CDU 1950–1973*, Düsseldorf, 1981

Bürklin, Wilhelm P., *Grüne Politik. Ideologische Zyklen, Wähler und Parteiensystem*, Opladen, 1984

——, *Wählerverhalten und Wertewandel*, Opladen, 1988

Dalton, Russel J., '"The West German party system between two ages"', in J. Russell Dalton, Scott C. Flanagan and Paul Allen Beck (eds), *Electoral Change in Advanced Industrial Democracies*, Princeton, 1984, pp. 104–33

Dettling, Warnfried (ed.), *Deutsche Parteien im Wandel*, Munich, 1983

Döring, Herbert, and Gordon Smith, *Party Government and Political Culture in Western Germany*, London, 1982

Döring, Herbert, 'Wählen Industriearbeiter zunehmend konservativ? Die Bundesrepublik Deutschland im Westeuropäischen Vergleich', *Archiv für Sozialgeschichte*, vol. 29, 1989

Falke, Wolfgang, *Die Mitglieder der CDU. Eine empirische Studie zum Verhältnis von Mitglieder- und Organisationsstruktur der CDU 1971–1977*, Berlin, 1982

Falter, Jürgen W., *Faktoren der Wahlenscheidung. Eine wahlsoziologische Analyse am Beispiel der saarländischen Landtagswahl 1970*, Cologne, 1973

——, 'Kontinuität und Neubeginn. Die Bundestagswahl 1949 zwischen Weimar und Bonn', *Politische Vierteljahresschrift*, vol. 22, 1981, pp. 236–63

——, 'Bayerns Uhren gehen wirklich anders. Politische Verhaltens- und Einstellungsunterschiede zwischen Bayern und dem Rest der Bundesrepublik', *Zeitschrift für Parlamentsfragen*, vol. 13, 1982, pp. 504–21

——, Christian Fenner and Michael T. Greven (eds), *Politische Willensbildung und Interessenvermittlung*, Opladen, 1984

—— (ed.), *Wahlen und politische Einstellung in der Bundesrepublik Deutschland: neuere Entwicklungen der Forschung*, Frankfurt, 1989

Faul, Erwin (ed.), *Wahlen und Wähler in Westdeutschland*, Villingen, 1960

Feist, Ursula, Manfred Güllner and Klaus Liepelt, 'Strukturelle Angleichung und ideologische Polarisierung. Die Mitgliedschaft von SPD und CDU/CSU zwischen den sechziger und siebziger Jahren', *Politische Vierteljahresschrift*, vol. 18, 1977, pp. 257–78

Feist, Ursula, and Klaus Liepelt, 'Eine neue Scheidelinie. Nichtmaterielle Leitbilder und ihre Dynamik für das Parteiensystem in der Bundesrepublik Deutschland', *Journal für Sozialforschung*, vol. 23, 1983, pp. 26–39

——, 'Modernisierung zu Lasten der Großen. Wie die deutschen Volksparteien ihre Integrationskraft verlieren', *Journal für Sozialforschung*, vol. 27, 1987, pp. 277–95

Fogt, Helmut, and Pavel Uttitz, 'Die Wähler der Grünen 1980–1983: Systemkritischer neuer Mittelstand', *Zeitschrift für Parlamentsfragen*, vol. 15, 1984, pp. 210–26

Gluchowski, P., 'Lebensstile und Wandel der Wählerschaft in der Bundesrepublik Deutschland', *Aus Politik und Zeitgeschichte, Beilage zur Wochenzeitschrift Das Parlament*, vol. B. 12, 1987, pp. 18–32

——, and Hans-Joachim Veen, 'Nivellierungstendenzen in den Wähler- und Mitgliedschaften von CDU/CSU und SPD 1959–1979', *Zeitschrift für Parlamentsfragen*, vol. 10, 1979, pp. 312–31

Greven, Michael T., *Parteimitglieder. Ein empirischer Essay über das Alltagsbewußtsein in Parteien*, Opladen, 1987

——, 'Entwicklungsphasen des Parteiensystems in der Bundesrepublik Deutschland', *Gegenwartskunde*, vol. 2, 1989, pp. 167–79

Haungs, P., and E. Jesse (eds), *Parteien in der Krise? In- und ausländische Perspektiven*, Cologne, 1987

Hein, Dieter, *Zwischen liberaler Milieupartei und Nationaler Sammlungsbewegung. Gründung, Entwicklung und Struktur der Freien Demokratischen Partei 1945–1949*, Düsseldorf, 1985

Herzog, D., et al., *Politischer Wandel in West-Berlin. Wählerschaft und politische Führungsschicht Anfang der achtziger Jahre*, Opladen, 1987

Hoffmann, Hans-Jürgen, and Jürgen Krautwig, 'Die Landtagswahlen 1987/88 in der Bundesrepublik Deutschland: Kontinuität der Trends', *Journal für Sozialforschung*, vol. 28, 1988, pp. 193–215

Hofmann-Göttig, Joachim, *Die jungen Wähler. Zur Interpretation der Jungwählerdaten der Repräsentativen Wahlstatistik für Bundestag, Landtage und Europaparlament 1953–1984*, Frankfurt and New York, 1984

——, 'Die Neue Rechte: Die Männerparteien', *Aus Politik und Zeitgeschichte Beilage zur Wochenzeitschrift Das Parlament*, vol. B 41–2, 1989, pp. 21–31

Holtmann, Everhard, *Politik und Nichtpolitik. Lokale Erscheinungsformen politischer Kultur im frühen Nachkriegsdeutschland*, Opladen, 1987

——, 'Die neuen Lassalleaner. SPD und HJ-Generation nach 1945', in Martin Broszat et al. (eds), *Von Stalingrad zur Währungsreform. Zur Sozialgeschichte des Umbruchs in Deutschland*, Munich, 1988, pp. 169–210

Hoschka, Peter, and Hermann Schunck, 'Stabilität regionaler Wählerstrukturen in der Bundesrepublik', *Politische Vierteljahresschrift*, vol. 18, 1977, pp. 279–300

Jesse, Eckhard, *Wahlrecht zwischen Kontinuität und Reform. Eine Analyse der Wahlrechtsdiskussion und der Wahlrechtsänderungen in der Bundesrepublik Deutschland 1949–1982*, Düsseldorf, 1985

——, 'Die Bundestagswahlen von 1972 bis 1987 im Spiegel der Repräsentativen Wahlstatistik', *Zeitschrift für Parlamentsfragen*, vol. 18, 1987, pp. 232–42

——, *Wahlen. Bundesrepublik Deutschland im Vergleich*, Berlin, 1988

Jung, H., *Wirtschaftliche Einstellungen und Wahlverhalten in der Bundesrepublik*, Paderborn, 1982

Kaase, Max (ed.), 'Wahlsoziologie heute. Analysen aus Anlaß der Bundestagswahl 1976', *Politische Vierteljahresschrift*, vol. 18, 1977

Kaase, Max, and Klaus von Beyme (eds), *Elections & Parties*, Beverly Hills, 1978

Kaase, Max, and Hans-Dieter Klingemann (eds), *Wahlen und politisches System. Analysen aus Anlaß der Bundestagswahl 1980*, Opladen, 1983

Kaase, Max, and Hans-Dieter Klingemann (eds), *Wahlen und Wähler Analysen aus Anlaß der Bundestagswahl 1987*, Opladen, 1990

Kaltefleiter, Werner, 'Eine kritische Wahl. Anmerkungen zur Bundestagswahl 1983', *Aus Politik und Zeitgeschichte. Beilage zur Wochenzeitung Das Parlament*, vol. B 14, 1983, pp. 3–17

——, *Parteien im Umbruch. Ein Beitrag zur politischen Geschichte der Bundesrepublik Deutschland*, Düsseldorf, 1984

Kaste, Hermann, and Joachim Raschke, 'Zur Politik der Volkspartei', in Wolf-Dieter Narr (ed.), *Auf dem Weg zum Einparteienstaat*, Opladen, 1977, pp. 26–74

Klingemann, Hans-Dieter, *Bestimmungsgründe der Wahlentscheidung. Eine regionale Wahlanalyse*, Meisenheim, Glan, 1969

——, 'Politische und soziale Bedingungen der Wählerbewegungen zur NPD. Fallstudien Baden-Württemberg', *Sozialwissenschaftliches Jahrbuch für Politik*, vol. 2, 1971, pp. 563–601

——, 'West Germany', in Ivor Crewe and David Denver (eds), *Electoral Change in Western Democracies. Patterns and Sources of Electoral Volatility*, London, 1985, pp. 230–62

——, and Max Kaase (eds), *Wahlen und politischer Prozeß. Analysen aus Anlaß der Bundestagswahl 1983*, Opladen, 1986

Klotzbach, Kurt, *Der Weg zur Staatspartei. Programmatik, praktische Politik und Organisation der deutschen Sozialdemokratie 1945–1965*, Berlin, 1982

Kocka, Jürgen, and Michael Prinz, 'Vom "neuen Mittelstand" zum angestellten Arbeitnehmer', in Werner Conze and Rainer M. Lepsius (eds), *Sozialgeschichte der Bundesrepublik Deutschland. Beiträge zum Kontinuitätsproblem*, Stuttgart, 1983, pp. 210–55

Kohlsche, Andreas, *Wählerverhalten und Sozialstruktur in Schleswig-Holstein und Hamburg von 1947 bis 1983*, Opladen, 1985

Kolinsky, Eva (ed.), *The Greens in West Germany. Organisation and Policy Making*, Oxford, 1989

Konrad Adenauer Stiftung (ed.), *Kommunales Wahlverhalten*, Bonn, 1976

Kort-Krieger, Ute, 'Der realistische Wähler. Problemlösungskapazität von Parteien im Urteil ihrer Anhänger', *Politische Vierteljahresschrift*, vol. 27, 1986, pp. 290–310

Krockow, Christian Graf von (ed.), *Brauchen wir ein neues Parteiensystem*, Frankfurt, 1983

——, and Peter Lösche (eds), *Parteien in der Krise. Das Parteiensystem der Bundesrepublik und der Aufstand des Bürgerwillens*, Munich, 1986

Küchler, Manfred, 'Was leistet die empirische Wahlsoziologie?', *Politische Vierteljahresschrift*, vol. 18, 1977, pp. 145–68

——, 'Interessenwahrnehmungen und Wahlverhalten. Perspektiven und Ergebnisse der neueren Wahlforschung', *Zeitschrift für Politik* (new series), vol. 27, 1980, pp. 277–90

Kühr, Herbert (ed.), *Vom Milieu zur Volkspartei. Funktionen und Wandlungen der Parteien im kommunalen und regionalen Bereich*, Königstein, 1979

——, and Klaus Simon, *Lokalpartei und vorpolitischer Raum*, Melle, 1982

Leggewie, Claus, *Die Republikaner. Phantombild der neuen Rechten*, Berlin, 1989

Lepsius, M. Rainer, 'Sozialstruktur und soziale Schichtung in der Bundesrepublik Deutschland', in Richard Löwenthal and Hans-Peter Schwartz (eds), *Die zweite Republik. 25 Jahre Bundesrepublik Deutschland – eine Bilanz*, Stuttgart, 1974, pp. 263–88

——, 'Die Bundesrepublik Deutschland in der Kontinuität und Diskontinuität historischer Entwicklungen: Einige methodische Überlegungen', in Werner Conze und M. Rainer Lepsius (eds), *Sozialgeschichte der Bundesrepublik Deutschland*, Stuttgart, 1983, pp. 11–19

Lepsky, Norbert, 'Die Republikaner', *Aus Politik und Zeitgeschichte. Beilage zur Wochenzeitung Das Parlament*, vol. 18, B 41–2, 1989, pp. 3–9

Linz, Juan, *The Social Bases of German Politics*, Ph. D., New York, 1958

——, 'Cleavage and Consensus in West German Politics: The Early Fifties', in S. M. Lipset and Stein Rokkan (eds), *Party Systems and Voter Alignments:*

Cross-National Perspectives, New York, 1967, pp. 283–321

Merkl, Peter H., 'West Germany', in Peter H. Merkl (ed.), *Western European Party Systems. Trends and Prospects*, New York, 1980, pp. 21–60

Mielke, Gerd, *Sozialer Wandel und politische Dominanz in Baden-Württemberg. Eine politikwissenschaftlich-statistische Analyse des Zusammenhangs von Sozialstruktur und Wahlverhalten in einer ländlichen Region*, Berlin, 1987

Mintzel, Alf, 'Conservatism and Christian Democracy in the Federal Republic of Germany', in Zig Layton-Herny (ed.), *Conservative Politics in Western Europe*, London, 1982, pp. 131–59

——, *Die Volkspartei. Typus und Wirklichkeit*, Opladen, 1983

——, 'Gehen Bayerns Uhren wirklich anders?', *Zeitschrift für Parlamentsfragen*, vol. 18, 1987, pp. 77–93

——, and Heinrich Oberreuter (eds), *Parteien in der Bundesrepublik Deutschland*, Bonn, 1989

Mintzel, Alf, 'Großparteien im Parteienstaat der Bundesrepublik', *Aus Politik und Zeitgeschichte. Beilage zur Wochenzeitung Das Parlament*, vol. B 11, 1989, pp. 3–14

Müller-Rommel, Ferdinand, *Innerparteiliche Gruppierungen in der SPD. Eine empirische Studie über informell-organisierte Gruppierungen von 1969–1980*, Opladen, 1982

——, 'Zum Verhältnis von neuen sozialen Bewegungen und neuen Konfliktdimensionen in den politischen Systemen Westeuropas: Eine Empirische Analyse', *Journal für Sozialforschung*, vol. 24, 1984, pp. 441–54

Naßmacher, Karl-Heinz, *Parteien im Abstieg. Wiederbegründung und Niedergang von DP, DZP und FDP in den Jahren 1945–1965*, Opladen, 1989

Norpoth, Helmut, *Wählerverhalten in der Bundesrepublik. Arbeitsbuch zur sozial- und politikwissenshaftlichen Lehre*, Frankfurt, 1980

Oberndörfer, Dieter (ed.), *Wählerverhalten in der Bundesrepublik Deutschland. Studien zu ausgewählten Problemen der Wahlforschung aus Anlaß der Bundestagswahl 1976*, Berlin, 1978

Oberndörfer, Dieter, Hans Rattinger and Karl Schmitt (eds), *Wirtschaftlicher Wandel, religiöser Wandel und Wertwandel. Folgen für das politische Verhalten in der Bundesrepublik Deutschland*, Berlin, 1985

Oberndörfer, Dieter, Karl Schmitt and Gerd Mielke, *Parteien und regionale politische Kultur in der Bundesrepublik Deutschland*, Berlin, 1989

Obernreuther, Heinrich, *Parteien zwischen Nestwärme und Funktionskälte*, Zürich and Osnabrück, 1983

Pappi, Franz Urban, 'Parteiensystem und Sozialstruktur in der Bundesrepublik', *Politische Vierteljahresschrift*, vol. 14, 1973, pp. 191–213

——, 'Sozialstruktur, gesellschaftliche Wertorientierungen und Wahlabsicht', *Politische Vierteljahresschrift*, vol. 18, 1977, pp. 195–229

——, 'Konstanz und Wandel der Hauptspannungslinien in der Bundesrepublik', in Joachim Matthes (ed.), *Sozialer Wandel in Westeuropa*, Frankfurt, 1979, pp. 465–79

——, and Michael Terwey, 'The German Electorate: Old Cleavages and New Political Conflicts', in Herbert Döring and Gordon Smith (eds), *Party*

Government and Political Culture in Western Germany, London, 1982, pp. 174–96

Pappi, Franz Urban, 'Die konfessionell-religiöse Konfliktlinie in der deutschen Wählerschaft. Entstehung, Stabilität und Wandel', in Dieter Oberndörfer et al. (eds), *Wirtschaftlicher Wandel und Wertwandel. Folgen für das politische Verhalten in der Bundesrepublik*, Berlin, 1985, pp. 263–90

——, and Peter Mnich, 'Social Structure and Party Choice in the Federal Republic of Germany since the 1960's', in Mark N. Franklin et al. (eds), *Electoral Change*, London, 1988

Pappi, Franz Urban, 'Die Anhänger der neuen sozialen Bewegungen im Parteiensystem der Bundesrepublik, *Aus Politik und Zeitgeschichte, Beilage zur Wochenzeitung Das Parlament*, vol. B 26, 1989, pp. 17–27

——, 'Germany', in Mark N. Franklin, Thomas T. Mackie and Henry Valen, *Electoral Change: Responses to Evolving Social and Attitudinal Structures in Western Countries*, Cambridge, 1989

Paterson, William E., 'West Germany. Between Party Apparatus and Basis Democracy', in Alan Ware (ed.), *Political Parties. Electoral Change and Structural Response*, Oxford, 1987, pp. 158–82

Plassner, Fritz, *Parteien unter Stress. Zur Dynamik der Parteiensysteme in Österreich, der Bundesrepublik Deutschland und den Vereinigten Staaten*, Vienna, 1987

Raschke, Joachim, *Soziale Bewegungen*, Frankfurt, 1985

Rattinger, Hans, 'Empirische Wahlforschung auf der Suche nach dem rationalen Wähler. Politische Sachfragen als Bestimmungsfaktoren des Wahlverhaltens in der Bundesrepublik und in den Vereinigten Staaten', *Zeitschrift für Politik*, vol. 27, 1980, pp. 44–58.

——, *Wirtschaftliche Konjunktur und politische Wahlen in der Bundesrepublik Deutschland*, Berlin, 1980

Reigrotzki, Erich, *Soziale Verflechtungen in der Bundesrepublik. Elemente der sozialen Teilnahme in Kirche, Politik, Organisationen und Freizeit*, Tübingen, 1956

Ritter, Gerhard A., and Merith Niehuss, *Wahlen in der Bundesrepublik Deutschland. Bundestags- und Landtagswahlen 1946–1987*, Munich, 1987

Rohe, Karl, 'Vom sozialdemokratischen Armenhaus zur Wagenburg der SPD. Politischer Strukturwandel in einer Industrieregion nach dem Zweiten Weltkrieg', *Geschichte und Gesellschaft*, vol. 13, 1987, pp. 508–33

Roth, Dieter, 'Sind die Republikaner die fünfte Partei?', *Aus Politik und Zeitgeschichte. Beilage zur Wochenzeitung Das Parlament*, vol. 18, B 41–2, 1989, pp. 12–18

Rucht, Dieter, 'Zum Verhältnis von sozialen Bewegungen und Politischen Parteien', *Journal für Sozialforschung*, vol. 27, 1987, pp. 297–313

Rudzio, Wolfgang, 'Wahlverhalten und kommunalpolitisches Personal in ausgewählten Oldenburger Gemeinden. Aspekte politisch-sozialer Milieustrukturen', in Wolfgang Günther (ed.), *Sozialer und politischer Wandel in Oldenburg. Studien zur Regionalgeschichte vom 17. bis 20. Jahrhundert*, Oldenburg, 1981, pp. 253–97

Sahner, Heinz, *Politische Tradition, Sozialstruktur und Parteisystem in Schleswig-Holstein. Ein Beitrag zur Replikation von Rudolf Heberles: Landbevölkerung und*

Nationalsozialismus, Meisenheim, Glan, 1972

Sarcinelli, Ulrich, *Symbolische Politik. Zur Bedeutung symbolischen Handelns in der Wahlkampfkommunikation der Bundesrepublik Deutschland*, Opladen, 1987

Schacht, Konrad, *Wahlentscheidung im Dienstleistungszentrum. Analysen zur Frankfurter Kommunalwahl vom 22. März 1981*, Opladen, 1986

——, 'Alte Partei und neue Schichten. Zu den Chancen der SPD in den Dienstleistungsstädten', *Die neue Gesellschaft*, vol. 34, 1987, pp. 358–62

Schmidt, Ute, 'Katholische Arbeiterbewegung zwischen Integralismus und Interkonfessionalismus: Wandlungen eines Milieus', in Rolf Ebbighausen and Friedrich Tiemann (eds), *Das Ende der Arbeiterbewegung in Deutschland? Ein Diskussionsband für Theo Pirker*, Opladen, 1984, pp. 216–39

——, *Zentrum oder CDU. Politischer Katholizismus zwischen Tradition und Anpassung*, Opladen, 1987

Schmitt, Karl, 'Inwieweit bestimmt auch heute noch die Konfession das Wahlverhalten? Konfession, Parteien und politisches Verhalten in der Bundesrepublik', in Hans-Georg Wehling (ed.), *Konfession eine Nebensache? Politische, soziale und kulturelle Ausprägungen religiöser Untersuchiede in Deutschland*, Stuttgart, 1984, pp. 21–57

——, *Konfession und politisches Verhalten in der Bundesrepublik Deutschland*, Berlin, 1989

Schönbohm, Wulf, *Die CDU wird moderne Volkspartei. Selbstverständnis, Mitglieder, Organisation und Apparat 1950–1980*, Stuttgart, 1985

Schoof, Peter, *Wahlbeteiligung und Sozialstruktur in der Bundesrepublik Deutschland. Eine politikwissenchaftlich-statistische Aggregatdatenanalyse sozialstruktureller und ökonomischer Bestimmungsfaktoren der Wahlbeteiligung bei Bundes-und Landtagswahlen zwischen 1972 und 1976*, Frankfurt, 1980

Schultze, Rainer-Olaf, 'Wählerverhalten und Parteiensystem in der Bundesrepublik Deutschland', in Hans-Georg Wehling (ed.), *Westeuropas Parteiensystem im Wandel*, Stuttgart, 1983, pp. 45–82

Serfas, Günther, *'Lieber Freiheit ohne Einheit als Einheit ohne Freiheit'. Der Neubeginn der Demokratischen Volkspartei in Württemberg-Baden 1945/46*, Heidelberg, 1986

Stöss, Richard (ed.), *Parteien-Handbuch. Die Parteien der Bundesrepublik Deutschland 1945–1980*, 2 vols, Opladen, 1983/84

——, *Die neue Rechte in der Bundesrepublik*, Opladen, 1989

——, *Politics Against Democracy: Right Extremism in West Germany*, Oxford, 1990

Veen, Hans-Joachim and Peter Gluchowski, 'Tendenzen der Nivellierung und Polarisierung in den Wählerschaften von CDU/CSU und SPD von 1959–1983. Eine Fortschreibung', *Zeitschrift für Parlamentsfragen*, vol. 14, 1983, pp. 545–55

——, 'Sozialstrukturelle Nivellierung bei politischer Polarisierung – Wandlungen und Konstanten in den Wählerstrukturen der Parteien 1953–1987', *Zeitschrift für Parlamentsfragen*, vol. 19, 1988, pp. 225–48

Veiders, Wolfgang W., *Großstadt und Umland. Eine Mehrebenenanalyse des Wahlverhaltens im Großraum Köln/Bonn*, Ph. D., Freiburg, 1978

Weber, Hermann, 'Traditionslinien und Neubeginn der deutschen Parteien

1945 – am Beispiel der "Arbeiterparteien"', in Max Kaase (ed.), *Politische Wissenschaft und politische Ordnung*, Wiesbaden, 1986, pp. 305–38

Weinacht, Paul-Ludwig (ed.), *Die CDU in Baden-Württemberg und ihre Geschichte*, Stuttgart, 1978

Wiesendahl, Elmar, *Parteien und Demokratie. Eine soziologische Analyse paradigmatischer Ansätze zur Parteienforschung*, Opladen, 1980

Wildenmann, Rudolf, 'Die soziale Basis der Herrschaft Konrad Adenauers', in Dieter Blumenwitz et al. (eds), *Konrad Adenauer und seine Zeit*, 2 vols, Stuttgart, 1976, pp. 275–84

——, *Volksparteien. Ratlose Riesen? Eine Studie unter Mitarbeit von Werner Kaltefleiter et al.*, Baden-Baden, 1989

About the Contributors

Jürgen W. Falter: born 1944; Professor of Political Science and Comparative Research on Fascism, Free University of Berlin; 1977–8 Kennedy Memorial Fellow, Harvard University; 1980–1 Visiting Professor, Johns Hopkins University (Bologna Center). Recent publications: *Wahlem und Abstimmungen in der Weimarer Republik*, Munich, 1986; (co ed.), *Politische Willensbildung und Interessenvermittlung*, Opladen, 1984; *Der 'Positivismusstreit' in der amerikanischen Politikwissenschaft*, Opladen, 1982.

Alf Mintzel: born 1935; Professor of Sociology, University of Passau; 1967–81 Assistant, Assistant Professor and Privatdozent, Central Institute for Social Science Research, Free University of Berlin. Recent publications: *Die CSU. Anatomie einer konservativen Partei*, Opladen, 1975, 1978; *Geschichte der CSU*, Opladen, 1977; *Die Stadt Hof in der Pressegeschichte des 16., 17. und 18. Jahrhunderts*, Hof, 1979; *Die Volkspartei. Typus und Wirklichkeit*, Opladen, 1984; (with Inge Lu Mintzel), *Es ist noch Zeit genug. Bilder und Gedichte*, Passau, 1989.

Merith Niehuss: born 1954; Akademische Rätin, University of Munich. Recent publications: *Arbeiterschaft in Krieg und Inflation*, Berlin, 1985; (with Gerhard A. Ritter), *Wahlen in der Bundesrepublik Deutschland*, Munich, 1987.

Franz Urban Pappi: born 1939; Professor of Sociology, University of Kiel. Recent publications: (editor and author), *Methoden der Netzwerkanalyse*, Munich, 1987. Articles on voting behaviour (spatial models, in J. Falter et al. (eds), *Wahlen und politische Einstellungen in der Bundesrepublik Deutschland*, Frankfurt, 1989), new social movements (in press), interlocking directorates (*Kölner Zeitschrift für Soziologie und Sozialpsychologie*, vol. 39, 1987, pp. 693–717).

Gerhard A. Ritter: born 1929; Professor of Modern History, University of Munich; Member of the Bavarian Academy of Science; Honorary Fellow of

St Antony's College, Oxford; 1965–6, 1972 Visiting Professor, University of Oxford; 1971–2 Visiting Professor, University of California (Berkeley); 1973 Visiting Professor, University of Tel Aviv; 1976–80 Chairman of the Association of German Historians. Recent publications: *Parlament und Demokratie in Großbritannien*, Göttingen, 1972; *Staat, Arbeiterschaft und Arbeiterbewegung in Deutschland*, Berlin and Bonn, 1980; *Die deutschen Parteien 1830–1914*, Göttingen, 1985; *Social Welfare in Germany and Britain. Origins and Developments*, Leamington Spa and New York, 1986; (with M. Niehuss), *Wahlen in der Bundesrepublik Deutschland. Bundestags- und Landtagswahlen 1946–1987*, Munich, 1987; *Der Sozialstaat. Entstehung und Entwicklung im internationalen Vergleich*, Munich, 1989.

Karl Rohe: born 1934; Professor of Political Science, University of Essen; 1987–8 Visiting Fellow, St Antony's College, Oxford. Recent publications: *Politik. Begriffe und Wirklichkeiten*, Stuttgart, 1978; (ed. with H. Kühr), *Politik und Gesellschaft im Ruhrgebiet. Beiträge zur regionalen Politikforschung*, Kronsberg, 1979; (ed.), *Die Westmächte und das Dritte Reich 1933–1939*, Paderborn, 1982; *Vom Revier zum Ruhrgebiet. Wahlen – Parteien – Politische Kultur*, Essen, 1986; (ed.), *Englischer Liberalismus im 19. und frühen 20. Jahrhundert*, Bochum, 1987.

Karl Schmitt: born 1944; Professor of Political Science, University of Cologne. Recent publications: *Politische Erziehung in der DDR*, Paderborn, 1980; (ed. with Dieter Oberndörfer), *Kirche und Demokratie*, Paderborn, 1983; (ed. with Dieter Oberndörfer and Hans Rattinger), *Wirtschaftlicher Wandel, religiöser Wandel und Wertwandel in der Bundesrepublik Deutschland*, Berlin, 1985; *Konfession und Wahlverhalten in der Bundesrepublik Deutschland*, Berlin, 1989.